CRITICAL APPROACHES TO WRITING ABOUT FILM

John E. Moscowitz

Broward Community College

Prentice Hall
Upper Saddle River, NJ 07458

Library of Congress Cataloging-in-Publication Data

Moscowitz, John E.
    Critical approaches to writing about film / John E. Moscowitz.
        p.   cm.
    Includes bibliographical references and index.
    ISBN 0-13-083707-5 (paper)
    1. Film criticism.   I. Title.
PN1995.M625   1999
791.43'01'5—dc21   99-31977
                                                                        CIP

Editorial director: Charlyce Jones Owen
Editor-in-chief: Leah Jewell
Acquisitions editor: Carrie Brandon
Editorial/production supervision
    and interior design: Mary Araneo
Senior managing editor: Bonnie Biller
Buyer: Mary Ann Gloriande
Editorial assistant: Gianna Caradonna
Photo researcher: Diana P. Gongora
Image specialist: Beth Boyd
Manager, Rights & Permissions: Kay Dellosa
Director, Image Resource Center: Melinda Reo
Marketing manager: Brandy Dawson
Cover designer: Robert Farrar-Wagner
Cover photo: *The Godfather.* Paramount Pictures, 1972.

Credits appear beginning on page 203, which constitutes a
continuation of this copyright page.

This book was set in 10/12 New Century Schoolbook by A & A Publishing
Services, Inc. and was printed and bound by Courier Companies, Inc.
The cover was printed by Phoenix Color Corp.

ISBN 0-13-083707-5

PRENTICE-HALL INTERNATIONAL (UK) LIMITED, London
PRENTICE-HALL OF AUSTRALIA PTY. LIMITED, Sydney
PRENTICE-HALL CANADA INC., Toronto
PRENTICE-HALL HISPANOAMERICANA, S.A., Mexico
PRENTICE-HALL OF INDIA PRIVATE LIMITED, New Delhi
PRENTICE-HALL OF JAPAN, INC., Tokyo
PEARSON EDUCATION ASIA PTE. LTD., Singapore
EDITORA PRENTICE-HALL DO BRASIL, LTDA., Rio de Janeiro

To

Dr. Kathryn Lynn Gerstman

Kathy has seen me through the many iterations of *Critical Approaches to Writing About Film*—those times of rejection and despair, agonizing decisions, and heady elation. She did so always with warmth, empathy, and encouragement. It is for these and other endearing qualities that this book is dedicated.

CONTENTS

Appendices

PREFACE

In conceptualizing *Critical Approaches to Writing About Film*, I perceived a need for a textbook that explored different approaches to writing about film. It could be used for such courses taught at numerous community colleges and four-year institutions as: Introduction to Film, Introduction to Cinema Studies, and Film as Literature. The last offering, Film as Literature—which originates in English departments for writing credit—especially needs different models of varied approaches, formats, and lengths inherent in written discussion of film. To that end, this text furnishes theory, discussion, and examples of written critiques, reviews, comparative analyses, and documented research projects about the cinema. Film techniques used to create motion pictures are integrated into numerous instructional paragraphs and sample papers.

The text considers those writing approaches best suited for analyzing a cinematic source in the college classroom. These include

- What perspective to take when reviewing a film,
- How to write reviews of the same film but of varying lengths,
- How to adopt a fitting tone when critiquing a movie,
- How to enhance English writing skills,
- What methods to use in writing comparative analyses, and
- How to research and create a documented essay on a motion picture.

Critical Approaches to Writing About Film employs various strategies, presentations, and conventions when considering these and other questions and topics suggested by the title. Sample presentations of written pieces examining both classic and more contemporary cinema encompass:

- Student-written essays of various lengths, formats, and approaches to specific films,
- Demonstrations by the author of techniques and perspectives taken to writing film reviews and comparative analyses, and
- Sample published pieces by professional reviewers.

The conventions incorporated when writing reviews or other critical pieces on film involve

- Devising lead-ins, plot overviews, and obligatory credits,
- Taking subjective stances and making evaluations,
- Presenting precursive and contemporary parallels and/or influences,
- Introducing and developing points of emphasis, and
- Creating effective concluding remarks.

To illustrate such concepts and their variations, sample passages or complete pieces immediately follow the text. Captioned photographs from the films being discussed are provided to aid the instruction as well. Lengthier examples are placed at the end of the chapter.

Comparative analysis is often used as a teaching tool. This writing approach and format has been helpful in

- Demonstrating multiple writing options on the same film,
- Illustrating how film adopts—and adapts—its literary source,
- Portraying remakes of film classics and showing how they differ from the original in terms of their treatment of and adjustment to new audiences.

Demonstration of proficiency in research techniques and forms are the norm in many higher education courses. Those that study the various aspects of cinema are no different. Therefore, this text shows how to

- Select researchable topics,
- Adopt proper tactics of organization for an individualized paper including the outline,
- Consider and use varied written and electronic sources,
- Amass and cull data,
- Streamline the documentation process through photocopying and color coding,

- Incorporate in-text citations and works cited page, and
- Prepare the initial and final drafts.

The book is divided into six chapters, two appendixes, and a glossary: chapter 1, "Preparation for and the Process of Film Criticism"; chapter 2, "Style and Structure in Film Criticism"; chapter 3, "Types of Film Criticism: The Review"; chapter 4, "Types of Film Criticism: The Critique"; chapter 5, "Types of Film Criticism: The Comparative Analysis"; chapter 6, "Types of Film Criticism: The Documented Research Paper"; appendix A, "Primary and Secondary Sources of Works Cited"; appendix B, "Quizzes, Questions, Essays, and Research Projects"; and "Glossary of Cinematic Terms," and "Index of Titles and Names."

As can be expected, each chapter builds on material previously presented. Appendix A documents all written or film material referred to in the text from primary and secondary critical sources. Appendix B provides testing tools and writing topics tailored for each of the six chapters. A glossary of cinematic terms is included as a helpful reference. Finally, *Critical Approaches to Writing About Film* is intended to be used as either a primary or supplementary text depending on how great the course's emphasis is on writing critically about film.

Acknowledgments

I would like to thank Jack Riggs of Georgia Perimeter College, Martin F. Nordern of the University of Massachusetts-Amherst, Darrell Costa of DeVry Institute of Technology-Pomona, and Jon Bentley of Albuquerque TVI, who reviewed and commented on this manuscript; Mary Araneo, who coordinated the production; Patrick Baeringer, Ann Birr, Arlene Mandel, Jim Sander, Kimberly Springer, Jodi Turchin, and Deborah Wade, who so graciously permitted the use of their Film as Literature papers to be reproduced and discussed in this book; Maggie Barbieri, Joan Polk, and Carrie Brandon, who made and then transferred editorial decisions and did the final permissions research and paperwork; Mary Jamieson, who did most of the early research on many of the films incorporated in this work; Gloria Johnson, who provided her research paper as a sample for discussion in this book; Bill McGrath, who furnished competent help along with an inexhaustible patience with my word-processing and software problems; Suzanne St. Laurent, who, as friend and departmental colleague, spent much time proofreading and making editorial suggestions of the rough draft; and Judy Weir, who did late research on films to help me meet my editorial deadlines.

John E. Moscowitz

1

PREPARATION FOR AND THE PROCESS OF FILM CRITICISM

Film has been provoking reaction via the written word ever since its earliest versions flickered hesitantly on the makeshift screens in the nineteenth century. Over the years, writing about film has become a cottage industry. Journalists write reviews and critical features about current and past movies. Authors pen popular books about cinema's history, its movers and shakers, and those whose faces have been projected larger-than-life before millions. Academics produce scholarly papers and theoretical monographs about the motion picture. Students labor to present their viewpoints in the form of reviews, critiques, comparative analyses, and research papers.

This chapter will present a methodical preparation for film criticism and suggest different procedures to take in that process. The mindset one adopts during the actual critiquing is important since one must distinguish between the objective and subjective components of film criticism and judge when one is more appropriate than the other. Various types of written cinematic criticism will be introduced including an awareness of the different audiences, approaches, styles, and lengths for reviews, critiques, comparative analyses, and documented research studies.

When writing about film, one should be acquainted with and willing to use appropriate cinematic terms. As you read this chapter—and subsequent chapters—please refer to the glossary of cinematic terms provided at the end of the book.

Preparation

We watch movies for entertainment and/or information. If we are going to analyze a film, however, we must be prepared to watch it critically, not passively.

Having a Purpose

Why does one critique a movie? The reasons vary yet are similar to those for critiquing a musical work, a play, a novel, or a nonfiction book; or, for that matter, critiquing an automobile, an airline service, a college course, a restaurant, and so on. Besides informing us as to what decisions to make, critiquing forces the writer to consider that concept or entity objectively: by amassing data, organizing it, analyzing its meaning, and making a series of evaluative judgments leading to its ultimate appraisal. Writing the critique is merely documenting the analytical and evaluative process on paper or electronically. In most critical analyses, there is also some subjectivity: yet, a skilled critic will be able to distinguish between what is objective (factual and nonopinionative) and what is subjective (intuitive and reflecting one's personal tastes) and when to use one or the other appropriately.

The reason why critical papers are assigned in any college course is to provide tangible proof of critical reading and/or critical viewing, followed by critical thinking and organizing, and, finally, critical writing. Relating what happened, when, and to whom in their proper order is merely factual recounting; why and how something occurred and if the presentation of such material works for the reader/viewer, on the other hand, is critical evaluation. It is that critical perspective in its various written formats that is the objective of many college courses, including those in literature and the arts, of which film is very much a member.

Why write a critical piece on a movie? Isn't film just an expression of mass culture for a mass audience—at its lowest common denominator—that is churned out indiscriminately? Or, as some have been heard to disparagingly comment, "Y'know, it's only a movie . . ." True, many poorly conceived, shoddily crafted, and exploitive films have been foisted on the public. But they should be branded as such by critics and reviewers. Excellent motion pictures have also been produced; such fine work should, therefore, also be identified and assessed. One must be reminded, as well, that a work being printed on paper and bound in cloth is no guarantee of quality. Like everything else creative, some efforts are inferior, many are average, and some are exceptional. Be reminded that the writing and editing of a book often involves only a handful of individuals, whereas the making of a motion picture employs hundreds—sometimes thousands—of people. They, in turn, must labor together under the relentless pressures of time, budget, and, in some instances, grueling geographic locations.

There is another reason for analyzing and discussing any work of art or literature and, especially, film. In many instances, a movie is a fairly accurate portrayal of life: of how the human condition is at present, was in the past, or, perhaps, will be in the future.

But if movies show life, does film always portray life accurately? Neutrally? Apolitically? Fairly? Of course not, and critical discussion, either oral or written, tries to distinguish accuracy from exaggeration, evenhandedness from bias, the real from the imaginary, and fact from opinion. In looking at a motion picture critically, we not only make more sense of the film but, perhaps, more sense of ourselves, the relationships that we have with others, and the multifaceted world at large.

Developing a Plan

Before watching a new film prior to writing its review, or before organizing your thoughts preceding the critiquing of a cinema classic, you must be aware of your intended *audience*. Is the review going to be a formal essay for your professor? An article in the campus newspaper? An informal verbal account of the movie for the film club? How long should it be? How knowledgeable is your audience? These and similar questions must be answered before you can proceed with development of a plan. Obviously, the longer the project, the more detailed the planning must be. It might involve seeing the movie once or twice or renting the video and taking notes. When working with older films, it may involve doing library or Internet research for previously written critical material. Since any given film can be reviewed or critiqued from dozens of perspectives, a fresh, honest, and personal perception can still be made even after conducting research.

The Tools and the Process

Once a plan of execution is decided upon, serious data gathering begins. For this, you need the obvious: a pencil with an eraser, a notepad, and a penlight. A battery-powered laptop computer would be a worthy substitute for the aforementioned materials when watching a video on a videocassette recorder (VCR), and, in this instance, a remote control device is strongly recommended.

Before we go any farther, we must first distinguish the *film review* from the other forms of written critical expression on cinema. The review makes an important distinction from the rest: it assumes that the reader may not be familiar with the movie in question and definitely has *not* seen it. For the other types of critical expression, the assumption is the opposite: namely, that the reader is somewhat familiar with the motion picture(s) in question and has seen it (them). The review, therefore, immediately poses some restrictions: the reviewer must not retell the entire plot and must not divulge the outcome of the climax and its denouement. There are times when these restrictions can be violated without integrally harming the review—as when evaluating some farces—but, in most cases, details of the climax and the ending must be avoided. (Other aspects of the written movie review will be discussed in depth in Chapter 3)

Taking Notes in the Cineplex

Critical viewing of a film is quite different from attending the local moviehouse with a box of popcorn in one hand and an enormous cup of soda in the other and kicking back to enjoy two hours of entertainment. That is casual movie viewing, and what you are left with afterwards are some impressions and reactions. Many of the subtleties have been missed because the watching has been passive rather than active. Active watching, however, is a crucial component of critical viewing. The process is analogous to reading for pleasure versus reading critically. Before the viewing can take place, you must have already asked yourself questions about your expectations of the film. These expectations could be determined by your familiarity with the following:

- The director's style, biases, preferred subject matter, and/or body of work;
- The actors and whether they are big name stars, an ensemble of character players, or a cast of virtual unknowns; and
- The genre's pronounced stylistic qualities—such as those found in the western, the comedy, or the action thriller (with its increasing dependency on special effects).

It may be that the movie is a "small" film with a low budget, an unrecognizable cast and director, and a movie title which gives no indication of its genre or theme. Certainly, the context of your expectations and prior knowledge would differ for such a film compared to the latest Steven Seagall action blockbuster.

For the initial viewing of a film at a local theater, it is best to go when the audience is scanty. Matinees and twilight shows are the best times, and the rates for admission are also lower than at later evening showings. First, get all the important credits written down before the film actually begins running. The poster advertising the film in the lobby or near the outdoor box office has information as to the stars, the director, producer, screenwriter, and other major contributors to the film. Additional credits can be obtained during the showing, from recent reviews in the local newspaper, or from such nationally circulated newspapers as *The New York Times,* which are often available at your local public or college library. Film credits can also be found from various Internet sources, especially the Internet Movie Database.

Find a seat away from others so that their rustlings or whispers won't distract you and your penlight and jottings won't annoy them. As the credits begin scrolling, make sure the list of actors is separate from the other credits since, eventually, you will be filling in the names of the characters the cast plays. As the movie unfolds, try to discern the setting. Sometimes, it is obvious: a seedy section in a wintry, contemporary San Francisco; or a tree-lined residential street with single-family homes during summer in the 1950s. (Automobiles and their license plates as well as clothing help fix the era.) In many films that are set in exotic locales or historical periods, either a voice-over or a line written across the screen announces the setting: "German East Africa, September 1915" (from *The African Queen*).

Next, try to identify the tone and genre of the film—humorous, suspenseful, exciting, or realistic—which, in turn, helps determine whether it is a comedy, mystery, thriller, or drama. Of course, through word-of-mouth, television trailers, or newspaper advertisements, you may already know the genre and tone. The music accompanying a movie often strongly suggests its tone.

As you scrutinize a film, you are absorbing and processing information and events as they unfurl on the screen while simultaneously silently questioning yourself about what you see. These would include inquiries about the relationship of the characters to each other as they are introduced or the significance of certain events that have occurred. You would also be aware of numerous visual and symbolic clues and try to comprehend their impact upon the plot or theme.

During the film's first half-hour, you may have no idea yet of what you are going to emphasize in your piece. Each review or critique, besides including the standard relevant information mentioned above (called *boilerplate*), emphasizes a few points and develops them. Such points will come gradually as you perceive patterns evolving in the film or get interested in particular aspects of the movie. These are the attributes that will make your review or critique different from someone else's.

If a class were assigned to write individual papers on *Babette's Feast* (1987), everyone would probably furnish similar boilerplate. Each would mention the setting (a remote Danish fishing village on the Jutland Peninsula in the mid-nineteenth century). Also included would be Gabriel Axel, the director who also wrote the screenplay adapted from the Isak Dinesen novel. The names of the cast and the characters they play would also be listed in the students' papers. Very likely, a short

Babette's Feast (1988) The rustic townspeople in the midst of dining on Babette's gourmet French meal.

paragraph would be written summarizing the film. (In fact, this would probably closely resemble what is typically written on the plastic jackets of movie videos.) But from this point on, the writers move in divergent directions. One student might concentrate on the opulence of Babette's banquet as compared to the blandness and simplicity of the villagers' normal fare. Another might expound on the use of the unsaturated color and its meaning in the film—with its dark blues and grays in the exterior shots, earth tones accentuated by the candlelight of the interiors, and the severe, somber hues of the clothing worn by both the men and women. Yet another student might discuss the juxtaposition of the widow Babette, a sophisticated and mysterious Parisian, set among these simple, God-fearing, unworldly denizens of the remote, seaside Danish hamlet. Someone else might analyze the motifs of sacrifice and gratitude as manifested by the two sisters, Martina and Philippa, and their housekeeper-cook, Babette. Finally, someone might deliberate on how the title of the film functions both symbolically and thematically.

I have just skimmed the surface of topics that could be written on this thought-provoking, heartwarming motion picture. This will become clearer when the different types of critical writing done on film is presented in greater detail in succeeding chapters.

Throughout the movie, you take notes and jot down words of anything that may be useful to you later on. Do not worry about organization at this juncture. At the movie's finale, you can still glean much useful information as the credits scroll by before the theater's houselights come up. It is best to see the film again, either later that day or the next. If seeing a film once more is not possible, then within twelve hours of the initial screening—while the film's images, insights, and the connections between them are still vivid—study your notes carefully, reorganize them, and write the rough draft.

In summary, the process for viewing a film critically in a theater follows these chronological steps:

1. Attend a performance at a time when crowds are smallest: weekday matinees or twilight showings.
2. On your notepad, copy any useful information from the movie poster of your film in the theater.
3. Using a penlight and pencil, jot down useful information in a notepad from the opening credits.
4. Discern the setting, tone, and genre as soon as possible.
5. Comprehend the interplay of the characters and their relationships to each other and the plot.
6. Focus on one or two aspects of the film that you could develop.
7. Write down anything you find important during the film.
8. Glean information from the closing credits.
9. See the film again within twenty-four hours. If this is not possible, within twelve hours read and reorganize your notes and write your first draft.

Using the VCR

The videocassette recorder has revolutionized how we see movies on television. No longer need viewers be victimized by network censors and their arbitrary edits; no longer need film enthusiasts be bombarded indiscriminately by mind-numbing advertisements at an increasing pace as the movie rolls toward the climax; no longer need movie fans be chained to their easy chairs and couches, daring not to leave for two minutes and miss an important segment.

In fact, the preferred technology for a review or any other critical essay would be the VCR (or more recent devices such as laser disks and digital video disks [DVDs]). Using such a device, you can stop the film wherever and whenever you want to, freeze a frame, or use the rewind and play buttons either to see some piece of action again or catch the exact wording of an important exchange of dialogue. You can see a passage repeatedly to search for any subtleties in characterization, theme, or symbolism that may have eluded you previously.

Since the video of a film has been made and released after both the first and second run engagements, and since there is already a wealth of information available in periodicals and on the Internet, you can use such technology for not only writing a review but any other critical assignment. Writing a review is an exercise in a type of format and really is not contingent on the release date. In fact, you may be assigned to write a review on *Gone with the Wind*, even though it made the first of its many runs in 1939.

The methodology that you use preparing to view a videotape, then seeing it, and, finally, writing about it is similar to that which you use when watching a film critically in the theater. The suggestion, again, is to do preliminary research to get all the necessary information involving the cast and credits beforehand. Of course, you may opt to rewind and freeze a frame a few times to obtain that data from the introductory and final credits. Again, as the film unfurls, you want to discern the setting, the tone, and the genre. In time, a number of aspects of the film will intrigue you so that you follow and then develop them into the main thrusts of your review or other critical piece.

The attitude that you take during a critical VCR viewing (or in a theater, for that matter) should be interrogatory. You must keep questioning the meaning of what you see and jot down these interrogations. They can always be answered after the showing has ended, when you review your notes. From the opening moments to the final credits, you should be generating questions about such typical aspects of a film as the

- Movie's title and its significance,
- Format of the opening credits—whether there is static background behind them or action is transpiring—and its effect,
- Purpose of the film's opening minutes regarding establishment of setting, theme, mood, characterization, and/or tone,
- References to other films,
- Patterns indicative of the director's style,
- Impact of lighting, music, sound, special effects, camera shots, costuming, and set design on the film,
- Strengths and weaknesses in casting,
- Lapses, if any, in continuity,
- Sloppiness, complexity, or tightness of plot, and
- Effectiveness and validity of the final scene and ending shot.

It is always best to write the rough draft while the film is still fresh in your mind. If you own the video or have borrowed it for a considerable length of time, the immediacy for writing the first draft is lessened considerably—you may not even want to write a draft until you have seen the video an additional time or two. However, if it is rented from the local video mart, you probably will want to view it again within twenty-four hours and then write the initial version.

For writing a lengthy critical paper, you will want to view the video a few times and then integrate your critical viewing notes with your other research. This would consist of copies of reviews, plot summaries, excerpts from articles, books, and the like from the library since you will want to combine your impressions and insights with those of other critics, reviewers, and scholars. Make sure to give credit when appropriate and employ standard documentation practices.

In summary, the process for viewing a film critically on a VCR follows these chronological steps:

1. Gather other reviews, plot summaries, lists of credits and the like and have them available for your viewing.
2. Start the video: on your notepad, jot down any useful information that adds to what you already have. Especially important would be what you can gather about setting, tone, and genre.
3. Note the interplay of the characters and their relationships to each other and the plot.
4. Focus on one or two aspects of the film that you could develop.
5. If doing a comparative study, note the parallels as they unfold.
6. As you watch, jot down anything else that you could conceivably use later on in your paper. Do not hesitate to use the rewind, play, and freeze frame functions of your VCR for accuracy in quotes and cinematic subtleties to catch and incorporate later on in your first draft.
7. Glean information from the closing credits.
8. See the video again within twenty-four hours. If you own it, see it an additional time or two before writing the first draft.
9. Read, integrate, and document additional source material—reviews and critical pieces—with your notes and insights as you compose your first draft.
10. Proofread, edit, and write your final draft on your word processor or computer.

2

Style and Structure
in Film Criticism

Once you have done the research, amassed the data, and seen the film—either at the theater or at home on a VCR—you are ready to write. For a shorter piece of 300 words or less, an outline (which is strongly suggested for a longer paper) is optional. In almost whatever type of paper you write, you will include *boilerplate,* such as the following:

- Title of the film,
- Date of release (if not recent),
- Director and perhaps additional contributors,
- Literary source if not an original screenplay,
- Leading cast members,
- Main theme (basically, what the film is about), and
- Genre.

In the heart of your paper, you will state some insights and develop them fully about the movie in question. During the course of the paper, you will also make some evaluative judgments about the film in general, or some specific aspects of it, or both. Subjectivity is part of any film criticism because so much of this form of writing has to deal with one's personal interpretations and preferences.

The Subjective Attitude

As already stated, subjectivity is an essential element of the review and, to only a slightly lesser degree, of any other type of critical essay; thus, it should be incorporated into your piece. By definition, any of the four types of critical work—review, critique, comparative analysis, or documented research paper—must do more than merely summarize the plot.

The key word is *analyze*. All four types of critical papers mentioned above and covered by this book in Chapters 3 through 6 analyze aspects of a film.

Objectivity Coexisting with Subjectivity

Comprehending the difference between the objective and the subjective is the key point. Any critical piece has both in varying degrees. Subjectivity is more than just a declarative judgment; subjectivity expresses an opinion, suggests an impression. Objectivity, however, is based on incontrovertible fact. Much of the following statement is obviously subjective and judgmental; those words that make it so are in bold print.

> *Schindler's List*, made by Steven Spielberg in 1993, **was not only one of the most important films of that year but will prove to be a landmark in the history of modern filmmaking.**

Compare it with following short paragraph below, which is entirely objective:

> Director Steven Spielberg's *Schindler's List*, released in 1993, won a host of Academy Awards and other cinematic honors for that year. It garnered Oscars for Best Picture, Best Director, and Best Actor (Liam Neeson) among others.

Add the following bold print phrase after "among others" in the last sentence above, and the otherwise objective paragraph ends on a subjective note:

> . . . among others, **making it the most important film of that year, and, because of its subject matter, one of the most significant motion pictures of any year.**

The use of adjectives, adjective phrases, adverbs as well as nouns can change an objective statement into one that is subjective. Specific word choice is most important since the connotative weight that certain words convey adds subjectivity. (This concept will be expanded upon in the next major section of this chapter, Word Choice and Sentence Mix). Those words below in bold print are subjective; remove them, and the short paragraph becomes objective.

> In 1993, Steven Spielberg's **most significant effort to date,** *Schindler's List* told the **unlikely** but true story of a German industrialist who risked his life to save his **dedicated and doomed** Jew-

ish employees, and, simultaneously, **effectively** subverted the **juggernaut** of the **Nazi war machine**.

Making Judgments

Evaluative (subjective) statements and words can be made any time or any place within your paper. Since the reader should be able to recognize by the context of the sentence and your word choice when you are making a subjective statement, you should avoid such comments as: "I think," "in my opinion," "I believe," and the like, except for emphasis. It is understood by the reader that what you are expressing is what you think or believe or is your opinion.

In comparing the following two paragraphs, the second is stronger because the subjective opinion is clearly understood. However, in the first example, statements of the "I/my" phrases (in boldface) are too numerous and unnecessary.

> **I didn't know that much about classical music, much less Mozart's body of musical work, yet I was able to recognize his genius** in Milos Foreman's *Amadeus* (1983). **My musical naivete proved no impediment to enjoying** his masterful melodies and orchestrations. From his earliest compositions and performances to those written just before his untimely death, **I was amazed** at the volume, richness, and breadth of Mozart's musical accomplishments—**despite my being so untutored in classical music.**

In the paragraph above, the I/my phrases weaken the impact of the flow of words and make the whole paragraph more tentative and more conditional than it need be. It also unwittingly shifts the emphasis away from the material being discussed to the insufficiencies of the writer.

The paragraph below, although admitting the writer's ignorance of classical music (but without using an I/my phrase), focuses less on the critic's shortcomings and more on the genius of the title subject of the film.

> Unfamiliarity with much of the music of Mozart poses no impediment to the appreciation of the genius of the man and his work. *Amadeus* (1983), the excellent Milos Foreman rendering of what drove Wolfgang Amadeus Mozart from his formative years as a child prodigy—displaying his unique talents as both composer and performer—until his premature death, is an enthralling cinematic experience. Despite a lack of fundamental knowledge of classical music, one could still appreciate and be astounded by the richness and breadth of his

melodic and orchestral accomplishments. That they were made in such a relatively short lifetime makes him even more remarkable.

Important as evaluative proclamations may be, evidence to support such claims is even more so. You may be expressing an opinion, but backing it up with instances from the film or elsewhere makes your piece more compelling and complete. Such evidence supporting your judgments need not be in the same paragraph as long as they eventually appear in your paper.

As an example, the following few paragraphs, although not a complete review, make some subjective statements that are supported with enough evidence from the film to give credence to those assertions.

Barry Levinson is a director known for his occasional motion picture journeys to the city of his roots, Baltimore, Maryland—especially the Baltimore of the past. *Diner* (1982), *Tin Men* (1987), and *Avalon* (1990) are all bittersweet reminiscences of former times experienced by Levinson himself or his family in that city. Even a popular current television series *Homicide*, which Levinson produces, is set and shot on location in his hometown. However, it is *Diner* that best captures the nostalgia and the wistfulness of a middle-aged moviemaker towards the failed dreams of youth.

Diner (1992) Kevin Bacon, Mickey Rourke, Daniel Stern, and Tim Daly in the opening interior scene at the Fells Point Diner.

The title is very apropos since the action begins, ends, and constantly returns to the meeting place of the main male characters of this ensemble film. The setting is December 1959, and Levinson has faithfully recreated the ambience of the "Silent Generation" of the 1950s. The tight skirts, snug pants, tab collar shirts, and thin ties along with either young men's short hair or swept back "wet" hairstyles, specific rock n' roll tunes, and large-finned automobiles redolent of those times are all accurately in evidence. More important than these material representations are the thoughts, biases, philosophies, and dreams that get bandied about over hamburgers, french fries with gravy, slices of pie and mugs of coffee.

The fellows are in their early twenties, and all, to varying degrees, either are drifting or uncomfortable with the choices that they have made or are about to make. Eddie (Steve Guttenberg) is to be married in a few weeks and, being a secret virgin, is scared stiff of the wedding night; Shrevie (Daniel Stern) is already married to Beth (Ellen Barkin), and both are finding that they have little in common; and Boogie (Mickey Rourke) is a hairdresser by day, sometime law student by night, and compulsive womanizer and gambler all the time in between. The other characters are searching for that ineffable something to give direction, stability, and maturity to their lives. Yet, there is a sense that life is slipping by them and the best years of their lives are past. Their precious friendship is the connection to those better times. Their almost nightly meetings at the Fells Point Diner and talks about football, rock n' roll, and sex provides the glue that keeps their friendship together.

Notice how the second and third paragraphs develop the assertions made in the first paragraph. Highlighting an incident or two and then concluding remarks would complete this review. It should be mentioned, however, that the first paragraph could serve as a launching pad for a comparative analysis where the two other Levinson films that are mentioned would be discussed showing the common elements of all three motion pictures. (More on the comparative analysis paper will be covered in Chapter 5.)

How Much to Retell

One of the problems that many students have—regardless of the type of critical writing project—is knowing when to turn off the faucet of plot summarizing. Size of the piece should determine the amount of plot summation. Any of the four critical forms discussed in this book—movie review, critique (critical analysis), comparative analysis, and documented research paper—uses plot summaries, but only the *précis* or *synopsis* summarizes the entire plot in detail. A critical work is not synonymous with the précis. A précis explains what has transpired, not why. On the other hand, the four critical forms, since they are analytical, definitely address themselves as to the "why and how" as well as to the "what."

No matter which of the four forms you use, before writing the first draft, you must decide what you are going to say about a film. What is the point(s) of your critical essay? Although boilerplate such as production credits, actors, setting, genre, tone, plot summary, and the like will be included, unless one of these aspects is to be greatly expanded as the emphasis of your paper—for example, the psychological effects of the jungle setting on the soldiers in *Platoon*—you still have to develop a focus in your paper. Boilerplate is not a substitute for such a focus but a required adjunct.

The review that follows on *Glengarry Glen Ross* (1992) provides the necessary boilerplate but also identifies its main thrust in the opening paragraph. It further develops the theme in the second paragraph. Every subsequent paragraph is still tied to the paper's emphasis, even though one section will focus on the plot, another on the actors, and a third on the setting. Yet, they all reinforce the focus of the review—namely, this film's portrayal of hell. Both the title of the piece and its conclusion also are indicative of the point that this review is making.

Hell, Version of: America in the Nineties

Director James Foley opens *Glengarry Glen Ross* with a rainy night in a dingy section of Brooklyn, immediately establishing a somber disquieting mood for the film. The camera pans across a seedy commercial street framed by elevated train tracks and moves into a shabby real estate office. Its inhabitants—a number of middle-aged to elderly burned-out salesmen—are soon given one of the profanest and most memorable tongue lashings in recent screen history by Blake (played most effectively by Alec Baldwin), a hotshot sales executive from the head office, downtown. They are threatened with consignment to hell and its ultimate torment: being fired. In reality, though, they are already there and have been for years.

Dante Alighieri wrote *The Inferno* at a time when Europe was emerging from the Dark Ages and perceived his concentric-circled hell as a netherworld swarming with demons, furies, and other vengeful denizens. Inflicting continuous torture upon those souls eternally damned, these supernatural oppressors seemed credible enough to the medieval mind. Centuries later, Jean Paul Sartre saw no need to venture below the crust of planet Earth for his vision of the infernal regions. His play, *No Exit*, portrays hell to be already

Glengarry Glen Ross (1992) Jack Lemmon in his riveting role as Levene, one of the members of an exceptional ensemble cast.

well-established right here on the surface and peopled entirely with other humans. David Mamet's drama and subsequent filmscript of *Glengarry Glen Ross* sees a portion of hell in a sleazy branch real-estate office circa today [1992]. The damned and their hellhounds share the same occupation: real estate sales.

Sinners, no doubt, but, nonetheless, hardworking professionals, they are all clawing to survive in a business where deceit elbows out truth, survival tramples collegiality, and "What-have-you SOLD-for-us-lately?" is measured in nanoseconds. The characters are skill-fully played by a cast that should garner more than its fair share of Oscar nominations. There is Moss (Ed Harris): envious, hot-headed, a no-crap-taking guy but not much of a closer, and desperate enough to plan a burglary of his own office to steal and sell prime real estate leads; Aaronow (Alan Arkin): who has few original thoughts nor the guts to be the heist's co-perpetrator; Levene (Jack Lemmon): smarmy, desperately inventive, pathetic, at times the Lomanesque old timer who, nevertheless goes for the jugular when backed into a corner; and, finally, Roma (Al Pacino): a seemingly world-weary philosopher who subtly transforms into a shark whenever the scent of a sale enters his waters.

All of these men do show flashes of humanity and camaraderie, especially in their contempt for (and fear of) the main office. But uniting against a common enemy gets short shrift when numero uno in sales for the month will get a new Cadillac; the man in second place, a set of steak knives; and the rest, pink slips. Mention must be made of the fine performance of Kevin Spacey as the office manager who is the lightning rod for the threats from headquarters above and the derision of his salesmen below.

The climax is electrifying, with most of the principals giving an acting *tour de force* that demonstrates numerous mood swings in just a few minutes. Most turn on each other when the enemy no longer is the company but their fellow salesmen. They struggle frantically: some to keep their jobs, others to keep out of prison.

Materialism, greed, betrayal, corruption, fraud, and mendacity parade across the screen in the stirring finale. The actual burglar is found out, but none of them really profits from the discovery. Instead, they all will suffer, being even more entrenched in the hell of their own making.

In the review of *Glengarry Glen Ross* above, the theme is that the real estate agency is a glimpse of contemporary hell and that the agents and their manager are both sufferers and tormentors in it. The title of of the review, "Hell, Version of: America in the Nineties," suggests the theme. Although the climax and ending of *Glengarry Glen Ross* are alluded to, the statements are generalized enough so as not to diminish the impact on anyone who sees the movie for the first time after reading the review. Both the climax and the denouement are mentioned, however, since they are connected to the theme of the review.

To further help you make the decision when to stop plot summarization and begin analysis, the following is a précis of *Quest for Fire* (1982). Notice how no analysis or personal opinion interferes with the narrative. This synopsis, if presented as a critique, would be unacceptable because of its lack of analysis. It would fall short as a review because it does not make any evaluation of the movie, goes into too much detail about each adventure and its respective climax, and then gives away the denouement.

Quest for Fire

Based on the French novel by J-H. Rosny, *La Guerre du feu*, the film by Jean-Jacques Annoud, *Quest for Fire* looks at a prehistoric society. It received special assistance from anthropologist Desmond Morris for accuracy in movements and gestures by Cro-Magnons, Neanderthals, and other hominids of that age and from Anthony Burgess, who served in a comparable capacity for prehistoric verbal communication. The action is also preceded by the following prologue:

> 80,000 years ago, man's survival in a vast uncharted land, depended on the possession of fire.
>
> For those early humans, fire was an object of great mystery, since no one had mastered its creation. Fire had to be stolen from nature, it had to be kept alive—sheltered from the wind and rain, guarded from rival tribes.
>
> Fire was a symbol of power and a means of survival. The tribe who possessed fire, possessed life.

The film begins with a tribe of cave people, the Ulam, going about their daily routines around a large bonfire at the mouth of a very high and craggy cave. The shelter sits in the midst of a hardwood forest during what seems to be November. They are suddenly attacked by a band of man-apes who are naked and very strong. The man-apes use found objects—such as stones and heavy sticks—as weapons. Those attacked, however, have more human features, wear animal skins, and use crude tools made of wood and stone. They also have a designated fire bearer to carry glowing embers from place to place in a portable contraption made from an animal skull and hide. They are driven from their cave and flee through the woods where they are harassed by a pack of wolves. Clambering across a bog, they extricate themselves from the ravenous animals but soon are marooned on an islet of a river delta.

They try to start a fire. Naoh (Everett McGill) attempts to blow the ember into a flame, but it dies. He is blamed and exiled until he and two companions, Amakar (Ron Perlman) and Gaw (Najeer El-Kadi), bring back fire.

A series of adventures befall them. First, they are attacked by two saber-toothed tigers, where the men's only escape is to climb a solitary tree. While waiting for their predators to finally abandon them—their prey—the three eat the leaves of the tree. A confrontation later with another tribe of man-apes ensues; these folk, however, wear animal skins, have fire, and devour human flesh. The trio create a ruse and are able to steal some hefty burning sticks. Joining them is Ika (Rae Dawn Chong), a hostage of the cannibals, who is from yet another people but escaped her captors during the raid. The four find a number of boulders and rocks leaning haphazardly against one another as shelter. They wake to find the angry man-apes on a ridge in front of them and a herd of woolly mammoths approaching them from the rear. They manage to befriend the multi-ton beasts with handfuls of grass which then return the favor by attacking the man-apes. They then continue their return to their own clan. Ika, however, eventually leaves the three others to rejoin her tribe—an Iron Age people with huts made of wooden frames having animal skins and dried mud over them, simple household utensils and pottery, and short iron spears as primary weapons. Ika's people soon capture the three wanderers.

The trio escape the forced hospitality of this tribe and are once again joined by Ika. During their brief stay, however, the three cave-fellows have been taught to make a fire with two sticks using the drill method. They meet a renegade party from their own tribe, fight, and dispatch them with those metal spears. The plot comes full circle when they find the remnants of their people on that same grassy islet and bring them fire. The film ends with the same opening shot of a solitary blaze on a ledge in the rocky wilderness at night.

In summary, the précis is quite different from the review or the critical analysis (critique). The précis above introduces the characters sequentially and provides the plotline for the film. However, with the exception of the prologue scrolled across the screen, the précis doesn't touch upon theme, mood, and tone nor furnish any other analytical remarks.

Adopting a Tone

The tone you adopt in a critical paper already is a subjective element of the critique and, especially, the review. Often in reviewing a comedy, the tone the reviewer adopts is light, even humorous. In fact, reviews are usually slightly more informal in word choice and tone than critiques or other critical forms. Perhaps, the most serious, no-nonsense tones are reserved for the documented research paper. *Tone,* as we are using it here, means the critic's or writer's voice. Make sure that the tone you adopt for a critical piece is appropriate for the subject of the film, the tone of the film, and your reaction to and evaluation of the film. Notice the jaunty, sarcastic tone employed in the opening sentence that reviews the troubling and provocative motion picture *Sophie's Choice* (1982):

> Watch Meryl Streep as she reaches into her bag of ethno-imitative tricks and takes a stab at a Polish accent . . . in the midst of a WW2 concentration camp no less!

The Alan J. Pakula film with its extensive flashbacks by Sophie (Meryl Streep) of her torturous life in a Nazi concentration camp would not be fitting for such a jocular tone—even if the critic feels her performance, for example, is greatly wanting. The intent and texture of the film militate against such a casual tone for the following reasons:

- The tone of the novel by William Styron from which the movie is based is serious;
- The tone of the film itself is serious; and
- The tone of the performances of Meryl Streep and Kevin Kline, its principal characters, is serious.

Therefore, the review could be expected to be no less so—even if the critic sees the end product as flawed.

The use of irony and sarcasm is a double-edged sword. On one hand, it can make for an effective and entertaining review; on the other, it may betray some deep biases of the critic about the subject matter, the type of film subgenre, or the personnel involved—especially the director and actors. Irony, parody, and sarcasm can be compelling—especially when a film is being panned; but again, if the use of these tonal elements is excessive or unfair and the evidence provided is unconvincing, employing such a tone can backfire. Pretentious words and lengthy, torturously structured sentences are also inappropriate. Your main objective is to communicate your opinion and to justify it clearly and convincingly: using jargon, obfuscating ideas, and selecting sophisticated, multisyllabic words to impress your readers will not accomplish your original intended goals.

The review below is riddled with errors in tone and function. It gives away key information about the climax—especially for the genre, a romance/thriller. Its language is excessive in panning the film: the critic does not like it—which is the reviewer's prerogative—but gets too personal and sarcastic condemning its principal players. Even the title borders on the distasteful. The words and phrases that are capitalized below need to be revised. If they were to be, the review—although negatively critical—would, at least, be fairer and more credible. Ironically, the film—*The Bodyguard*—was a sizable hit the year of its release (1992) and in the video rental market thereafter.

Kevin Does Whitney . . . Or Does He?

The CONTROVERSIAL CASTING MAKES FOR A BOX OFFICE DUD: IS AMERICA REALLY READY TO SEE TACITURN, ALL-AMERICAN, WASP, LEADING MAN KEVIN COSTNER AND SULTRY, AFRICAN AMERICAN, MEGASTAR SONGSTRESS

WHITNEY HOUSTON AS CELLULOID LOVERS? I THINK NOT. He, as the ex-Secret Service man hired to be bodyguard/security chief, and she, as the headstrong, fabulously successful singer/ actress? Hired gun falls for his boss; glamorous client desires her protector? NAH!

Oddly enough, race plays almost no part in this movie. The fact that Houston's character, Rachel Marron, is black is incidental. Race is never discussed in *The Bodyguard*: no nuances are made about it; acceptance by family or friends because of it isn't at stake; and the failure of their relationship is not at all affected by it. Rather, the issue is a matter of lifestyle: excessive wealth versus modest income, celebrity versus privacy, one set of professional contacts versus another. It would be wonderful if our country were as colorblind as this film makes it out to be. Certainly, the advance publicity for the film centered around its shock value because of our undercurrent of racial division and intolerance. Echoes of Spike Lee's *Jungle Fever*.

Perhaps the movie fails because of the wooden performances of its principals. There are no sparks between them. IT IS DOUBT-FUL THAT THE SCANDAL RAGS HAVE MUCH DIRT TO WAL-LOW IN ON THIS FLICK. The love affair is unbelievable on the screen because the acting and dialogue make it so implausible. WHITNEY, BABE, STICK TO SINGING . . . PLEASE! AND, KEVIN, GUY, SHOULDN'T WE BE MORE CAREFUL CHOOSING SCRIPTS?

As for the plot, it improves after one is able—WITH GREAT EFFORT—to ignore the miscasting (which, incidentally, extends to some of the supporting characters as well). Someone does want very much to kill Rachel. Frank Farmer (Costner) comes on board to rad-ically improve security at her opulent Beverly Hillsish estate and hire competent additional staff. She resents his quiet, take-charge manner over her domain until the attempts on her life become more obvious and daring. Her burgeoning fear quickly engenders a CURI-OUS (TO THIS VIEWER, AT LEAST) passion for him. After their token date she seduces him IN PERHAPS THE MOST TEPID CIN-EMATIC BEDROOM SCENE WITNESSED IN MANY YEARS. But the morning after, he has an ethical problem: if he gets involved with the person he is hired to protect, his effectiveness as a human shield is greatly compromised. It just isn't professional—SO MUCH FOR THE LIBIDO.

In time, there are three obvious suspects—Rachel's sister Niki; her former head of security, now reduced to strong-arm gorilla Tony; and a fanatic fan, who shall go unnamed. However, DISCLOSURE

OF THE REAL KILLER, PORTMAN, ALSO AN EX-SECRET SERVICE OPERATIVE, IS INTENDED TO BE A SURPRISE.

The climactic finale, ALTHOUGH ULTIMATELY PREDICTABLE, has some nice touches. Frank divines that another attempt will take place, this time at the Oscar awards where Rachel is a presenter as well as a multi-categoried nominee. HE FEARS IT MAY BE SUCCESSFUL. The action sequences do work and also VINDICATE FARMER FROM his innermost guilt: HAVING NOT BEEN THERE TO PROTECT RONALD REAGAN WHEN THE PRESIDENT WAS SHOT. (IT SHOULD BE MENTIONED THAT HE REALLY WAS NOT DERELICT IN HIS DUTIES; HE WAS ATTENDING HIS MOTHER'S FUNERAL AT THE TIME OF THE ASSASSINATION ATTEMPT.)

The Bodyguard, produced and written by Lawrence Kasdan and directed by Mick Jackson, DOES NOTHING FOR THE CAREERS OF ITS TWO STARS. Whitney Houston's acting debut vehicle is unfortunate—SHE CAN SING AND CHARM BUT SHE SURE CAN'T ACT! And Kevin Costner—a master in the use of silence, facial expressions, and body gestures to convey frustration, tension, and fear—IS BORED AND BORING. OBVIOUSLY, KEVIN HAS RIPPED US ALL OFF BY MERELY GOING THROUGH THE MOTIONS WHILE COLLECTING, NO DOUBT, A SUBSTANTIAL PAYCHECK.

A fairer review for the film that avoids sarcasm and *ad hominem* (personal) attacks is the rewritten version below. Note that it also doesn't give away the person attempting to kill the singer. In a "whodunit" or "who is trying to do it," the reviewer does not disclose all.

Kevin and Whitney . . . Graded "D" in Chemistry

The casting of the film from the outset is its most obvious flaw. Kevin Costner's taciturn, stoic rendering of an ex–Secret Service man hired to be the personal bodyguard/security chief plays opposite Whitney Houston's crafting of a headstrong, fabulously successful singer/actress. Hired guy falls for his boss; glamorous client desires her protector—no, the chemistry just isn't there.

Oddly enough, race plays almost no part in this movie. The fact that Houston's character, Rachel Marron, is black is incidental. Race is never discussed in *The Bodyguard*: no nuances are made about it; acceptance by family or friends because of it isn't at stake; and the failure of their relationship is not at all affected by it. Rather, the issue is a matter of lifestyle: excessive wealth versus modest income, celebrity versus privacy, one set of professional contacts versus another. It would be wonderful if our country were as color blind as this film makes it out to be. Certainly, the advance publicity for the film appealed to the shock value because of our undercurrent of racial division and intolerance. Echoes of Spike Lee's *Jungle Fever*.

The movie fails because of the wooden performances of its principals. There are no sparks between them. The love affair is unbelievable on the screen because the acting and dialogue make it so implausible. Ms. Houston shows little of the fire and talent so evident as a singer/entertainer in her attempt at acting. Mr. Costner should not have chosen this script as a vehicle for his onscreen abilities.

As for the plot, it improves after one is able to ignore the miscasting (which, incidentally, extends to some of the supporting characters as well). Someone does want very much to kill Rachel. Frank Farmer (Costner) comes on board to radically improve security at her opulent Beverly Hillsish estate and hire competent additional staff. She resents his quiet, take-charge manner over her domain until the attempts on her life become more obvious and daring. Her burgeoning fear quickly engenders a passion for him. After their token date she seduces him unconvincingly in a rather tepid bedroom scene. But the morning after, he has an ethical problem: if he gets involved with the person he is hired to protect, his effectiveness as a human shield is greatly compromised. It just isn't professional.

In time, there are three obvious suspects: Niki, Rachel's sister; Tony, her former head of security, now reduced to strong-arm gorilla; and a fanatic fan, who shall go unnamed. However, the possibility is also raised that someone other than the trio may be the real killer.

The climactic finale has some nice touches. It takes place amidst the glamour and glitz of the Oscar awards where Rachel is a presenter as well as a multi-categoried nominee. Frank expects another attempt on Rachel's life. The action sequences that result do work as Farmer deals with his innermost guilt and the fear it spawns.

The Bodyguard is produced and written by Lawrence Kasdan and directed by Mick Jackson. Whitney Houston's acting debut is marred by her pallid performance in this mystery/thriller. And Kevin Costner—a master in the use of silence, facial expressions, and body gestures to convey frustration, tension, and fear—just goes through the motions in his role.

Although the review pans the film, the sarcasm and *ad hominem* attacks are eliminated, making the criticism fairer and more plausible. Following, in contrast, is a review of *Honeymoon in Vegas* (1992). Note that the tone is breezy as it pokes fun at some aspects of the film. After reading the piece, you should be left with the impression that the reviewer liked the film and took liberties with it fairly, even affectionately.

Vegas, Kauai, and Elvis Too!

Elvis lives! (or at least do dozens of Presley impersonators conventioning in Las Vegas). Elvis' music and the aforementioned wannabes are part of the strong supporting cameo cast making this Andrew Bergman film one of the most entertaining—and hilarious—comedies of 1992. The plot is improbable. But who says that a funny flick such as *Honeymoon in Vegas* has to mirror life?

Predictably, there is a love triangle that is the source of the conflict and subsequent action for most of the movie. Jack Singer (Nicholas Cage) plays a New York private detective not averse to placing a bet or two and very much in love with Betsy (Sarah Jessica Parker), a pert elementary school teacher. The problem is that he is petrified of marriage while her patience and biological clock are running out. His phobia stems from the deathbed wish of his mother (the indomitable Anne Bancroft) that he never marry. Betsy finally gives Jack an ultimatum for marriage and suggests that he sleep on it (but alone). He responds by impetuously flying her off to Las Vegas for immediate matrimony.

The couple are soon ensconced in the over-opulent, neo-nouveau-riche-Casablanca-by-way-of-Hollywood Ali Baba Honeymoon Suite at Bally's Resort. There may not be forty thieves around, but one is more than sufficient in the person of megabuck gambler/gangster Tommy Corman (versatile James Caan). He intends to steal not only Jack's money but also fiancée Betsy—who uncannily resembles the hoodlum's dead wife Donna. Corman inveigles Singer into a "harmless" (and rigged) poker game just hours before the intended nuptials. Besides a huge sum of money that Singer does not have, Corman ends up "winning" Betsy for the weekend: not in glitzy Las Vegas, Nevada, however, but in Edenesque Kauai, the Hawaiian Islands.

The plot now approaches imaginative farce as Jack tries to dissuade her from leaving with the lecherous lord of larcenous legerdemain. He misses catching up to Corman's white stretch limousine by ten yards and dejectedly returns to New York. Then impulse rules, and he flies off to Kauai to win back his honey. But the marriage-minded mobster easily thwarts him.

Eventually, it is back to Vegas for the climax. The denouement is pure Hollywood happy ending with a number of ingenious twists, the cleverest of which is Jack's joining the Flying Elvis Presley Skydivers (Utah chapter)as a desperate move to reach Vegas. Ultimately, he plunges by parachute with them to the entrance of Bally's: the fitting finale not only to the film but also to the Elvis festival of lookalikes. In so risking his life for his love, Jack predictably gets his lady's hand in marriage with the skydivers witnessing the ceremony.

The movie has a number of brilliant comical touches. One has Peter Boyle as Chief Orman, a long-haired New Ager singing the "Bali Hai" aria from *South Pacific*. Another has a host of Elvis impersonators providing the background music for the initial meeting of Corman and Betsy in the nightclub—the fact that one Elvis is Filipino, another black, and the third a six-year-old Chicano, just adds to the incongruity.

Mention must be made of Nicholas Cage's outstanding performance. His work in *Moonstruck, Peggy Sue Got Married*, and *Raising Arizona* provides an inkling, but *Honeymoon in Vegas* should confirm his standing as one of our best comedic actors on the screen today.

The tone in the review above is consistent with the subject matter, namely a quick-paced comedy. Note that the title of the review not only gives an indication of some of the movie's features but hints at the reviewer's tone as well. Although the climax and ending are mentioned, they are necessary to support the contention that this is an "entertaining," "improbable," and "imaginative farce." Obviously, in reviews of farces, there is a bit more leeway about giving away the climax and the ending.

Word Choice and Sentence Mix

In all forms of writing, the words chosen and the sentence flow determine effective writing: it is not only what you say (substance) but how you say it (style). To put together well-written sentences, paragraphs, and papers means being able to

- Recognize the differences between the denotative and connotative meanings of words,
- Select the most specific (concrete) word to convey your intended meaning,
- Avoid using clichéd phrases at all times, and
- Vary both sentence length and structure to avoid repetitiveness in sentence patterns.

Denotation and Connotation

The *denotative* meaning of a word is its dictionary and more inclusive definition. Thus, such words as *actor, player, trouper, thespian, performer, impersonator, mime,* and *mummer* are all synonyms in their denotative meanings. However, *connotative* meanings refer to the associations that words carry and are actually more restrictive. Each of the denotative synonyms for *actor* listed above have entirely different associations from each other and thus different connotations (connotative meanings):

- Player: one who acts in a movie or play;
- Trouper: one who is a member of a cast of a play or movie;
- Thespian: now a somewhat pretentious word for a stage actor;
- Performer: one who takes part in any type of public performance be it on stage, in a nightclub, on film; he/she can be an actor, dancer, singer, comic, impressionist, musician, or professional athlete for that matter;
- Impersonator: one who imitates someone else—another performer, politician, or celebrity—often for comical effect;
- Mime: one who silently imitates certain human acts, gestures, and expressions; and
- Mummer: now one of a group of people in similar elaborate costumes who march in parades often playing instruments.

Misuse of words connotatively can be quite embarrassing and unintentionally funny. Imagine someone saying in praise of the following actress' comedic talents, "My favorite mummer of the last decade or so is Goldie Hawn: she really makes me laugh." Or, imagine someone marveling at the classical acting skills of Sir Laurence Olivier: "His abilities as a Shakespearean impersonator were unrivaled in his prime."

It is important to use synonyms to make your writing more interesting to the reader. However, the connotative accuracy of your choices is equally vital. Therefore, when you consult a thesaurus to find a synonym or that "perfect" word for your intended meaning, make sure that you select a word that you are familiar with in your reading and have used before in your writing.

Specific Wording

Overdependence on generalized terms makes for inferior writing. In everything you write—not only film critiques—you want to be as concrete as possible. Concreteness usually leads to accuracy, whereas overgeneralization not only makes for dull reading but may also contribute to misinterpretation. In the following introductory paragraph of a critique, those words that are too broad and need to be more specific are boldfaced; the title of the film is italicized.

> *Gone with the Wind,* **a memorable endeavor made some decades ago about Americans at war, was highly acclaimed. Derived from the bestseller, it contains all that the moviegoer can desire. It has been faithfully produced from its literary source and has had top notch direction, screenwriting, acting, cinematography, and such. No wonder it has been such a cinematic favorite!**

As can be clearly seen, this opening paragraph is too vague and broad. The only concrete features are the production's name; we are not even told that it is a motion picture. The following paragraph, however, converts every vague statement above into one far more specific. Now it is the concrete words and phrases that are in boldface.

> The **David O. Selznick production** of *Gone with the Wind* **(1939)**—that **sprawling epic** of the **American Civil War**—to **many moviegoers, is still the greatest American movie of all time.** No wonder! **Based on the Margaret Mitchell runaway bestseller of the same name, it contains all of the elements of the historical romance novel—a great love story, opulent settings, events of historic importance, the gamut of human emotions, set pieces typical of the era —here translated so well into cinema. Its faithfulness to the book's plot, characters, setting, tone, and themes, has not gone unnoticed and unrewarded. It has amassed no less than nine Academy Awards. The winners include: Victor Fleming for direction, Sidney Howard for the screenplay, Vivien Leigh (as Scarlet O'Hara) for best actress and Hattie McDaniel (as Mammy) for best supporting actress, Ernest Haller and Ray Rennahan for cinematography, Hal C. Kern and James E. Newcom for editing, William Cameron Menzies for production design and, finally, Lyle Wheeler for art direction.**

Cliché Avoidance

All good writing avoids clichés, trite expressions, and unoriginal figurative language. This is especially so if the paper is trying to adopt a serious, more formal tone. Film clichés include, among others:

a cast of thousands	silver screen
movie mogul	boffo
blockbuster	a film the whole family will enjoy
sex symbol	heartwarming saga
action-packed	whodunit
movie (film) siren	film (screen) starlet
girl (boy) crazy	riding off into the sunset
Tinseltown	hooker with the heart of gold
blazing six-guns	oatburner
shocker	on the edge of your seat
chills and thrills	box office hit
two thumbs up	boulevard of broken dreams
rogue cop	the lovely [person's name]
sidekick	meanwhile, back at the ranch
bloodlust	blood curdling scream
damsel in distress	hot number
bobbysoxers	the "heat"

And, these are just the "tip of the iceberg" (yet another cliché). Just to show how prevalent they are, the following is a partial list of clichés that have become film titles; occasionally, a film title itself emerges into a cliché:

a dog's life	not a pretty picture
a face in the crowd	odd man out
against all odds	one from the heart
all that jazz	on the town
battle of the sexes	over the edge
born yesterday	rebel without a cause
catch-22	shadow of a doubt
do the right thing	shoot the moon
duck soup	take the money and run
forbidden fruit	the best years of our lives
going places	the right stuff
it's a wonderful life	the way of the world
kiss of death	till the end of time
life at the top	you can't take it with you

Variance of Sentence Length and Structure

A well-written paragraph will contain sentences of varied lengths and structures. Sentences that follow the same predictable pattern of structure and/or length eventually make the piece boring. Sentences that are long with complicated structures, if continued, will make the paragraph ponderous and unwieldy. Sentences that are short which follow the same sentence pattern make the paragraph choppy and juvenile.

Below are three paragraphs that say the same thing substantively. Each, however, varies greatly from the others in sentence length and structure.

> 1
>
> Having two of Hollywood's most gifted and versatile actors, Robin Williams and Robert De Niro, appearing together in the same movie was a treat for theater audiences in 1990 and surely both a pleasure and challenge for director Penny Marshall. In her adaptation of Oliver Sacks' novel *Awakenings*, Marshall reverses our expectations in having Robin Williams play Dr. Malcolm Sayer, a painfully shy psychiatrist and Robert De Niro portray Leonard Lowe, a catatonic patient of long standing in a psychiatric hospital. In Leonard's emergence from his catatonia—a condition caused after contraction of encephalitis during an epidemic in his childhood—he surprises everyone and delights Dr. Sayer especially with the nimbleness of his mind and his thirst for sensory experience and knowledge about the world.

This first paragraph, with its lengthy sentences (at least forty words each) and complicated structures makes for laborious reading.

> 2
>
> Robin Williams and Robert De Niro appear in a movie together for the first time. Penny Marshall as director made the movie in 1990. She adapted Oliver Sacks' novel *Awakenings* into a film of the same name. Williams plays Dr. Malcolm Sayer, a painfully shy psychiatrist. De Niro portrays Leonard Lowe, a catatonic patient at a psychiatric hospital. Leonard contracted encephalitis during an epidemic in his childhood. He surprises everyone and delights Dr. Sayer with the nimbleness of his mind. Lowe has a thirst for sensory experience and knowledge about the world.

The second paragraph becomes boring because of the uniformity of its declarative statements and structural predictability (subject-verb-object pattern).

> 3
>
> In 1990, theater audiences could delight in watching two of Hollywood's most gifted and versatile actors Robin Williams and Robert De

Niro appearing together in the same movie. No doubt, it was both a pleasure and challenge for director Penny Marshall. Adapting Oliver Sacks' semiautobiographic novel *Awakenings* for the screen, she reversed our expectations. She had Williams play Dr. Malcolm Sayer, a painfully shy psychiatrist, while Robert De Niro portrayed Leonard Lowe, a catatonic patient. Leonard was a resident of long standing at Bainbridge, a psychiatric hospital. Making some incisive observations about his patients' conditions, Dr. Sayer devised different therapeutic procedures for them. When Leonard suddenly emerged from his catatonia—contracted from encephalitis during childhood—everyone was stunned. Dr. Sayer was especially delighted with the nimbleness of Lowe's mind. Leonard had a reawakened thirst for sensory experience and a burgeoning desire for knowledge about the world he had suddenly rejoined.

The third paragraph is similar in essence to the other two in what it says but does so in a manner that is more readable. Notice that its sentences vary both in length and structure.

Main Components

A critical work on the cinema—be it short review or lengthy research paper—will be organized to contain the standard components of the essay. To capture the reader and introduce the primary emphasis or direction of the paper is the function of the *lead-in sentence(s)*. The lead-in is so closely connected to the *introduction* of the piece that we will look at them together. The *topic sentence* is the focal point of any paragraph. Since it is the keystone sentence of the paragraph, all other sentences either derive from, lead to, or elaborate upon the topic sentence. The topic sentence is common to all paragraphs of the essay and, therefore, will be discussed in this subsection. Eventually, either in the introductory paragraph or soon thereafter, the *main point* or *thesis* of the entire essay is made. Once the thesis is stated, the *subordinate points* or *minor inferences* about it are presented to support and strengthen its assertion(s). Just as your paper needs lead-ins and the introduction at the outset, it also requires a *conclusion (concluding remarks)* at its completion. These can take many forms, just as with introductory statements.

The Lead-In/Introduction

Both writing and film share yet another element in common: the use of lead-ins and introductions. Whether it is an essay, short story, novel, or play, the reader/audience must be "hooked" early. In a movie, during the first ten to fifteen minutes, we should be getting engrossed; if not, the director and scriptwriter are in danger of losing us. In a critical essay, there is no excuse for a factual but dull opening paragraph. Even if the writer feels the need to serve the boilerplate and then get it quickly out of the way, somewhere in that initial paragraph should be a statement that is enticing, challenging, fascinating, disturbing, entertaining, or funny and builds a bridge to the main concern of the essay. There is no set format to follow, only common objectives. In each sample paragraph or two below, the lead-in both captures the reader's interest and moves arterially toward the heart of the paper.

The first sample of a lead-in is an excerpt of the review by *New York Times* critic Bosley Crowther of the French-Brazilian film, *Black Orpheus*.

> All tangled up in the madness of a Rio de Janeiro carnival, full of intoxicating samba music, frenzied dancing and violent costumes, the Frenchman Marcel Camus presents us a melancholy tale in his color film, "Black Orpheus" ("Orfeu Negro") . . . .

Black Orpheus (1959) Exterior shot of costumed crowds in the midst of Rio de Janeiro's Carnival.

Crowther captures the reader's interest in this short paragraph by juxtaposing the frantic gaiety of Rio during carnival—with all its music, colors, and action—with a melancholy plot. Nevertheless, he also includes the important boilerplate of the movie's title and the director's name and nationality.

The next review's lead-in was written by Roger Greenspun on *American Graffiti*, the little 1973 film about teenagers that launched the careers of so many.

> At dusk the cars begin to congregate. The drivers, kids in their teens, meet and greet and happily insult one another. A few couples, going steady, may pair off. There is a high school dance, but there is also the lure of the main street to cruise up and down, exchanging pleasantries, looking for dates, for excitement, an impromptu race, even a little danger. Every radio in town is turned in to Wolfman Jack with his line of eerie patter and all the latest hits—"Sixteen Candles," "The Book of Love" . . . It is early in the fall of 1962, somewhere in northern California.
>
> Two of the boys, Curt Henderson [Richard Dreyfuss] and Steve Bolander [Ron Howard], headed east to college, are uneasy at the prospect. John Milner [Paul Le Mat], champion drag racer, is 22—old enough to know he's headed nowhere, except up to the neon-lighted circle of Mel's Drive-In and perhaps the stillness of the automobile graveyard at the edge of town. Those are roughly the perimeters of George Lucas's "American Graffiti," which examines that much of America as it lives for about 12 hours, from an evening to the following morning.

Greenspun's review goes to pains to establish the setting using the present tense for immediacy. He creates the ambience as the film unfolds describing typical activities and music in his first paragraph. The last sentence of the paragraph establishes the specific time and place. Three of the characters and the director are introduced in the next paragraph as is the main concern of the film.

Critic A. H. Weiler's review of director Sidney Lumet's courtroom—or, more correctly, jury room—film *Twelve Angry Men* (1957) uses yet a different type of lead-in:

> Although cameras have been focused on jurors before, it is difficult to recall a more incisely revealing record of the stuff of which "peers" can be made than is presented in "12 Angry Men."
>
> For Reginald Rose's excellent film elaboration of his fine television play of 1954 . . . is a penetrating, sensitive and sometimes shocking dissection of the hearts and minds of men who obviously are something less than gods. It makes for taut, absorbing and compelling drama that reaches far beyond the close confines of its jury room setting.

Besides establishing the setting and mentioning the subgenre of motion picture, Weiler's introduction also makes such subjective remarks as "incisively revealing" and "excellent film elaboration," which introduce early some judgments of the movie. Also identified is the faithful approach taken in the adaptation of the Reginald Rose television play.

The Topic Sentence

The topic sentence can be found anyplace in a paragraph. In the subsequent paragraphs, the topic sentence is in bold print. Note that the topic sentence although found in a different position in each paragraph has all the other sentences of the paragraph relating to it.

The first example makes reference to Otto Preminger's *Carmen Jones*. The topic sentence clearly appears at the outset of the paragraph in bold print. The tone is straightforward and factual.

> **Once again, director Otto Preminger assembled a virtually all-black cast to bring an opera to life on the screen.** Earlier, the libretto for Bizet's *Carmen* had been re-written and updated with new English lyrics for the arias by Oscar Hammerstein II to become the 1943 opera *Carmen Jones*. Together with Preminger, Hammerstein made it into a highly acclaimed film event in 1954. In 1959, the director—this time with producer Samuel Goldwyn—brought the George Gershwin–Ira Gershwin–DuBose Heyward beloved folk opera *Porgy and Bess* to movie theaters around the nation. The film headlined Sidney Poitier as Porgy and Sammy Davis, Jr., as Sportin' Life; it also starred four notable holdovers from the earlier opera: Dorothy Dandridge (Bess), Diahann Carroll (Clara), Pearl Bailey (Maria), and Brock Peters (Crown).

The second example looks at *Body Heat*. Not only does the topic sentence appear towards the end of the paragraph, but the piece also whimsically adopts and maintains an extended metaphor throughout.

> Begin with a healthy dollop of sweltering South Florida in the summer. Mix beach surf and venetian blinds with multiple quantities of iced tea. Then garnish with palm fronds and the play of their shadows to establish the setting and intensify the mood. Take this mood and add a sultry femme fatale (Kathleen Turner) along with an incompetent lawyer (William Hurt) who conspires to murder her husband (Richard Crenna). Shake vigorously. **You now have *Body Heat*: Lawrence Kasdan's film noir cocktail, Florida style.** His 1981 directorial debut mixes the semitropical drink rather well in this two-hour version of his own screenplay.

The Main Point (Thesis)

Some critical essays on film follow the standard thesis statement pattern of the thesis being immediately followed by the minor inferences. All occur within the same sentence or the minor inferences come quickly on the thesis' heels in the next sentence. In many comparative papers and research studies, however, the thesis may not be introduced so obviously in this manner and follow such an orthodox pattern. In the movie review, with so much important boilerplate to be presented, the thesis could be considered as that personal insight or those few points that the writer wants to develop. Often the title—if it is not identical to the motion picture—will allude to the thesis.

In the review of *Glengarry Glen Ross* (appearing earlier in this chapter), the thesis is that the real estate agency is a glimpse of contemporary hell, and that the agents and their managers are both the sufferers and the tormentors in it. The title of the review, "Hell, Version of: America in the Nineties," points to that theme.

Each of the four paragraphs below contains a thesis statement about John Hancock's wonderful motion picture *Bang the Drum Slowly*. All four examples use the orthodox thesis statement pattern with three of the versions having the minor inferences incorporated into the same sentence. However, Example 2 has the minor inferences following immediately in the next sentence. The thesis itself is capitalized while the minor inferences are be in bold print.

1
John Hancock's *BANG THE DRUM SLOWLY* (1974) IS ABOUT FRIENDSHIP AND BASEBALL AND MORTALITY all looked at with **humor, poignance, and understatement.**

2
Taken from the Mark Harris book of the same name, *BANG THE DRUM SLOWLY* IS DIRECTOR JOHN HANCOCK'S 1974 FILM THAT REVOLVES AROUND BASEBALL, FRIENDSHIP, AND MORTALITY. He does so with **humor, poignance and understatement**.

3
BANG THE DRUM SLOWLY, a small 1974 film by John Hancock, is **funny, poignant, and understated** as it LOOKS AT FRIENDSHIP AND MORTALITY IN THE WORLD OF PROFESSIONAL BASEBALL.

4
The motifs of FRIENDSHIP AND MORTALITY DOMINATE JOHN HANCOCK'S *BANG THE DRUM SLOWLY*, the **understated,**

poignant, yet funny little film set in the world of Major League baseball.

The following segment below, on the same movie, places the thesis statement in one sentence with the minor inferences in the next. Both are placed within the larger context of an introductory paragraph.

When we think of Major League baseball today, not only superbly gifted athletes come to mind but also a world ruled by multi-year, multi-million dollar contracts, product endorsements, and increasing alienation from the fans. Twenty-five years ago, professional baseball players focused more on the team and on the game, and on their contributions to one and their performances in the other, respectively. Released in 1974, *Bang the Drum Slowly* is a small film by John Hancock which looks at the game from that earlier perspective. THE FILM, ESSENTIALLY, DELVES INTO THE MOTIFS OF FRIENDSHIP AND MORTALITY in a baseball setting. It does so in **a manner that is both funny yet poignant, and always understated**.

The first three sentences are used as lead-ins to the central idea, namely, the film's focusing upon the motifs of friendship and mortality in the world of professional baseball. However, the minor inferences concentrate on the tones of understatement, humor, and poignancy in developing those motifs.

Subordinate Points and Examples

Subordinate points (minor inferences) elaborate on the thesis. They do so by using scenes or incidents of the film as *concrete examples* of these points. Since the examples derive from or refer back to the subordinate points, they should be seen as clearly connected to the thesis statement.

The following paragraphs build upon the introductory paragraph previously presented for *Bang the Drum Slowly* and expand the subordinate points of the thesis. Through anecdote and example, they concern themselves with the humor, poignancy, and understatement that run throughout the film and characterize it.

The friendship between Henry Wiggens (Michael Moriarty) and Bruce Pearson (Robert De Niro) seems quite unlikely, incongruous, even comical at first. Henry is the urbane, ace pitcher from New York City. Bruce, on the other hand, comes from a small town in Georgia and perennially has to fight for a place on the roster as a catcher. Physically, they are like Mutt and Jeff: Henry, is tall and rangy; Bruce is average in height and slight in build. Yet there is a bond between

Bang the Drum Slowly (1974) Michael Moriarty and Robert De Niro at their lockers in a poignant film of friendship and mortality in a big league baseball setting.

them and it is introduced during the opening credits as we see them jogging around the perimeter of the ballfield during a team practice. This bond strengthens as the movie progresses.

The film opens on a note of pathos which is curiously restrained. In fact, throughout the film, humor, poignancy, and understatement are interwoven like a three-stranded rope. Henry and Bruce are leaving the Mayo Clinic in Rochester, Minnesota. Bruce has been diagnosed with Hodgkin's disease, a form of cancer. They are driving on a road silently flanked by fields flecked with snow. Bruce is impassive while Henry glances at him occasionally. Henry's voice-over declares:

"Actually, he got over it fairly quick. You might not think so, but it's true. You're drivin' along with a man who's been told he's dyin', yet everything keeps goin' along. I mean, it's been hard enough roomin' with him when he's well. He chews this disgustin' tobacco; he's pissed in the sink; and, as a catcher, he's a million dollars worth of promise with two cents on delivery. Most people didn't even know he was with the club. He was almost too dumb to play a joke on and now he'd been played the biggest joke of all."

They arrive at Bruce's parents and their son declares he's fine. Later, though, while fishing with Henry, he confesses that he is confounded at how earlier as a kid he almost drowned, then avoided death in Vietnam, and narrowly missed getting killed by a truck. But now, without taking risks, he's got a fatal disease. He laconically sums up his condition: "I been handed a shit deal, boy. I'm doomed." He mispronounces "doomed" as if it has two syllables. That night, he is seen burning his clippings in a bonfire.

The Conclusion

There are many approaches for writing a convincing concluding paragraph or section. Too often, students restate the thesis, which makes for a humdrum and repetitious ending since so much of the paper already has been devoted to stating then justifying or proving the thesis and its minor inferences. Actually, the options one has for writing a conclusion are as varied as those of the introduction, especially when writing about film.

A series of excerpts from some professional reviews best illustrate the different ways one can handle an ending. Note, as you read the reviews, how often there is a connection between the opening remarks and the concluding statements. This is not at all repetition but, rather, coming full circle.

Bosley Crowther, in his review, decidedly did not like Jean-Luc Godard's *Breathless* (1980). His initial paragraphs castigate the film and his final opinions reaffirm many of his earlier views.

> As sordid as is the French film, "Breathless," . . . —and sordid is really a mild word for the pile-up of gross indecencies—it is withal a fascinating communication of the savage ways and moods of some of the rootless young people of Europe (and America) today.
>
> Made by Jean-Luc Godard, one of the newest and youngest of the "new wave" directors who seem to have taken over the cinema in France, it goes at its unattractive subject in an eccentric photographic style that sharply conveys the nervous tempo and the emotional erraticalness of the story it tells. And through the American actress, Jean Seberg, and a hypnotically ugly new young man by the name of Jean-Paul Belmondo, it projects two downright fearsome characters.

Now for Crowther's conclusion:

> All of this, and its sickening implications, M. Godard has got into this film, which progresses in a style of disconnected cutting that might be described as "pictorial cacophony." A musical score of erratic tonal qualities emphasizes the eccentric moods. And in M. Belmondo we see an actor who is the most effective cigarette-mouther and thumb-to-lip rubber since time began.
>
> Say this, in sum, for "Breathless": it is certainly no cliché, in any area or sense of the word. It is more a chunk of raw drama, graphically and artfully torn with appropriately ragged edges out of the tough underbelly of modern metropolitan life.

Crowther takes a different approach structurally in his review of Czechoslovakian director Jiri Menzel's *Closely Watched Trains* (1966). For most of his piece, the critic talks about the quality of the burgeoning number of Czech film directors, the plot and themes of the World War II era film, and compares it somewhat to Jan Kadar's *The Shop on Main Street*. He uses his concluding section, however, for commenting on the personnel—both in front of and behind the cameras—who made this film.

> In Vaclav Neckar he has a most laconic, amusing and touching lad to play his diffident hero, and in Josef Somr he has an actor of lovely skills and very subtle suggestions to play the train dispatcher. Vladimir Valenta as the stationmaster, Vlastimil Brodsky as a Nazi official and Jitka Bendova as the passing conductor are also excellent in a splendid cast.
>
> Jiri Sust's economical yet perfectly applied musical score adds a great deal to the expression of this picture. It has good English subtitles.

Harry Pearson, Jr., ends his *Films in Review* column on Robert Zemeckis' *Forrest Gump* (1994) by asking a host of rhetorical questions, thus illustrating yet another approach for concluding critical writing on film. Pearson also makes reference to a drifting feather—and its inherent symbolism—that floats through the air during the opening credits and initial sequence of the film.

> Seeing this movie is like having your life pass before your eyes. Weren't we, like Forrest, unaware of the consequences of the assassinations of our leaders during the sixties, of the consequences of the flower power "liberation" and the Vietnam War? We, like the feather, drifted through these events without realizing their significance and/or being able to understand the impact they might have upon us and the life of the nation. Combine these flashbacks with most of the best tunes of the era and a genuinely felt sense of the time and

place . . . in subdued color and crystalline widescreen photography and you get to feeling a kind of melancholia, a regret for all the things that you have, unwittingly, let pass you by. A regret for the roads not taken. And in Gump's case, not even recognized.

What follows is a critique of *Of Mice and Men,* written under the assumption that the reader is familiar with the film, which was released in 1992. As a result, the movie's ending and its significance are discussed. A number of aspects of this critique should be noted:

- The function of the title,
- The lead-in sentences,
- The thesis statement at the end of the introductory paragraph,
- The plot summary to illustrate the motifs which are the minor inferences (subordinate points) of the thesis statement,
- The integration of credits (boilerplate) and evaluative remarks, and
- The concluding comment referring back to the last thematic motif.

Love, Loyalty, and Death on the Bum

The sound of hound dogs frantically chasing human quarry frames this latest film adaptation of John Steinbeck's classic novel *Of Mice and Men*. Shot in Central California's Santa Ynez Valley—not too far away from Salinas, "Steinbeck Country"—the film successfully creates the verisimilitude of America suffering under the relentless grip of the Great Depression. So many of Steinbeck's other works share the same setting; yet this story is particularly poignant because it focuses on a rather unique friendship between its two male characters, George and Lenny. For quite some time, both have been riding the rails in search of work: be it swinging a pick, harvesting a crop, or loading a wagon. But this is more than a slice of life tale of two migrant workers on the bum during hard times. Rather, *Of Mice and Men* is a sensitively executed film encompassing all the motifs of the novel: loyalty, love, violence, desperation and loneliness.

Lenny is a simpleton—big-hearted and extremely strong-bodied—whose naivete and miscomprehension of his enormous physical power often get him in trouble. It is always the smaller, wiry-bodied and sharp-witted George who has to extricate him from problems. The loyalty and love that Lenny has for George is obvious, but it is George's return of these emotions—no matter how grudgingly shown—that makes their relationship truly remarkable.

Escaping a lynch-mob because of Lenny's unintentional molesting of a young woman, the two hop a freight to Salinas, California, and get work on a large ranch nearby. For a while, things go smoothly. George becomes less distrusting and more personable, and at least Lenny's prodigious strength earns him respect. But his size also earns him the enmity of Curley, the ranch owner's hotheaded son. That Curley also has a restless, openly seductive wife doesn't help matters. The villains—bully and temptress respectively—are clearly drawn, and the ensuing crisis is inevitable. Despite Curley and wife getting their just desserts—he a mangled hand and she a broken neck—it is George and Lenny who ultimately suffer. Their dream of stability and security in the form of a small spread of their own is crushed after Lenny's accidental killing of Curley's wife in the barn.

It is George's unwillingness to let Lenny suffer the terrors of a desperado—running away from those who would kill him without his fully fathoming why—that makes the conclusion. As a final act of love, George grants Lenny a permanent cessation of his fears: firing a bullet into the back of the head of the unsuspecting man.

The movie is a convincing vehicle for multitalented Gary Sinese as its director, producer, co-writer, and star (in the role of George). But it is the performance of John Malkovich as Lenny that is especially heart-rending. Obviously, Malkovich has done much research in order to understand the minds and mimic the motions of those who have childlike intellects residing in bodies of adults. Thus, the actor's gestures, rationalizations, and emotional outbursts while playing the role ring particularly true. Casey Siemaszko as Curley has measured well the demands of this important supporting role while Sherrilyn Fenn has the right blend of sultriness and wistfulness to be fully credible as his wife. However, it is Ray Walston who gives the most memorable rendering of the supporting cast. It is as Candy—the old, crippled ranch hand who insinuates himself into George and Lenny's dream and whose hard-earned savings can make it reality—that Walston embodies the desperate loneliness of those who live without family, possessions, and hope.

The title of the critique, "Love, Loyalty, and Death on the Bum," relates to three motifs that run through the film; thus, it serves a unifying function. Various permutations of love permeate the film: the fraternal love between George and Lenny, the possessive love of Curly for his wife, and the love that Lenny has for animals. The loyalty that George and Lenny have to each other is both admirable and touching. At the end, when death comes to Lenny, he is "on the run"; since he is no longer employed—having been forced to revert to his hobo status—he is also "on the bum" when killed.

The lead-in sentences of the introductory paragraph operate in various capacities. The first sentence captures the attention of the reader as it describes "hound dogs chasing human quarry." Then it segues into establishing the setting and expounding a bit about "Steinbeck Country." It also mentions the historical era when the Great Depression gripped most of America, a time that pervades most of John Steinbeck's literary works.

The next to last sentence of the paragraph serves as a bridge to it: "But this is more than a slice of life tale of two migrant workers on the bum during hard times." It connects the previously stated rest of the paragraph to the final sentence which serves as the thesis statement: "Rather, *Of Mice and Men* is a sensitively executed film encompassing all the motifs of the novel: loyalty, love, violence, desperation, and loneliness."

The third paragraph acts as a plot summary. The major events are sequentially but briefly presented. The motifs of love, loyalty, and violence are illustrated by events that occur. Another motif from the thesis statement, desperation, is demonstrated in the paragraph that follows as well as the initial paragraph of the critique.

The integration of credits with evaluative commentary comprises most of the final paragraph. The "multitalented" Gary Sinese and exceptional acting of John Malkovich are showcased here. Finally, the paragraph concludes with mention of the last motif, loneliness, as demonstrated by Ray Walston's portrayal of Candy, the "old, crippled ranch hand . . . [who] embodies the desperate loneliness of those who live without family, possessions, and hope."

Revision Techniques

Every rough draft has to be converted into a first draft and then proofread, edited, rewritten, honed, and polished before it can be submitted to a professor or a publisher. Such revision techniques can be broken down into two component areas: proofreading and self-editing. The differences between them are not so much in kind as they are in degree; of the two, however, self-editing is the far more time-consuming, disciplined endeavor.

Proofreading

Proofreading basically is a one-step process. In a way, it is the mirror image of brainstorming. In brainstorming, you write down a number of ideas and keywords about a topic before organizing them into a recognizable pattern or outline prior to creating the rough draft. With proofreading, after allowing a number of hours to elapse since the initial writing, you make a first pass at rereading the draft and correcting mistakes as you go along. In this procedure, typographical errors and others in spelling, capitalization, punctuation, and other mechanical miscues are discerned and rectified. If using a hard copy, errors are underlined or circled and corrected as close by as possible using a pen or pencil in a color other than black. If working on a computer or word processor, corrections are made on the spot leaving no evidence of the previous oversights.

An effective method of proofreading is to do so at the sentence level—not the paragraph level—to catch the maximum number of mechanical slips. Although you read each sentence from its first word to its last, you *start from the last sentence of the paper and work your way back to the first sentence.* This method is utilized so that continuity between sentences is broken, ensuring that each sentence is isolated from the rest. It is in trying to correct sentences for mechanical errors that the contexts of the other sentences actually get in the way. If you were to read for errors normally—that is, from the beginning of your essay through its conclusion—your eyes would occasionally trick you into perceiving something as correct (because you expect it to be) when, actually, it is wrong. Remember, proofing for mechanical errors is not the same as rereading for content flaws, which will be discussed in the next subsection on self-editing.

The sample paragraph below is the introduction for a review of John Cassavetes' unconventional film *Shadows,* released in 1961. The paragraph is rife with errors.

What does one make of a seemingly scriptless, plotless, directorless movie? Where the only sense of purpose must be provided by the self? Where the only cardinal principal is improvisation? This could be a receipt for disastrer, but in the hands of John Cassavetes—technically the director but perhaps a more correct term would be the facilitator and inspirer—somehow this formula for anarchy works. That the cast are virtually unknown is no reflection on there talent or potential. The production of *Shadows* at times does get out of hand, but for every instance of chaos is a moment of keen insight, of a subtle valid nuance that marks great acting.

Below we see what happens to the paragraph after a quick proof-reading. All the necessary corrections have been incorporated into the text below and are in bold print.

> What does one make of a seemingly scriptless, plotless, directorless movie? Where the only sense of purpose must be provided by the self? Where the only cardinal **principle** is improvisation? This could be a **recipe** for **disaster.** **Yet**, in the **loose-reined** hands of John Cassavetes—technically the director but perhaps a more **accurate** term would be facilitator **or supervisor**—somehow this formula for anarchy works. That the cast **members** are virtually unknown is no reflection on **their** talent or potential. The production of **Shadows, at times,** does get out of **hand. But** for every instance of **chaos, there** is a moment of keen **insight;** of **subtle,** valid nuance that marks great acting.

Self-Editing

Self-editing (rewriting) is a more time-consuming, deliberate procedure than proofwriting. Rewriting involves heavy revision: where not only are random errors discovered and made right, but numerous words are changed, various sentences are restructured, certain ideas are deleted or added, and the document as a whole is scrutinized for possible major reorganization. One brief read-through is not sufficient. Each rereading can have specific and limited objectives, among them

- Conformity of margins and spacing,
- Consistency of typographical fonts and print conventions,
- Consistency of theme and emphasis,
- Accuracy of details and statistics,
- Correction of errors in spelling, punctuation, grammar, capitalization, usage, subject verb agreement, and tense agreement,
- Completeness and balance of the whole,
- Conformity of style and tone,
- Lack of confusion between objective and subjective elements,
- Clarity at the sentence and paragraph levels, and
- Admixture of sentence lengths and structures.

With this in mind, we turn to a relatively short review of the 1992 thriller *Sneakers* by Phil Alden Robinson, who both directed and wrote the screenplay. We will first look at the initial draft of the review with its accompanying handwritten corrections and edits and then note the changes made in the rewritten final version.

From Hippies to Hackers

Sneakers is a motion picture that almost everyone enjoys: it appeals to all family members over 11 (or computer buffs even younger); although suspenseful, it is not too ~~heavy~~ *intense*; and, finally, for a refreshing change of pace, it is low on profanity and sexual situations. Sure, there are ~~good guys~~ *heroes* and ~~bad guys~~ *villains* of some complexity as well as some interesting themes that conflict, but as the credits scroll, movie patrons emerge into the lobby with smiles on their faces.

Director *and* screenwriter Phil Alden Robinson has ~~brought together~~ *assembled* a solid cast that, although not greatly challenged, seems to enjoy participating in this ultra-high-tech espionage thriller. Much of the movie revolves around the premise of what *has* happened to the dedicated, antiwar activists of the 60s once they've grown up. For one thing, the idealistic first generation of McLuhan's "global village" is now ~~middleaged~~ *middle-aged*; it has developed a more practical side: its members—having emerged as programmers, systems analysts, computer specialists—are, in a word, cyber-savvy. *not* that they have all become three-piece suited, button-downed IBMers or even jeans-and-sneakers Silicon Valley geeks. — *rewrite and reorganize*

During the first ~~reel~~ we see these former hippies as members of a unique security firm whose job has two phases: breaking into an office building or factory and then ~~it~~

developing a custom-made security system to thwart such *burglaries*. Robert Redford stars as Bish, the head of this unusual outfit. He is ably assisted by Dan Ackroyd (Mother), Sidney Poitier (Crease), David Strathairn (Whistler), and River Phoenix (Carl). All have interesting backgrounds (*read*: misfits) and specialized skills (some illegal when practiced) such as: safecracking, space age explosives, cryptography, forensic science, electronics that have made them collectively the top high-tech security company around.

As alluded to previously, they all have pasts and "too many secrets." Redford, in 1969, had broken into a government office to alter its computers, thus electronically trashing the Selective Service's draft records. His co-conspirer was one Cosmo. It turns out that Bish escaped the inevitable police raid while Cosmo was arrested, then jailed.

But fanaticism doesn't always mellow; idealism can be twisted into more malevolent ends. Now Cosmo (Ben Kingsley) is the head of PlayTronics, a mysterious "toy" company whose employees are heavily armed and wear paramilitary uniforms. Some of his men are, no doubt, ex-jailbirds like himself, but others are renegade members of the National Security Agency. That his intention is not merely to thrash Mattel or Fisher-Price at Christmastime is clearly evident. Instead, his goal is to possess the ultimate computer chip—"The Codebreaker"—which would enable him to access, then control any computer system he chooses.

Cosmo doesn't have the capabilities to develop such a chip, but is willing to ~~beg, borrow, or steal~~ *steal or even kill* for it. He tries to enlist the services of Bish's company. When ~~failing~~ *he fails*, the serious mayhem begins. Ironically enough, Redford and Company are pressed into the service of the FBI (personified by James Earl Jones) to get the Codebreaker chip. They have begrudgingly acquiesced after realizing that renegades from federal agencies wedded to thugs and fanatics are far more of a threat than other legitimate, though imperfect, government law enforcement groups. Bish's boys comprehend that they are involved in more than another caper; rather, *it is* a war for the ultimate power; worldwide control of information.

Even though Cosmo sees himself as a modern-day Robin Hood, his methods are evil; in truth, it is Redford and his merry band who more closely resemble the residents of the Sherwood Forest. ~~of "olden tymes gone by".~~ The climax boils down to a simple confrontation between good and evil.

Sneakers is heavy on plot yet ~~simple~~ *simplistic* in its themes and characterizations. However, it is precisely these qualities that make this, ~~ultimately~~ *essentially*, a pleasing though not intellectually arresting movie.

Now we look at the self-edited, revised, rewritten version. The changes run the gamut from typographical corrections to marginal adjustments to restructuring sentences to augmenting the original with additional material. The end product is tighter and flows more smoothly as well as is cleaned of its mechanical errors.

From Hippies to Hackers

Sneakers is a motion picture that almost everyone enjoys: it appeals to all family members over 11 (or computer buffs even younger); although suspenseful, it is not too intense; and, finally, for a refreshing change, it is sparse on profanity and sexual situations. Sure, there are heroes and villains of some complexity as well as some interesting themes that conflict, but by the time the credits scroll, movie patrons emerge into the lobby with smiles on their faces.

Director and screenwriter Phil Alden Robinson has assembled a sterling cast that, although not greatly challenged, seems to enjoy participating in this ultra high-tech espionage thriller. Much of the movie revolves around the premise of what happened to the dedicated, antiwar activists of the 60s once they've grown up. For one thing, the idealistic first generation of McLuhan's "global village" is now middle-aged; it has developed a more practical side: its members having emerged as programmers, systems analysts, computer specialists. Not that they all have become three-piece-suited, button-downed IBMers or even jeans-and-sneakers Silicon Valley geeks, but they all are, in a word, cyber-savvy.

During the first reel, we see these former hippies as members of a unique security firm whose job has two phases: breaking into an office building or factory and then developing a custom-made security system to thwart such burglaries. Robert Redford stars as Bish, the head of this unusual outfit. He is ably assisted by Dan Akroyd (Mother), Sidney Poitier (Crease), David Strathairn (Whistler), and River Phoenix (Carl). All have interesting backgrounds (read: misfits) and "specialized" skills (some illegal when practiced, such as: safecracking, space age explosives, cryptography, forensic science, electronics) that have made them collectively the top high-tech security company around.

As alluded to previously, they all have pasts and "too many secrets." Redford, in 1969, had broken into a government office to alter its computers, thus electronically trashing the Selective Service's draft records. His co-conspirator was one Cosmo. It turns out that Bish escaped the inevitable police raid, while Cosmo was arrested, then jailed.

But fanaticism doesn't always mellow; idealism can be twisted into more malevolent ends. Now Cosmo (Ben Kingsley) is the head of PlayTronics, a mysterious "toy" company whose employees are heavily armed and wear paramilitary uniforms. Some of his men are, no doubt, ex-convicts like himself, but others are renegade members of the National Security Agency. That his intention is not merely to thrash Mattel or Fisher-Price at Christmastime is clearly evident. Instead, his goal is to possess the ultimate computer chip—"The Codebreaker"—which would enable him to access then control any computer system he chooses.

Cosmo doesn't have the capabilities to develop such a chip, but is willing to steal or even kill for it. He tries to enlist the services of Bish's company. When he fails, the serious mayhem begins. Ironically enough, Redford and Company are pressed into the service of the FBI (personified by James Earl Jones) to get the Codebreaker chip. They have begrudgingly acquiesced after realizing that renegades from federal agencies wedded to thugs and fanatics are far more of a threat than other legitimate, though imperfect, government law enforcement groups. Bish's boys comprehend that they are involved in more than another caper; rather, it is a war for the ultimate power: worldwide control of information.

Even though Cosmo sees himself as a modern-day Robin Hood, his methods are evil; in truth, it is Bish and his merry band who more closely resemble the residents of the Sherwood Forest. The climax boils down to a simple confrontation between good and evil.

Sneakers is heavy on plot yet simplistic in its themes and characterizations. However, it is precisely these qualities that make this, essentially, a pleasing though not intellectually arresting movie.

This chapter has looked at the styles and structures employed in critiquing films. It first explored the different attitudes adopted in critical writing. Numerous excerpts and full-length examples illustrated such concerns as objectivity and subjectivity, judgment, plot summary, and tone. Word choice was deemed important especially in the areas of denotation and connotation, concreteness, and cliché avoidance. Sentence variation in structure and length was also discussed. The chapter then considered the main components of any critical paper including the lead-in sentence and introduction, the topic sentence, the thesis statement, subordinate points and examples, and the conclusion. Finally, revision techniques were mentioned: namely, proofreading and self-editing.

Chapters 3 through 6 look at specific types of film criticism. These include the review, the critical analysis, the comparative analysis, and the documented research paper respectively.

3

TYPES OF FILM CRITICISM:
THE REVIEW

The second chapter mentions that there are four modes of critical written expression about film that this text explores: the *review,* the *critical analysis* (also known as the *analytical critique*), the *comparative analysis,* and the *documented research paper.*

The *review* is the most popularized form of film criticism. We see examples of the review in student newspapers, the daily press, popular magazines, television, and the Internet, among others. The two most typical functions of a review are to *summarize* or *provide an overview* and *make an evaluation* of a movie, usually in release at either first- or second-run local theaters. Since the review is a type of critical format, it can be applied to any film regardless of release date. The review also makes an important assumption: that the reader has *not* seen the movie in question.

Audience and Format

Recognizing your audience is the first hurdle to jump when writing a review. Knowing your readership will help determine the tone, style, vocabulary level, and length of the critical piece. What you say and how you say it will differ depending on whether you direct your review toward sixth graders, the general adult public, or your college professor.

As stated above, the reviewer has the obligation to both summarize and evaluate the film. In so doing, the reviewer furnishes the necessary *boilerplate:* title, director, literary source (if there is one), other technical staff, genre, and major cast members. In addition, a plot synopsis gives the reader some idea as to what can be expected of the film. However, the critic must be sure to avoid detailing the climax and ending, especially in a thriller, suspense drama, or mystery. The reviewer is then expected to develop one or two aspects of the film that have had a particular impact on him or her. All of these elements are considered part of the overview section—a major responsibility of the critic. Without some subjective evaluation, however, the reviewer is basically dispensing a plot summary with screen credits and a few insights but little else. The readership expects more: Was it a decent film worthy of investing six or seven dollars per head? If so, why? If not, why not? Judgment is a requisite of the review. Such an evaluation, and perhaps a recommendation, must be made in a logical manner supported by convincing arguments and facts. In summary, the review should include these components:

- Boilerplate—title, director, literary source, other technical staff, genre, major cast members;
- Plot synopsis;
- Point(s) for development; and
- Evaluation/recommendation.

In the last chapter, you saw numerous samples of complete movie reviews. All contained the major components listed above, and all were directed to a college-level audience. Below, however, are three sample introductory paragraphs that review Sydney Pollack's 1982 hit *Tootsie*. The content differs somewhat in each, since it is determined by the maturity level and background knowledge of the audience to which it is directed. The first example is meant for sixth graders; the second is intended for a general adult public; and the third is addressed to a professor of film studies. All three reviews are written as if it were 1982 and the film were playing at local theaters.

(1) (Sixth Graders)
Michael Dorsey, played by Dustin Hoffman, has been an actor—on and off—in New York City for twenty years. Unemployed again, he is really eager to work on the stage or in front of a camera. To get a role in a television soap opera, Michael Dorsey has no choice but to become Dorothy Michaels. First, he shaves his face, arms, and legs. After that, he puts on make-up and a wig. Finally, slipping into women's clothing and high heels, Michael leaves for the tryout. When he gets the job soon after, the fun really begins in *Tootsie*, the zany comedy directed by Sydney Pollack.

(2) (General Adult Public)
"Method" actor Michael Dorsey (Dustin Hoffman) once again is pounding the New York streets looking for work and haunting the unemployment office. He knows he is talented and devoted to his craft: yet, after twenty years, Dorsey has been more off the stage than

on it and behind in his rent more often than in front of an audience. Desperate for acting work, he auditions for a soap opera as Dorothy Michaels—easily his most demanding acting stretch ever. We watch, fascinated, as Michael Dorsey transforms himself into Dorothy Michaels in *Tootsie*, the delightful Sydney Pollack comedy. He shaves appendages and face, plucks strategic hairs, applies cosmetics skillfully, sets a wig in place, and squeezes into undergarments, clothes, and high heels. When his convincing performance nets him the role, the fun not only begins, but we also gain some subtle insights into what it is like for a man to live the role he has created as a woman.

(3) (Professor of Film Studies)
The concept is not new: the ancient Greeks and the Elizabethans employed it. Earlier comedies of this century milked it for laughs. Thus, when director Sydney Pollack puts Dustin Hoffman in drag, we might expect yet another guffaw-filled, pratfall-laden, slapstick farce. Not so. We should expect more from Messrs. Hoffman and Pollack in *Tootsie*, and we get it. The tired premise has a few unique twists that make it fresh. Hoffman as Michael Dorsey is an unemployed New York City actor. A fanatical exponent of the "Method" school, he is almost unemployable as he questions every line and assails every director and playwright with his script interpretations. However, to end his twenty-year stint in thespian purgatory calls for radical measures: he commits to audition for a television soap opera as Dorothy Michaels—a decidedly desperate stretch. Yet, professional that he is, Michael skillfully transforms himself into Dorothy, reads the lines, and wins the role. Not only does the fun now really begin but so do inquiries into sexual identity reversal and what it entails.

Notice how the introductory paragraph directed toward sixth graders uses very direct language. Michael Dorsey's background and current problem are stated in the first two sentences. What he does to prepare for the audition takes up the bulk of the paragraph, but the last sentence serves as a segue to the rest of the review.

In the introductory paragraph aimed at an adult audience, the structural development is the same: we meet Michael Dorsey, learn of his chronic problem, witness the lengths he goes to for an audition, and then proceed to the rest of the review. But here, more details are given, using more mature language and more sophisticated sentence formation.

Finally, the third sample immediately adopts a scholarly tone, alluding to the theater of the ancient Greeks and the Elizabethans for historical comparisons. Eventually, Dorsey is psychologically dissected with examples of his extreme behavior which contribute to his somewhat chronic unemployablity. Despite additional concepts that are broached, the structure of the paragraph still resembles that of the other two.

Tone, Style, and Word Choice

A review, besides providing plot and boilerplate information on a movie as well as some personal insights and an evaluation of it, also adopts an attitude. It can be solemn, playful, sarcastic, scathing, or reverential. The style of language can be informal or formal. In an informal review, slang expressions and some liberties with sentence structure are more likely to be taken. This will also be reflected in the word choice and vocabulary level of the language. The formal review is more restrictive, eliminating use of slang and colloquialisms and most, if not all, nonstandard English terminology.

The Serious Review

A serious tone in a review is just that: sarcasm, double entendres, irony, overly clever word play, and a surfeit of slang should be in short supply. Critic Vincent Canby, in a positive review, adopts an earnest, straightforward tone as he introduces the Indian film *Distant Thunder*, made in 1973 by the subcontinent's preeminent director Satyajit Ray.

> The Bengali countryside is almost heavy with color, with golds, yellows, umbers, and especially with the greens of the rice fields. The village is tranquil. Caste is observed. It is part of the order of things. Occasionally, groups of airplanes are heard overhead, but they are remote as the war that, according to a village elder, "the king is fighting with the Germans and the Japanese." One villager reports the Germans have captured Singapore, but he is corrected. It's the Japanese who have captured Singapore, the man is told. Aside from a shortage of kerosene, the war, at first, doesn't seem to have much effect on the villagers in Satyajit Ray's fine, elegaic new film, "Distant Thunder" (Ashani Sanket). The movie . . . has the impact of an epic without seeming to mean to . . . .

Canby introduces the thematic irony that he would develop in the remainder of the review, namely: amidst this bucolic beauty and peace, a distant war is being fought which will affect the village eventually. His phrase, "the war, at first, doesn't seem to have much effect on the villagers," is ominous since it implies that as the film develops it will. It also serves as a transition to the rest of the review.

The Humorous Review

Humor is a tone that is frequently used in reviews. Its purpose can be to ridicule (as in the "pan") or to fondly poke fun at in a more positive vein. Often a humorous or light tone accompanies the critical remarks about a comedy or another genre movie with significant comical undertones. Such is the case in this introduction to a review of James Cameron's 1994 blockbuster *True Lies*.

> Take the sophistication, grace under pressure, and technical gadgetry of a James Bond flick. Then mix it with a Bruce Willis *Diehard* save-thousands-from-terrorists plot. Add a generous smattering of comic banter of a Mel Gibson/Danny Glover *Lethal Weapon* thriller. Follow with a heady dose of gratuitous violence, mayhem, and death à la Stallone's *Rambo*. Finally, toss in a dash of domestic sentimentality as found in, well, 25% of American movies. Now place this entire mélange under the unifying heat of a spoof and you have the formula for *True Lies*, the most successful adventure-thriller-action-comedy of the year.

The lead-in device identifies elements of other well-received action thrillers that have been taken to create this particular motion picture. The last sentence claims that these adoptions or influences—here compared to components of a chemical formula—do work extremely well in *True Lies*.

The Pan

A reviewer is not always going to enjoy what he or she sees nor believe it has many redeeming qualities. Some movies are poorly written or ineptly directed; others exhibit inferior acting. The public has a right to be warned about those films regarded as "turkeys," "bombs," and "flops." Below is an unsympathetic review—a *pan*—of the sequel to *Home Alone*. Made in 1992, it is entitled *Home Alone 2: Lost in New York*. It is followed by Renata Adler's pan of the western *The Good, the Bad, and the Ugly*.

Laughing All the Way to the Bank/II

It was the blockbuster of blockbusters for 1990; it won critical acclaim despite being obviously produced for mass commercial appeal; it created America's latest child megastar, Macaulay Culkin. If any doubt remains, these kudos belong to the original *Home Alone*.

As with any sequel, the question arises as to whether the second can equal or even surpass the first. This film tries—very hard. All the players are in place: John Heard, Catherine O'Hara, Daniel

Stern, and Joe Pesci. The same creative duo of John Hughes (writer) and Chris Columbus (director) pull out all the stops to match their first effort. The studio moguls open their wallets wide, sparing no production expenses to generate the same market impact as its predecessor. Yet . . .

The subtitle to *Home Alone/2* is *Lost in New York*, and, indeed, the film does just that—it gets lost in Gotham. To begin with, as in most comedies, an audience is asked to suspend its disbelief. But there are too many ex–New Yorkers around and people who know that city to go unbothered indefinitely by how quickly and easily Culkin does Manhattan. He seems to visit every major landmark in the course of just one afternoon. As an "accidental tourist," no less!

Once again, it is the Christmas season. Now some treacly sentimentality can be expected, but the movie dishes up enough sugary goo to send half the audience running to their dentists after the show.

The premise of the film has the Chicago-based extended family leaving for a Miami Yuletide holiday. Unfortunately, at the airport, Kevin (Culkin) mistakes a lookalike for his father and following him, boards a plane bound for La Guardia, not Miami International. Thus, the bulk of his adventures is in the streets, alleys, and abandoned buildings of the Big Apple.

Joe Pesci and Dan Stern team up to reprise their roles as the two bumbling thieves bent on vengeance against little Kevin. The violence is even more excessive and implausible in this version. Stern alone is hit by a brick—tossed by his unflappable ten-year-old nemesis—in the same place on the forehead no less than five times with just momentary disability. Both burgling bozos suffer thirty-foot falls onto pavement or construction debris, yet repeatedly spring back into vindictive action like *Terminator* cyborgs. The boundless creativity of the violence coupled with the resilience of the victims make some scenes resemble more a Saturday morning cartoon show than a "family comedy"—sort of human embodiments of the Road Runner and Wiley Coyote.

Today, though, "something for the whole family to enjoy" seems to be rather permissively defined. Therefore, kids, during the holiday season will, no doubt, fill the theaters. Two hours later, they will leave the popcorn-encrusted auditoria with their needs for slapstick comedy and exaggerated screen mayhem sated.

Home Alone/2 is cute and clever. Nevertheless, despite its efforts, it ultimately cannot escape the dreaded "Sequel Syndrome."

Notice that at the outset, the title of the review hints at the tone of this critical piece and its evaluation of the film. The second paragraph introduces the general problem of any sequel: the tough act to follow. Yet, despite all the efforts to match and even surpass the original, it fails. The third paragraph begins to identify the whys and hows of the film's shortcomings. Each succeeding paragraph identifies additional defects or excesses that hurt the film. Along the way, the general premise, the plot, and the players are mentioned. Finally, in the last sentence, the movie is consigned to the growing heap of the Sequel Syndrome.

Pans are not confined to comedies that are excessive or just fall short of expectations. Critic Renata Adler loathed Sergio Leone's 1966 "spagehtti western" *The Good, the Bad, and the Ugly* and states her opinion forthrightly in her review.

The Good, The Bad, and the Ugly

"The Burn, the Gouge, and the Mangle" (its screen name is simply inappropriate) must be the most expensive, pious and repellent movie in the history of its peculiar genre. If 42nd Street is lined with little pushcarts of sadism, this film, which opened yesterday at the Trans-Lux 85th Street and the DeMille, is an entire supermarket.

The plot—and in their eagerness to mutilate someone, the writers continually lose track of it—seems to run as follows:

A man whose pseudonym is Bill Carson, and who owns a clam-shaped snuffbox, knows the whereabouts of $200,000. Three characters, Burn (Clint Eastwood), Gouge (Lee Van Cleef), and the Mexican, Mangle (Eli Wallach)—whose names in the film are Joe, Setenza, and Tuco, respectively—are anxious to get hold of it. Ultimately, Clint Eastwood gets it. The action takes place in the West during the Civil War. That is all. It lasts two and a half slow hours.

The movie entitled "The Good, the Bad, and the Ugly" forgets all about Bill Carson for an hour. Then, he makes a brief appearance, rolling his one eye (any number of characters in the movie have lost an eye, or an arm, or a leg, or two legs), and dies, covered with blood and flies and making rasping noises, in incredible agony. Before expiring, he divulges the location of the cemetery in which the money is buried to Mangle, and the gravesite to Burn.

The sole purpose of the snuffbox is to enable Gouge to jam Mangle's fingers quite painfully in it. Gouge himself is missing a joint of a finger in his gun hand. The camera dwells on this detail lovingly.

Eli Wallach, as the Mexican, has a wound over his left eye, which

The Good,the Bad, and the Ugly (1966)   Eli Wallach as Tuco, the Mexican desperado, ready to wreak more mayhem.

heals and reopens throughout the film for no apparent reason. He is throttled three times, sun-scorched, and once so severely beaten by Van Cleef that anyone who would voluntarily remain in the theater beyond this scene (while he might be a mild, sweet person in his private life) is not someone I should care to meet, in any capacity, ever.

Wallach rolls his eyes, makes hideous gastrointestinal noises to convey shades of emotion, and laughs incessantly. Among his feldspar teeth, there is one capped with what looks like a molten paper clip. He also forgets, from time to time, what sort of ethnic part he is playing; and particularly when he is called to shout, his Mexican is laced with Riverdale.

Van Cleef's acting consists of displaying a stubble of beard and narrowing his eyes. Aside from various other shootings and beatings he administers, he shoots one man through a salad bowl (although most of the movie takes place in arid country, there are an awful lot of salads and vegetables) and another through a pillow. In the end, he is shot.

There is scarcely a moment's respite from the pain. Most of the scars and wounds are administered about the face, and even Eastwood, as the hero, spends a good part of the movie with his face blistered. His face and voice are expressionless throughout.

Several of the actors are Italian, and their voices are dubbed. There are some irrelevant battle scenes, as though, near the end of the movie, the writers and the director, Sergio Leone, hoped that it might pass for anti-war. "Never so many men were wasted so badly," Eastwood says. And there is a completely meaningless sequence with a bridge—as though it might pass for "San Luis Rey" or "Kwai." Sometimes, it all tries to pass for funny.

The film is the third of a trilogy ("A Fistful of Dollars" and "A Few Dollars More" preceded it.) There are immortal lines in the special context. One, just when it appears there is going to be a nonviolent moment in the film, from an officer who is preaching against brutality: "Sergeant," he begins, "gangrene is eating my leg away. Also my eye." Another, when Eastwood surprises Wallach in the bathtub: "Put your drawers on and take your gun off," he says.

Renata Adler's critical digs at *The Good, the Bad, and the Ugly* run rampant throughout her review. Her initial sentence pillories the movie by renaming it "The Burn, the Gouge, and the Mangle." She calls it "repellent" because of its excessive sadism. After a brief synopsis of the plot, she identifies those set pieces that exhibit the gratuitous violence that she condemns so strongly. She also castigates the acting of some of its principals—namely, Eli Wallach, Lee Van Cleef, and Clint Eastwood—in the interpretations of their roles. The fact that the supporting cast and all the extras are Italian and have their words dubbed she perceives as a further weakening of the film.

The Rave Review

The *rave review* is one that applauds a movie on multiple fronts. The screenplay, the direction, the acting, the set design, and the music score all seem exceptional. Films that get raves—especially those from the distinguished critics of the big newspapers, magazines, and trade journals—usually get nominated and win Academy Awards as well as other prestigious cinematic honors. Most reviews, as can be guessed, however, fall somewhere in the spectrum between the pan and the rave. To illustrate examples of the rave review, two films are considered: William Wyler's *The Best Years of Our Lives* and Frank Capra's *You Can't Take It with You*. Besides the two full-length reviews by Bosley Crowther and

Frank S. Nugent, respectively, much shorter reviews of those films that appear on the World Wide Web are presented and analyzed.

William Wyler's *The Best Years of Our Lives* has quite a pedigree: screenplay by Pulitzer Prize–winning playwright Robert E. Sherwood, based on the novel *Glory for Me* by celebrated author MacKinlay Kantor, and produced by Samuel Goldwyn, who pulled out all the stops to assemble a cast of some of Hollywood's premier talents.

The Best Years of Our Lives

It is seldom that there comes a motion picture that can be wholly and enthusiastically endorsed not only as superlative entertainment but as food for quiet and humanizing thought. Yet such a one opened at the Astor last evening. It is "The Best Years of Our Lives." Having to do with a subject of large moment—the veteran home from the war—and cut, as it were, from the heart-wood of contemporary American life, this film from the Samuel Goldwyn studio does a great deal more, even, than the above. It gives off a warm glow of affection for everyday, down-to-earth folks.

These are some fancy recommendations to be tossing boldly forth about a film which runs close to three hours and covers a lot of humanity in that time. Films of such bulky proportions usually turn out the other way. But this one is plainly a labor not only of understanding but of love from three men who put their hearts into it— and from several others who gave it their best work. William Wyler, who directed, was surely drawing upon the wells of his richest talent and experience with men of the Air Forces during the war. And Robert H. Sherwood, who wrote the screen play from a story by MacKinlay Kantor, called "Glory for Me," was certainly giving genuine reflection to his observations as a public pulse-feeler these last six years. Likewise, Mr. Goldwyn, who produced, must have seen this film to be the fulfillment of high responsibility. All their efforts are rewarded eminently.

For "The Best Years of Our Lives" catches the drama of veterans returning home from war as no film—or play or novel that we've yet heard of—has managed to do. In telling the stories of three veterans who come back to the same home town—one a middle-aged sergeant, one an air officer and one a sailor who has lost both hands—it fully reflects the delicate tensions, the deep anxieties and the gnawing despairs that surely have been experienced by most such fellows who have been through the same routine. It visions the overflowing humors and the curious pathos of such returns, and it honestly and sensitively images the terrible loneliness of the man who has been hurt—hurt not only physically but in the recesses of his self-esteem.

Not alone in such accurate little touches as the first words of the sergeant's joyful wife when he arrives home unexpectedly, "I look terrible!" or the uncontrollable sob of the sailor's mother when she first sees her son's mechanical "hands" is this picture irresistibly affecting and eloquent of truth. It is in its deeper and broader understanding of the mutual embarrassment between the veteran and his well-intentioned loved ones that the film throws its real dramatic power.

Especially in the readjustments of the sailor who uses prosthetic "hooks" and the airman who faces deflation from bombardier to soda-jerker is the drama intense. The middle-aged sergeant finds adjustment fairly simple, with a wife, two grown-up kids and a good job, but the younger and more disrupted fellows are the ones who really get it in the teeth. In working out their solutions Mr. Sherwood and Mr. Wyler have achieved some of the most beautiful and inspiring demonstrations of human fortitude that we have had in films.

And by demonstrating frankly and openly the psychological blocks and the physical realities that go with prosthetic devices they have done a noble public service of great need.

It is wholly impossible—and unnecessary—to single out any one of the performers for special mention. Frederic March is magnificent as the sergeant who breaks the ice with his family by taking his wife and daughter on a titanic binge. His humor is sweeping yet subtle, his irony is as keen as a knife and he is altogether genuine. This is the best acting job he has ever done. Dana Andrews is likewise incisive as the Air Forces captain who goes through a grueling mill, and a newcomer, Harold Russell, is incredibly fine as the sailor who has lost his hands. Mr. Russell, who actually did lose his hands in the service and does use "hooks," has responded to the tactful and restrained direction of Mr. Wyler in a most sensitive style.

As the wife of the sergeant, Myrna Loy is charmingly reticent and Teresa Wright gives a lovely, quiet performance as their daughter who falls in love with the airman. Virginia Mayo is brassy and brutal as the latter's two-timing wife and Cathy O'Donnell, a new, young actress, plays the sailor's fiancée tenderly. Hoagy Carmichael, Roman Bohnen and Ray Collins will have to do with a warm nod. For everyone gives a "best" performance in this best film this year from Hollywood.

From the first sentence on it is clear that we are reading a rave review. The rest of the fairly lengthy piece supports this claim with superlatives about the acting, the direction, and the script of this exceptional motion picture. Crowther applauds the film for exposing a very timely issue of that era: the problems of the returning World War II veteran. That this motion picture does so with such humanity and realism, enabling it to reach the audience at once and keep it engrossed for the entire three hours running time is especially remarkable.

Two other rave reviews—much shorter in length—of *The Best Years of Our Lives* follow. The first, written without a byline in 1946 and during the film's initial run, originally appeared in the cinema trade publication *Boxoffice Magazine*. Now it is found in *Boxoffice Online Reviews*.

The Best Years of Our Lives

Goldwyn–RKO 172 mins.
It's priceless—one of those pictures every producer hopes to make. It's close to the everyday lives of millions of men at present—their postwar readjustment problems; it's as human as your next door neighbor. It has romance, pathos and humor, and more—it is garnished by some of the most unexpected humor. These situations pop up and furnish some mirth-shaking moments. Frederic March, as the banker-father of a family of two, who comes back from the war the way he went—a sergeant—gives one of the finest performances of his career, and Myrna Loy, his wife in the picture, runs a close second. Dana Andrews, former soda jerker back as a captain, is forceful, virile and convincing, and a new find, Cathy O'Donnell, gets a flying start on the road to stardom. Her emotional shadings in moments of pathos are something to behold. William Wyler directed.

SELLING ANGLES
Every once in a while Sam Goldwyn turns out a masterpiece. This is one. It's small town life with no theatricalism—simply told and so honest it is heartwarming. Put everything you have behind that new girl, Cathy O'Donnell. She's wonderful. The tieups with stores, banks and juke parlors are so obvious they're waiting to be tested. You can play it from one of three angles or all three—romance, comedy, tears.

CATCHLINES
They're Home, Boys . . . See What Happens to Them. After the War

The Best Years of Our Lives (1946)   Harold Russell, Dana Andrews, and Frederic March as three veterans returning from war facing their uncertain peacetime futures.

What? They Do Some Rehabilitating and They Are Rehabilitated . . . Some Come Back to Happy Families . . . Some Face New Problems. Watch the Boys Face Life Again . . . And Conquer It. Laugh With Them, Cry With Them, Too, If You Feel Like It . . . And You Probably Will.

Reviewed: December 7, 1946

This review, although bursting with praise, is geared to a far smaller and more specialized audience than Crowther's *New York Times* piece. By being directed to film distributors, theater owners, and others in the movie business, it focuses on certain aspects of the film that, because they have great merit, can also lend themselves to a great deal of positive publicity.

Also via the Web is the capsule review of *The Best Years of Our Lives* from the *Mr. Showbiz Movie Guide*, which evaluates classics as well as contemporary cinema. It rated the film a 91 out of 100, and David Mermelstein, the reviewer, made the comments that follow:

The seminal World War II film (which won the Best Picture Academy Award) chronicles the lives of three vets during America's difficult adjustment back to peacetime. Viewing grand themes through an intimate prism, the film frankly confronts the difficulties that vets and those close to them encountered when worlds were once more turned upside down. Real-life vet Harold Russell (who lost his hands in the war) won a Best Supporting Actor Oscar for his role as the crippled soldier, while the excellent Frederic March garnered the Best Actor prize as a well-off family man trying to reacclimate to a sedentary life.

One of the challenges of any filmmaker is to successfully convert one medium to another: a short story or novel into cinema, or a stage drama into a motion picture. Frank S. Nugent's highly complimentary review of Frank Capra's conversion of the George S. Kaufman–Moss Hart Broadway hit, *You Can't Take It with You*, concentrates on that aspect of the film.

You Can't Take It with You

Pulitzer Prize plays do not grow on bushes, a circumstance which is bound to complicate their grafting to the cinema. "You Can't Take It with You" was a tremendously amusing play. George Kaufman and Moss Hart, who wrote it, had just three curtains to make, one set to cover them all and an irresistibly comic panel of characters. Brevity was not merely the spice of their wit, but the salvation of it. Everything happened so quickly, and so humorously, that only post-mortem reflections suggested that the dramatists might have been raising a towering, but essentially fragile, structure. Grandpa Vanderhof himself was an inexcusably anachronistic figure: no one, these days, can afford not to pay an income tax.

Columbia's film of the play, which moved into the Music Hall yesterday, has had to justify that Pulitzer award. Simply because it is a motion picture, and not a play, it has had to explore the Kaufman–Hart characters more thoroughly than the playwrights had need to. Instead of three curtains, there had to be a flowing narrative; instead of one set, there had to be a dozen (or more); instead of seeing things always through the direct, but nonetheless distorted, eyes of the amazing Vanderhofs and Sycamores, there had to be a certain respect for the viewpoint of the abused and ultra-rich Kirbys.

Frank Capra, its director, and Robert Riskin, its adapter, have vindicated that Pulitzer award, even at the expense of comedy. The characters Messrs. Kaufman and Hart invented were not unidimensional after all. When you look them through, as the picture does, you discover they were people, not caricatures. The playwrights drew their outlines; the picture has filled them in. Vanderhofs, Sycamores and Kirbys all have substance now. Beyond doubt, none of them is quite so funny—except possibly the hungry Russian, the lit'ry Mrs. Sycamore, the ballet-dancing Essie—but they are far more likable, far more human.

Humans, of course, are not as laughable as caricatures of humans. "You Can't Take It with You" is not as comic on the screen as it was on the stage. At least, not in its total effect. When it chooses to be funny it can be as funny as the dickens. But it chooses, too, on the screen, to be serious and, at times, moral and sentimental. Grandpa Vanderhof's philosophy was in defense of simple enjoyment of life. On the stage, its application was pretty comic; in reality, even in the reality of the screen, it can become pretty serious.

Mr. Riskin has done a lot with the story, chiefly in deference to the feelings of the Kirbys of the world, but it remains the high-spirited fable of the Sycamore girl and the Kirby boy who had to introduce their families to each other. The Kirby Srs. were from Wall Street and Park Avenue. The Sycamores and Vanderhofs were a long line of amiable lunatics: Grandpa, who quit work one day thirty-five years before because it wasn't fun; Mrs. Sycamore, who wrote endless plays because some one left a typewriter on her doorstep; Mr. Sycamore and Mr. De Pinna, who made their own fireworks; Essie, who danced; and Ed, who fooled around with a homemade printing press and revolutionary circulars. The Sycamores. and Vanderhofs were always sitting on gunpowder kegs. There were bound to be sparks when the flinty Kirbys came to call.

It's a grand picture, which will disappoint only the most superficial admirers of the play. Columbia, besides contributing the services of its famous writing-directing team, has chosen its cast with miraculous wisdom. Lionel Barrymore's Grandpa is the least bit of a let-down after Henry Travers's playing of the role on Broadway, but we're willing to admit our dissatisfaction may be due to the fact that Mr. Travers's Grandpa came first. Beyond that prejudicial doubt we enthusiastically admire every one everything—Jean Arthur's Alice Sycamore, James Stewart's honest young Kirby, Edward Arnold's badgered tycoon, Spring Byington's delightful Penny, Donald Meek's Mr. Poppins (a new one on Mr. Kaufman) and all the other names on the long cast sheet. And, before we forget it, "You Can't Take It with You" jumps smack into the list of the year's best.

What critic Frank S. Nugent does in his review is make mention of the play's receipt of the Pulitzer Prize repeatedly. He does this to illustrate how highly considered the original drama was and, thus, how great the achievements of its movie adaptation. Throughout his article, he compares aspects of the film with parallels in the play. In almost all cases, the motion picture fares very well.

Two short reviews, among others, of *You Can't Take It with You* appear on the Internet. *At-A-Glance Film Reviews* by "Sam" offers a glowing review.

You Can't Take It with You (1938)

Ratings
Sam: * * * * *
Reviews and Comments

Sam: In this brilliant screen adaptation of Kaufman and Hart's stage play of the same name, Jean Arthur plays Alice Sycamore, one of the only normal members of her eccentric family. She wants to marry her boss, Tony Kirby (Jimmy Stewart), but the class difference is an obstacle. The Kirby family is of the stereotypical stiff, humorless upper class. The two families make arrangements to have dinner, and Alice is worried sick that Tony's family won't approve of the engagement afterward.

I dare not give anything away, but suffice it to say that all heck breaks out. The chaos and havoc is a hoot, in the best tradition of the screwball comedies of the thirties. Sparkling dialogue, a breakneck pace, and the occasional quiet moment of profound introspection are all parts of what make this riotous film the classic that it is. (It even won a Best Picture Oscar, one of the few comedies to earn the honor.) Although the ensemble cast is superb throughout, keep an eye on Edward Arnold, who plays Tony's father. His moving performance is one of his best—and central to the film's success.

Jonathan Rosenbaum's *On Film Brief Reviews* from the *Chicago Reader's* raves are considerably more restrained. He finds the comedy, at times, somewhat dated.

Frank Capra and Robert Riskin's reductive, relatively conformist version of the Kaufman and Hart farce about an eccentric family (Lionel Barrymore, Jean Arthur, Misha Auer, Spring Byington) coming into contact with a rich one (Edward Arnold, Mary Forbes, James Stewart) won best-picture and best-director Oscars in 1938. There are still some laughs and entertainment to be found here, but forget about fidelity to the original.

Not all raves are universally shared. Some pictures are highly controversial and elicit strong feelings both pro and con. One such film is Neil LaBute's *Your Friends and Neighbors* (1998). Condemned by some in the strongest terms, it is lauded by others as the following review by the *Chicago Sun-Times'* columnist and PBS film commentator Roger Ebert attests.

Your Friends and Neighbors

* * * * (R)
Cary: Jason Patric
Man: Ben Stiller
His partner: Catherine Keener
Man: Aaron Eckhart
His wife: Amy Brenneman
Artist's rep: Nastassja Kinski
Written and directed by Neil LaBute. Running time: 100 minutes.
Classified R (for explicit dialogue).

Neil LaBute's "Your Friends and Neighbors" is a film about monstrous selfishness—about people whose minds are focused exclusively on their own needs. They use the language of sharing and caring when it suits them, but only to their own ends. Here is the most revealing exchange in the film:

> *Are you, like, a good person?*
> *Hey! I'm eating lunch!*

The movie looks at sexual behavior with a sharp, unforgiving cynicism. And yet it's not really about sex. It's about power, about forcing your will on another, about having what you want when you want it. Sex is only the medium of exchange. LaBute is merciless. His previous film, "In the Company of Men," was about two men who play a cruel trick on a woman. In this film, the trick is played on all the characters, by the society that raised and surrounded them. They've been emotionally short-changed and will never hear a lot of the notes on the human piano.

LaBute's "Your Friends and Neighbors" is to "In the Company of Men" as Quentin Tarantino's "Pulp Fiction" was to "Reservoir Dogs." In both cases, the second film reveals the full scope of the talent, and the director, given greater resources, paints what he earlier sketched. In LaBute's world, the characters are deeply wounded and resentful, they are locked onto their own egos, they are like infants for which everything is either *me!* or *mine!* Sometimes this can be very funny—for the audience, not for them.

Of course they have fashionable exteriors. They live in good "spaces," they have good jobs, they eat in trendy restaurants and are well dressed. They look good. They know that. And yet there is some kind of a wall closing them off from one another. Early in the film, the character played by Aaron Eckhart frankly confesses that he is his own favorite sexual partner. A character played by Catherine Keener can't stand it when her partner (Ben Stiller) talks during sex, and later, after sex with Nastassja Kinski, when she's asked, "What did you like best?" she replies, "I liked the silence best."

Ben Stiller and Keener are a couple; Eckhart and Amy Brenneman are a couple. In addition to Kinski, who works as an artist's assistant, there is another single character, played by Jason Patric. During the course of the movie these people will cheat on and with one another in various ways.

A plot summary, describing who does what and with whom, would be pointless. The underlying truth is that no one cares for or about anybody else very much, and all of the fooling around is just an exercise in selfishness.

The other day I spent a long time looking at the penguins in the Shedd Aquarium. Every once in a while two of them would square off into a squawking fit over which rock they were entitled to stand on. Big deal. Meanwhile, they're helpless captives inside a system that has cut them off from their full natures, and they don't even know it. Same thing in this movie.

LaBute, who writes and directs, is an intriguing new talent. His emphasis is on writing: As a director, he is functional, straightforward and uncluttered. As a writer, he composes dialogue that can be funny, heartless and satirical, all at once. He doesn't insist on the funny moments, because they might distort the tone, but they're fine, as when the Keener character tells Kinski she's a writer—"if you read the sides of a tampon box." She writes ad copy, in other words. Later, in a store, Kinski reads the sides of a tampon box and asks, "Did you write this?" It's like she's picking up an author's latest volume in a bookstore, although in this case the medium is carefully chosen.

The Jason Patric character, too, makes his living off the physical expression of sex: He's possibly a gynecologist (that's hinted, but left vague). The Eckhart character, who pleasures himself as no other person can, is cheating on his wife with . . . himself, and he likes the look of his lover. The Brenneman character is enraged to be treated like an object by her new lover, but of course is treated like one by Eckhart, her husband. And treats him like one. Only the Kinski character seems adrift, as if she wants to be nice and is a little puzzled that Keener can't seem to receive on that frequency.

LaBute deliberately isolates these characters with identification with any particular city, so we can't categorize them and distance ourselves with an easy statement like, "Look at how they behave in Los Angeles." They live in a generic, affluent America. There are no exteriors in the movie. The interiors are modern homes, restaurants, exercise clubs, offices, bedrooms, book stores. These people are not someone else. In the immortal words of Pogo, "We have met the enemy, and he is us."

This is a movie with the impact of the original stage production of Edward Albee's "Who's Afraid of Virginia Woolf." It has a similar form, but is more cruel and unforgiving than "Carnal Knowledge." Mamet has written some stuff like this. It contains hardly any nudity and no physical violence, but the MPAA at first slapped it with an NC-17 rating, perhaps in an oblique tribute to its power (on appeal, it got an R). It's the kind of date movie that makes you want to go home alone.

Roger Ebert's review covers quite a bit of ground. After dispensing with the four-star evaluation before the text begins, he first launches into the theme of the film: the extreme selfishness of all its characters. This selfishness is manifested in sexual desire and gratification with no love, compassion, or consideration for the other party under the sheets.

The critic then points out the influences on and parallels between LaBute's current film and other notable movies, namely his own *In the Company of Men* and Quentin Tarantino's *Pulp Fiction*. The egotistic, self-absorbed, and sometimes cruel characters are neither happy nor satisfied despite their comfortable and stylish residences paid for through good jobs with hefty incomes.

Ebert sees LaBute's considerable writing skills as the strong suit of this film. Clever, biting, and funny, LaBute's dialogue goes far in developing these despicable yet fascinating groups of contemporary people. As the audience condemns these characters for their morally bankrupt lives it becomes increasingly unsettled as it realizes those on screen have emerged from the same stuff as those in the theater seats and the distances between the two is uncomfortably short.

The Mixed Review

Predictably, most reviews of films fall somewhere between the pan and the rave. A critical piece will praise some features of a given movie and castigate others. Often, comparisons are made between the current film under review and its antecedents, identifying the film as a derivative of earlier—perhaps better—screen entries, or comparing it to other—and superior—works of the filmmaker. The reviewer continues to move back and forth: lauding the acting here, condemning the writing there; applauding well-conceived sequences in one paragraph, chastising the director's inconsistency in the next. The review is mixed and thus is a compilation of a movie that is "disappointing," or "falls short," but, nevertheless, has its "good points" and "flashes of brilliance."

Many critics, besides their written reviews, employ a rating system that immediately summarizes their overall evaluation of a motion picture. It is most comparable to an educator's grading system, but instead of letter grades—A, B, C, D, and F—usually stars are used (as with restaurants and hotels). Thus, an excellent or outstanding movie typically gets four stars (* * * *), a good film rates three (* * *), a mediocre entry deserves a modest two (* *), a poor cinematic feature nets a mere one (*); and a miserably executed reel of celluloid earns no stars whatsoever ( ). Some reviewers get so fine as to include pluses or even minuses (B+, A–). Others, in their definitions of ratings, provide "catchier" expressions than such standard terms as "excellent," "fair," or "poor." These substitutes would include "Don't miss!" "Worth a chance," and "Save your money," among others.

Two 1997 films, *Mad City* and *A Thousand Acres* exemplify this mixed-bag type of review. Each film has its strong qualities but also glaring weaknesses that would consign it to indifference. (Of course, what is dismissed by one reviewer or even panned by another can get high accolades from a third.)

Mad City was made by legendary Greek director Costa Gavras, most well-known in this country for his 1969 masterpiece *Z*. Although his return to American cineplexes is welcome, it is, nevertheless, less than fulfilling as *Newsweek* critic Jack Kroll indicates.

Media Is the Monster: Hoffman and Travolta Go Live on the Evening News

The Greek-born director Costa Gavras became a world figure in 1969 with the fiercely exciting "Z," the true story of a political murder that brought down the repressive Greek regime. "Z's" explosive mix of speed, action and dialogue gave ideology an emotional heat absent from the screen since the great Soviet directors. His subsequent films made Costa Gavras a one-man school of the politically committed movie. But the end of the cold war has dampened his fires. His American films of the '80s, like "Betrayed" and "Music Box," had little impact. "Mad City" strikes a spark, but the flame sputters.

In "Mad City," Costa Gavras takes aim at that bullet-riddled target the media. Max Brackett (Dustin Hoffman), a former hotshot national TV reporter who had an on-camera fight with his anchor, has been banished to a local California station. Max sees his way out of the hinterland when a schoolkids' outing at the local museum turns into a hostage situation. A laid-off guard, Sam Baily (John Travolta), turns up with a rifle and dynamite. When he accidentally wounds a guard, the local media swarm to the scene. But the slick Max takes control, coaching the dimwitted Baily and wrangling exclusive access from the cops. His former anchor, Kevin Hollander (Alan Alda), shows up and pulls rank, offering Max a network job if he moves to the background.

The result is tragic, fueled by media lust for a mini-Waco. TV execs adjust their coverage to the shifting polls of sympathy for Sam, the $8-an-hour guy with a family to support. Camera crews force their way everywhere. Interviews are inane, some edited to falsify context. Larry King does his remote like the Wizard of Disaster. Watching "Mad City" is like watching a thousand similar TV stories. Such familiarity kills impact. The genius of Oliver Stone, however controversial, in movies like "Natural Born Killers," has been to leap beyond reality , taking it to such a pitch of mad surrealism that he touches the profound pathology of a media-driven culture. And long before Stone, Billy Wilder's 1951 "The Big Carnival" (which is the source for Tom Matthews's "Mad City" screenplay) was a Swiftian take on a cynical reporter milking a small-town disaster to further his career.

Hoffman's Max is a corporate dilution of the Kirk Douglas character in "The Big Carnival." Travolta is more interesting. He's done a De Niro, gaining weight so that his potbelly and mutton-chopped jowls seem like the very protoplasm of a loser. Calming his kid hostages with Indian stories and junk food, Travolta's Sam focuses the residue of Costa Gavras's once raging social concern. But "Mad City" is not mad enough.

Jack Kroll's review basically is about a film by a great international director whose latest effort falls far short of greatness: "'Mad City' strikes a spark, but the flame sputters." The premise and themes revolve around abuses by "the media" on the gullible American public. As of late, news manipulation has been the source of a spate of films both made for television and theater audiences. After giving a plot summary that leads up to the climax but stops there, Kroll compares the film to two others: the recent *Natural Born Killers* by Oliver Stone (1994) and Billy Wilder's *The Big Carnival* (1951). In both comparisons, *Mad City* comes a distant second. Although the acting is praised—especially that done by John Travolta—*Mad City* offers only "the residue of Costa Gavras' s once raging social concern but . . . is not mad enough."

Just by adding an "s" to the word *mixed-review,* we mean something somewhat different than a film that is both praised and skewered by the same critic. The term "mixed reviews" signifies a movie of which the critics are, more or less, equally divided among those who award it a "thumbs up" and those who dismiss it with a "thumbs down."

Film critic David Ansen views Jocelyn Moorhouse's *A Thousand Acres* mainly in a positive light. The film is based on the celebrated Jane Smiley novel. His review especially praises the acting performances of Michelle Pfeiffer and Jessica Lange.

A Powerful Duet from the Heartland: Pfeiffer and Lange Triumph in *A Thousand Acres*

There are many ways in which *A Thousand Acres,* Jocelyn Moorhouse's film of the Jane Smiley novel, doesn't do justice to the Pulitzer Prize–winning book. But anyone in search of a powerful emotional experience, and anyone who wants to see two of the juiciest performances of the year, shouldn't miss it. Michelle Pfeiffer and Jessica Lange—both of whom, remember, were written off at the start of their careers as disposable Hollywood blondes—have done as much to light up American movies in the past two decades as any other actors I can think of. Paired as the Cook sisters, Rose (Pfeiffer) and Ginny (Lange), in this loose transposition of "King Lear" to the Iowa farmlands, they make an incandescent team.

Rose and Ginny are two of three daughters of a powerful and revered Iowa farmer named Larry Cook (Jason Robards). The third daughter, Caroline (Jennifer Jason Leigh), has become a lawyer in the city. The tragic events in Smiley's novel, as in "Lear," are set off when the patriarch quixotically announces his plans to divide his land among his three offspring. But Smiley turns Shakespeare on its head—for the heroines here are those archvillainesses Goneril and Regan, and the Lear figure is a malevolent patriarch who has

A Thousand Acres (1997) Jessica Lange, Michelle Pfeiffer, and Jennifer Jason Leigh while at a picnic on their father's Iowa farm.

inflicted ghastly psychological damage on his children. From under the family's Grant Wood surface, poisonous fumes rise.

Rose, the mother of two, recovering from a mastectomy, is a woman fueled by rage ("The more pissed off I feel, the better I am"), while the childless Ginny, passive and repressed, tries to smooth over the buried antagonisms that are wrenching this deeply dysfunctional family apart. These complex, fully realized women are Smiley's triumph, and Lange and Pfeiffer, playing an eloquent emotional duet, bring them vividly to life.

Moorhouse and her fellow Australian screenwriter Laura Jones succeed where it counts, capturing the close, sometimes bitterly fraught relationship between the sisters. The men in the tale—Rose's unstable husband (Kevin Anderson), Ginny's virtuous but obtuse mate (Keith Carradine) and the neighbor's seductive son Jess (John Firth)—are merely sketched in. The storytelling, full of dark secrets and impassioned outbursts, can seem melodramatic at times, and Moorhouse doesn't have much feel for the Iowa landscape or for the community that demonizes the two sisters. But if the movie is not all it could have been, when Pfeiffer and Lange are on the screen, you don't want to be anywhere else.

By coincidence, the two stars had neighboring offices at Orison Pictures back in 1992, when both received early galleys of Smiley's novel. They immediately turned to each other and smiled: this was the project they had been waiting for. "In the beginning we didn't really decide who was going to play what character," says Pfeiffer, who admits she always wanted to play Rose. "I loved her struggle, I loved her fight. She had this uncontrollable urge to speak the truth. This movie scared me a lot. This was one that I knew I could fail on in a big way." Lange was scared, too, at the prospect of playing Ginny. "Ginny's passive. I've never had to play a character like that before. At the beginning of the film I used to walk around the set and say, 'God, I haven't got a clue what I'm doing here.' But I always had the novel as my guideline. I kept it with me every second of the day."

Though it was a five-year struggle to get the movie made, the shoot itself, according to the stars, was mainly harmonious. "Jessica and I didn't know each other very well before this movie. I didn't even really talk to her until we were literally walking to the set to do our first scene together. But the work was effortless." Lange agrees: "There was not one moment in that suspended reality that I didn't believe that she was Rose and that she was my sister."

The problems came after the shooting ended, when Moorhouse ("How to Make an American Quilt") turned in her cut. Everyone was disappointed. The story meandered; the emotion got lost. The producers hired an outside editor to come in and work alongside Moorhouse's editor. The director stormed off, threatening to take her name off the movie.

With the input of the stars and the producers a new version emerged. "My feeling was the storytelling was not clear," says Lange of that first cut. "I had no problem shooting with Jocelyn," says Pfeiffer. "Postproduction was the hard thing. It may have been that she was too close to it. We were all too close to it. It took bringing in a new editor who was objective and brutal. It's still Jocelyn's movie."

In this age of the auteur, interfering with a director's "vision" is a great heresy. But in the real world, not all directors are created equal, and not all directors are always right. Movies are a collaborative art. Whatever Moorhouse's side of the story is (she declined to be interviewed), she has kept her name on the picture, and she deserves credit for creating the conditions that allowed Pfeiffer and Lange's magic to blossom. It may have taken fights to get there, but the movie still feels like a labor of love.

For the most part, David Ansen's review is quite complimentary to the movie. The acting performances alone of the two principal females in the cast are excellent enough to carry the movie. Ansen is also intrigued with author Jane Smiley's premise of taking Shakespeare's *King Lear* and totally changing it not only in terms of setting but also in the characterizations as well.

In contrast, we have the review written by *Time* magazine's Richard Schickel. He finds fault in almost every aspect of the production. His title and subtitle give an indication of what is to follow.

The Infirmities of Our Age: Shakespeare's *Lear* Gets Updated in *A Thousand Acres.* Result: Just Another Dysfunctional Family

Poor Shakespeare—obliged to motivate his tragedies with nothing more than seven terribly familiar sins and a smattering of Aristotle. How much richer his works might have been had the blessings of post-modernism been his. He might, for example, have been free to draw openly on incest as a theme instead of dropping little hints of it here and there for the scholars to ferret out 400 years later. And what about recovered memory? That's a dramatic device he never dreamed of.

You have to grant a certain credit to novelist Jane Smiley for the unapologetic boldness with which she appropriated the story of *King Lear* for her Pulitzer prize-winning novel, *A Thousand Acres,* resetting his mythical Britannic majesty and his fractious daughters on a modern Iowa farm. You also have to admire the nerve with which she attached pop-psych subtexts to her rearrangement, the daring with which she turned the whole works into a feminist tract.

It was the sober realism of her style that redeemed the novel, its weight and conviction that prevented readers from noticing (or caring) that by replacing noble enigmas with banal behaviorism, Smiley had downsized tragedy to melodrama. The movie version—bereft of diverting literary stratagems, relentlessly focused on whatnext narrative—takes it another step down—to soap opera.

It's not just that the Lear figure, played by Jason Robards, has been renamed Larry and dressed in coveralls, or that he decides to divide his realm among his daughters for tax purposes, although these devices have a certain flattening effect on the tale. The problem is that it is no longer his tragedy but his children's—Goneril, who he renamed Ginny and is played by Jessica Lange; and Regan, who's called Rose and impersonated by Michelle Pfeiffer; and Cordelia, known now as Caroline and acted by Jennifer Jason Leigh.

The first two, we eventually learn, were incestuously abused by their father when they were children. Rose, who has breast cancer, has never forgotten his long-ago depredations, but they have buried deep in Ginny's unconscious, from which her sister is determined to dig them out. All this is terribly up to date, "relevant" according to the vulgar standards set for us by the endlessly instructing voices of the media shrinks.

But sordid particulars and easy explanations are ever the enemy of tragedy. In this case they transform it—despite a lot of earnest acting of the kind that always seem to have its eye on a year-end prize—into nothing more than a revenge plot. They also rob it of grandeur and universality and deprive us of the pleasure of deriving our own meanings from its characters and events. We know what we think of child molesters, and we are aware of the dread consequences of their acts. On this matter we require no instruction. But a cracked old man, misjudging his powers and the nature of his children? Why yes, we can be moved to vivid identification with him, to pity and terror by his plight. Him we might someday become.

Richard Schickel is not overly impressed with the acting performances of its principal actors. While he sees the premise and "unapologetic boldness" of Smiley's novel and what it has done to Shakespeare's *King Lear,* he doesn't think it works in the Jocelyn Moorhouse film. (Interestingly, the director's name is never mentioned in the review). He sees no elements of a modern tragedy in the motion picture but rather sees its themes as analogous to a daytime talk show being expanded and placed on a twenty-foot screen.

Approaches

Besides boilerplate, some plot, and an evaluation, a review will emphasize some other aspect or two of the film to discuss and develop. This can be about any topic relevant to the film: how it reflects the political climate, the exceptional special effects, the impact of the cinematography, or the music score's enhancement of the mood. Most often, however, the review will center around one of the following:

- The storyline (plot);
- An idea, a theme, or an ideology; and
- The director or an actor (in terms of his or her trademarked style or previous body of work).

The Plot-Driven Review

The plot-driven review may disburse the boilerplate at the beginning, the conclusion, or throughout the piece. The same methodology can be used for the evaluative parts of the essay. However, the plot-driven review mainly concentrates on telling the story and making comments about it as it proceeds, mentioning those aspects of the movie that make it somewhat unique or interesting.

Robert Hatch's 1975 review of Sidney Lumet's *Dog Day Afternoon* appeared in *The Nation*. For the most part, it is a plot-driven appraisal of the film.

Sidney Lumet's *Dog Day Afternoon* is a picture that, for all its high comedy, social irony and bizarre excitement, does not quite accomplish what it sets out to do. I was entertained but somewhat less than satisfied, and I hope I can say that and still convey the idea that I think well of the film. Movie reviews today are too often rating services, and readers look for four-star banquets, forgetting that a one-star Michelin restaurant serves better food than they often eat.

The film is based on the magazine account of a one-day sensation that occurred in Brooklyn a few years ago—an attempted bank robbery that mobilized a large section of the New York police, agents of the FBI and the TV networks for fourteen hours of a hot summer afternoon and evening. The inventor of this ill-starred venture, as Lumet tells the story, is a young Brooklynite named Sonny (Al Pacino), whose most memorable characteristics are that he is singularly unfitted mentally and emotionally to rob a bank and that he is homosexual. He has taken this desperate way of raising money in order to finance a sex-change operation for his friend, at the moment recovering in the Bellevue psychiatric ward from an attempt at suicide. Sonny is also burdened with a very small but very possessive mother and with a wife and two small children. His companion in crime is Sal (John Cazale), an ex-convict whose intelligence and powers of self-control are alike unimpressive; he speaks with feeling of the human body as a sacred vessel of the Lord, but no one—least of all Sonny—knows what use he will make of an automatic rifle if his own vessel is seriously threatened.

Sonny is very bright, but sadly ill-organized, and for a bank robber hopelessly disinclined to make a nuisance of himself. The crime—conceived as one of those elegant, split-second capers—starts to fall apart at the very beginning and one senses that Sonny would be glad to call the whole thing off (especially when he discovers that there is very little cash in the bank that afternoon). But his somewhat boisterous activity in and around the tellers' counters has been noticed by people of the neighborhood and by now cops are deployed in solid ranks all up and down the street and on advantageous roofs; the cameras are poised and citizens of Brooklyn by the thousands have gathered to be entertained.

The police have brought to bear enough fire power to repel a military invasion, but cannot use it because Sonny and Sal have detained the bank manager, an elderly guard and eight or ten female tellers, cashiers, typists and clerks. Negotiations begin: Sonny steps outside from time to time to talk with the officer in charge, demanding at each appearance that the hundreds of guns being pointed at him be put out of sight. This earns him the cheers of the crowd, which he greatly enjoys—and which turn to cruel catcalls when the running broadcast carries the news of his homosexuality.

Meanwhile, the bank takes on the atmosphere of a community besieged, with Sonny and Sal gradually becoming part of that community. The women try to clean up Sonny's language, which is rather overburdened with the two most common four-letter words even for a Brooklyn boy under considerable stress. And Sonny worries about the health of his charges, calling for a doctor when the manager needs an insulin injection and sending out for pizzas and soda pop when the group gets hungry. The robbery is soon forgotten; they are all suffering from the same fatigue and they all have the same goal, which is to get out of the predicament with their skins intact. In this long central part of the picture the interest gradually shifts from the cops and robbers to the human relationships within the bank, and these are all tied in one way or another to the basic enigma of Sonny. He is obviously a charming, quick-witted, sassy-tongued city boy (after all, Pacino is playing him to the hilt and with evident delight) who, for all his ghoulish threats to throw a succession of corpses out into the street, is certainly going to hurt no one (unfortunately, the cops don't know him as well as do his charges, and no one has a clue as to what the taciturn Sal is thinking). But the difficulty here is that as one gets to know Sonny as more than a mannequin in a thriller, one wants to know him much more thoroughly; melodramatic thrills no longer seem to be the point of the film. What does he really feel for his hysterical friend in Bellevue; is he a decent husband and father; what does he do when he isn't robbing banks (he says he works in one, but Sonny isn't always truthful)? How, since he doesn't seem to suffer from megalomania, did he get the idea that he was up to armed robbery—what pushed him over the edge from an unconventional double life to a nutty project like that? You can think of a number of possible answers to these questions, but the film touches upon them only superficially, and then with clichés and sentimentality. There is a real Sonny, serving time somewhere, and some effort might have been made to find out what made him tick so erratically. But perhaps Lumet had neither the time nor the energy, within the framework of his pseudo-documentary thriller, to give his hero more than an immediate presence as a human being. It is exceedingly difficult to work psychological insights into the hugger-mugger of melodrama, and we must not complain too much if a good, fast-action picture fails to meet the standard set by Dostoevsky. Still, Lumet does suggest, increasingly as the story proceeds, that an engrossing study of human complexity lies just beneath the grotesque adventure, but he never gets around to displaying it.

Instead, Sonny recalls that fellows in his fix have sometimes traded hostages for a jet plane and safe passage to some country where the international laws of extradition are not observed. He proposes this expedient; the police jump at it; the FBI takes over, and the last section of the picture is an engrossing account of the arrival of an airlines limousine, the emergence of the hostages, walking awkwardly as a human wall around Sonny and Sal, a tense trip to Kennedy Airport, photographed from a low-flying helicopter, the appearance out of the night of the great jet and the last-minute double cross of the FBI.

By this time, once's allegiance is entirely to Sonny, and the final moments come as a scene of blackest treachery. Lumet's attitude toward the forces of law and order is interesting. He is amused at the spectacle of the regular police baffled by a crazy kid who waves a white handkerchief of truce while prancing up and down the sidewalk hurling insults at them. The law is present in such ludicrous numbers that even their chief can't keep track of them all, and one group, zealous for glory, almost sets Sonny and Sal to blazing away at their new friends in the bank. Still and all, Lumet seems to say, the cops of New York are a decent bunch of average Joes.

But toward the FBI he shows cold hatred. He represents them as emotionless straight arrows, prudish, self-righteous, beautifully tailored robots with death in their eyes. The fact is that, if we are to believe this account, they did free the hostages and without giving Sonny a transoceanic jet for his personal convenience. They also killed Sal, but, though I can't prove that that was necessary, I would not, from what I saw of him, have recommended trying to take him alive out of a crowd of innocent people. It isn't often that I feel impelled to defend the Bureau; but that's because, in my opinion, it is not good enough at discouraging armed robbery and much too ready to break the law in pursuit of mythical threats to the national security. Does Lumet seriously think that the FBI should have kept its word to Sonny? If that became general practice, we might soon run out of jets. But see the picture—it is less than perfect, but for the most part it is astonishingly good.

The focus of the extremely lengthy review above is a botched bank robbery that actually happened in Brooklyn fours years earlier. The review could be considered plot-driven despite its commentary on the director's decision to exclude deeper analysis of the principal character. It does praise the film for being exceptional within its genre, the action thriller. The review might be considered excessive in the amount of the plot that it divulges, however. The climax and shocking ending probably should have been omitted but, then again, Robert Hatch's point of how Lumet views so differently the two law enforcement agencies involved— the NYPD and the FBI—could not be introduced and developed. The review does end with a strong recommendation to the readership to see the film.

The Theme- , Idea- , or Ideology-Driven Review

Often a review will explore a theme or an idea or even an ideology that is central to a movie. Such is the case with *Scent of a Woman* (1992). The movie centers around two characters and the bond that is unexpectedly created between them. Thematically, it represents a movie subgenre and a common cinematic theme: the "buddy/road" film and the rite of passage respectively.

Two Tickets on This Rite of Passage

Typically, any serious film set in a prep school will involve some rite of passage for the youthful protagonist—whether it be dealing with sex, independence, ethics, or adulthood. However, what makes *Scent of a Woman*—directed by Martin Brest and adapted from the Italian novel *Il buio e il miele* by Giovanni Arpino—an unusual motion picture is the dual rite involving the mentor as well.

Scent of a Woman is also is a "buddy/road" film. At the outset, Charley Sims is a student at Baird, an exclusive prep school in New Hampshire. Played by newcomer Chris O'Donnell, he is cleancut, naive, hardworking, and bright. Unlike his fellow students, Charley is on scholarship, and his roots are firmly established in the faceless middle class. To the scions of wealth, privilege, and alumni, he is an outsider: to be befriended and used, but never to be accepted as an equal.

Not having the money to return to Oregon for Thanksgiving, Sims answers an ad to be a companion for a sightless man during the holiday. During his interview with the family, he meets and is verbally savaged by Lt. Colonel Frank Slade (in another exceptional performance by Al Pacino). Slade, a former Army Ranger, is bitter yet also insightful and, when he chooses to be, charming. He is introduced as a man who hates to be touched physically (and emotionally), yet because of his blindness, he has to manually grasp others.

Charley has additional concerns besides the prospects of tending to an irascible invalid for an extended weekend. Recently, he witnessed a malicious prank perpetrated by some schoolmates against Baird's Headmaster. The school's rigid honor code dictates that he tell all, yet the unwritten credo among students is that one never snitches on a classmate. One of Sims' "friends," George Willis (Bradley Seymour Hoffman), in on the prank, advises him: "We stick together. Us against them . . . stonewall everybody. Never leave any of us twisting in the wind." Except that this does not apply to Charley since he is not part of the rich and privileged clique, is quite expendable, and could be the one—if he cooperates with them—left "twisting in the wind."

As soon as Frank's family leaves for its Thanksgiving trip, the Colonel announces that Charley and he will be flying to New York City. The youth protests that the trip is beyond the terms of the agreement. Frank dismisses such reservations with a scathing, "Don't sharpshoot me, Peewee."

The trip to New York serves as a feeling-out period between the master and his novice as well as an airing of views. Frank's words are prophetic: "[The] weekend is just the start of your education." It does turn out to be a coming of age for Charley, with his values setting and maturing. What Frank does not tell Charley is the full intent of the excursion: Frank's last celebration of sensual pleasures before his ritualized suicide, or as he puts it: "All I want is one last tour of the battlefield."

In the probing and baiting that the Colonel undertakes during the journey from New Hampshire to Manhattan, he learns of Charley's impending dilemma at Baird. His sardonic advice: "To tell or not to tell: it's your ass. If you don't sing . . . have a nice day! . . . [There are] those who stand up and face the music and those who run for cover . . . cover is better."

They arrive in New York and stay at the Plaza Hotel. Frank, in a light-hearted mood, gives his companion tips on dancing, women, the good life. A few set pieces—the tango with Donna (Gabrielle Anwar), a beautiful society debutante, and the joyride in the rented red Ferrari convertible—create a bond between the cynical old rake and the idealistic young schoolboy.

For the actual Thanksgiving meal, Frank decides to visit his brother's family unannounced. His arrival is not greeted with enthused cries of surprise, however. Grown-up nephew Randy (Bradley Whitford) is even more corrosively hostile than his uncle. He sneers to Charley, "Why don't you take him to your family for dinner . . . [he was] an asshole before . . . now he's a blind asshole."

Back at the hotel, Baird is once again brought up and Frank's philosophizing is especially bitter: "Conscience is dead! Grow up! It's 'to hell with you, buddy.' Cheat on your wife; call your mother on Mother's Day. It's all crap."

However, Charley, still too trusting for his own good, insists he is not a squealer and calls George Willis for moral support. It is then that he learns that Willis' alumnus father will pull strings to hush his son's involvement. So much for honor.

Despite his cynicism, Frank, deep down, would not like to see Charley sell out. He sees integrity, or at least the seeds of it, in the youth.

Nevertheless, soon thereafter, Charley finds Frank, in his full dress uniform, ready to destroy himself with his government issued semi-automatic pistol. In a gut-wrenching scene, Charley dissuades him, if only for the time being. Frank refuses to give his young companion full credit for saving his life; instead, he states that what has kept him going is "the thought that one day . . . I can have a woman's arms and legs wrapped around me and I could wake up in the morning and she'd still be there."

The climactic scene of the movie has Frank suddenly appearing at Charley's public hearing at Baird as his advocate. The outcome of this stirring final set piece in the Baird chapel has to be imagined. Suffice it to say that at film's end, we see both characters have emerged through a life-enriching and honor-affirming experience cemented by the ties of true friendship.

The review shows how the eventual bonding that takes place during the various travels of young Charley Sims and aging curmudgeon Colonel Frank Slade makes it a buddy/road film—as claimed early in the second paragraph. The change in each character by movie's end—greater maturity for Charley and a re-embracing of life for the Colonel—supports the contention of the dual rite of passage made in the first paragraph.

Another aspect of the military mindset can be seen in Rob Reiner's *A Few Good Men,* also released in 1992. It exposes the chilling discrepancy between an outwardly espoused ideology and one that is secretly followed by those wielding significant power. The review that follows is an example of one that is ideology-driven.

Semper Fi . . . But Get a Good Lawyer

The United States Marine Corps: embodiment of the American patriotic ideal; last bastion where loyalty, love of country, and honor remain the rule and not the exception. A closed society whose own codes and laws are holy writ, impervious to civilian or even military accountability.

Or is it? A new breed in the military doesn't think so. Personified by Kaffee (Tom Cruise), a lieutenant in the Judge Advocates Group of the Navy, he is cynical, smart, and glib. Stationed in the heart of bureaucratic Washington, D.C., rather than some hardscrapple Leatherneck outpost, this type of naval officer is willing to compromise and cleverly plea bargain rather than sink in flames arguing on the stand for some glorious principle.

Suddenly, Kaffee's normal legal work is interrupted by a case requiring him to fly down to the Marine base at Guantanamo Bay in Cuba. He is assigned the defense of two gung-ho Marines accused of a barracks murder. He must interview the defendants and conduct a preliminary investigation. There he learns that this is a case that cuts to the very core of what it means to be a Marine in today's world. The dead man, Santiago, apparently had been far less than a perfect Marine, not tolerable especially at a forward station like "Gitmo." When he had informed on a fellow Marine, Pfc. Dawson, for a "fenceline shooting" (firing at an enemy sentry and thus risking retaliation, a fire fight, or an international incident), the need to harshly discipline Santiago was becoming imperative. Then when he went outside the chain of command to request a transfer, punishment was inevitable: a "Code Red" was set into motion.

(A Code Red is an informal, dangerous, and violent disciplinary action taken by fellow Marines under the sanction of, but officially denied by, a commanding officer for extreme cases of malingering, disloyalty, or negligence endangering fellow Marines. It is illegal under the Uniform Code of Military Justice.)

Two members of Santiago's unit—Dawson and Downey—had enacted the draconian disciplinary measures: they forcibly bound him, stuffed a sock into his mouth and secured it shut with duct tape. Before any extended pummeling or other physical abuse could occur, his lungs hemorrhaged. He died choking on his own blood.

During the Guantanamo visit, Kaffee confronts the base commander Colonel Jessep (Jack Nicholson) who belittles the other's youth, inexperience, and sheltered position. Jessep sermonizes "We're in the business of saving lives. . . . We follow orders or people die." A frontline position requires a Marine to put the unit, the Corps, God, and country first and foremost—never himself before the other four. Apparently, Santiago had trouble adhering to such an iron standard. Although Jessep denies ordering the Code Red, he had felt Santiago had to be "trained" rather than transferred, or the other men would be weakened and their lives put at risk. Santiago's immediate commander Lieutenant Kendrick (Keifer Sutherland) also denies involvement with the Code Red but echoes Jessep's sentiments stating that Santiago is dead because "He had no code. He had no honor."

Kaffee is not impressed with Jessep's professed patriotism nor with a code so rigid that it could lead to the death of a man like Santiago. He is supported in his views by the two other military lawyers working with him on the case, Lieutenant Weinberg (Kevin Pollak) and Lieutenant Commander Galloway (Demi Moore). It is they who prevail upon Kaffee to try the case rather than settle for a reduced charge.

In a dramatic courtroom climax, Kaffee calls Jessep to the stand. It is a showdown with no punches pulled. We see that Jessep "will stop at nothing to keep his honor" while his young adversary "will stop at nothing to find the truth." The outcome of their duel makes for a rousing climax of intense courtroom drama.

Nicholson's Colonel Jessep is one of the great movie performances of the year. He portrays a man who is sinister, zealous, clever, bullying, and convinced of his rightness even when it flouts the law he has sworn to uphold and defend. Tom Cruise does a masterful job as the foil to Nicholson's Jessep. Rob Reiner has skillfully directed a fine ensemble of players in this acting tour de force of Aaron Sorkin's script of his own hit play.

Since this is an ideology-driven review, some major concepts of a controversial military code are presented as the first paragraph. The second paragraph shows that this ideology is not universally held and introduces those characters who disavow it. The contending principles eventually become personified by two men who come into direct conflict in the movie's stirring climax.

The Auteur- or Actor-Driven Review

A number of reviews focus on the director or, as the French say, *auteur*. This type of director is very independent and uses a heavy hand in other aspects of filmmaking—especially writing and editing, but also cinematography and producing. In films by some strong directors (auteurs), actors are to be shaped like clay, to move as the filmmaker determines. To illustrate this concept, Lina Wertmuller and her film *Swept Away* are discussed.

Often films revolve around stars and are considered conveyances to showcase their talents or appeal. Such stars have the power to choose their scripts since they are strong box office draws. That is why we speak of a "Schwarzenegger film" or a "Stallone vehicle." If we go back in cinema history, especially to the comedies of the 1930s, we speak of the films of Mae West or W. C. Fields or the Marx Brothers— no one remembers who the directors were for their movies. For an example of the actor-driven review, we look at Woody Allen in *Manhattan Murder Mystery*. Although he did direct the film, the main thrust of the review is on his capacity as one of the great comic actors of our time.

Many consider Italian director Lina Wertmuller as the greatest female director of her era. She wrote all her own scripts, which usually had a consistency in their philosophical, political, and ideological content. Given great control of the films she made, Lina Wertmuller would be a strong example of a *femme auteur*. The following is an auteur-driven review of her 1974 film *Swept Away (By an Unusual Destiny in the Blue Sea of August)* and was written by Colin L. Westerbeck, Jr. in *Commonweal*.

Robinson Crusoe

In any film that takes place on a sailing boat—Victor Fleming's *Captains Courageous* (1937) and Roman Polanski's *Knife in the Water* (1963) come to mind first—the director is going to find the opportunities for beautiful photography irresistible. Lina Wertmuller's new film, *Swept Away by an Unusual Destiny in the Blue Sea of August*, is no exception. The film begins on a sailboat, and Ms. Wertmuller takes about every one of those opportunities she has to dazzle us with the scenery. During the day the boat nuzzles into the blue grottos of the Mediterranean coast. At dusk it glides before an orange and blue sunset. After nightfall, the mistress of the boat, Raffaela (Mariangela Melato), emerges from below decks into the brilliant, silvery backlighting of moonbeams bouncing off stainless fittings.

Even when Raffaela and one of her sailors, Gennarino (Giancarlo Giannini), get separated from the boat while out in a dinghy, life on the water remains a luxurious, stunning sight. As an aerial shot draws back from them lost at sea in their little boat, the camera picks up the swarming, iridescent highlights of the sun on the water. And when they at last fetch up on a deserted island, they are enfolded by green foliage, bleached limestone and pearl gray twilights. They are enshrouded in the sort of photography whose colors are so rich they seem actually to fill the air between us and the landscape we are looking at.

Yet none of this photography ever allows us to feel that Wertmuller only wants to send us pretty postcards. There's too much trouble in this paradise for us to get that impression. During the establishing shots at the very beginning of the film, before we get even close enough to make out who is speaking, we can hear Raffaela delivering a marathon diatribe against everything and everyone who isn't idle, feckless and fashionable like her. She is a rich bitch of the worst sort—the sort that flaunts it—and when she discovers that deckhand Gennarino is a Communist, she takes special delight in torturing him. When they are stranded and then marooned, it's like locking up a cobra and a mongoose in the same wicker basket. At first she continues to browbeat and bully him, but once they get to the island he's had enough. Now it's his turn, since she must depend on him for survival, to get his licks in. He makes her work for every morsel of food he provides, and slaps her around for good measure whenever he has the least excuse.

Thus Wertmuller's film becomes in large measure a contradiction, or at least a conflict, between what we see and what we hear.

Swept Away . . . (1974) The two principals—Giancarlo Giannini and Mariangela Melato—lost in a dinghy somewhere in the Mediterranean.

This is why the film is funny. All comedy is the result of some sort of incongruity or disproportion. The clown's shoes are too big and his hat is too small, the punchline of the joke is either an overstatement or an understatement, swatting a fly is wanton but blasting it with a cannon is hilarious. The incongruity that Wertmuller creates here is one between the visual and aural scales of her film. Again and again, as in those establishing shots at the beginning or that aerial shot of the dinghy, we see her characters from a great distance. Extreme long shots show us Raffaela's party lolling on the deck of the sailboat, or the tiny figures of her and Gennarino traipsing across their island. The scene in those shots is always lovely and tranquil, and the figures close together. Despite the distance from which we are watching, however, we hear the characters speak in these shots as if we were in their midst; and their dialogue is always pure discord. Raffaela is squawking about something, or Gennarino is, or each is shouting at the other simultaneously.

The disparity between the sights and sounds of the film makes us choose continually between believing what we hear and what we see. Those who choose the former think Wertmuller is full of passionate political commitments to socialism or feminism or revolutionism or whatever. This is unfortunate, especially since her popularity has been based on the misconception that she has such trendy commitments. (Perhaps because she sees where her bread is buttered, she has even encouraged this misconception.) The fact is that Ms. Wertmuller is not a politician: she's a filmmaker, and she knows that what we see is what must ultimately matter in a movie. Politics is the great subject of debate in her films, but what her characters have to say about politics is always just a lot of hot air and bombast. More than once Raffaela makes fiery speeches defying Gennarino, and in the next cut Wertmuller gets a laugh by showing her doing precisely what she was just inveighing against so eloquently.

Lina Wertmuller's comedy is really not a form of satire, then, but something much more personal and warm-blooded. To her the world is not as strident and disagreeable as it sounds in this film, but as beautiful and sensuous as it looks. When she suddenly jumps her camera off at a distance from her characters, it is in part to keep their ideological bickering in perspective—to show it as only a small hubbub in a very pleasing landscape. This is not to say, though, that Wertmuller is a sentimentalist, or that the rich pastel world she envisions here is without sadness. Like her two earlier films, *Love and Anarchy* and *The Seduction of Mimi*, this film ends unhappily because of the foolhardiness of a man.

Eventually, grudgingly, Gennarino's and Raffaela's loathing turns into love, but Gennarino is still too mistrustful to be satisfied with that. He effects their rescue so that she will have to prove her love for him by continuing it back in the civilized world. In a penultimate scene, he calls her at the hotel where she has been reunited with her husband. When she comes to the phone, he tells her he's calling from the gas station across the street and is looking right at her. But now that vision of them to which we have become accustomed is turned inside out. We no longer see them together and at a distance, arguing at the top of their voices. This time they speak softly and secretively as he explains how he's arranged to take her away again. He tells her nothing else matters, and she seems to assent. The trouble is that while they are saying these things, we are seeing them only in separate close-ups because they are no longer close enough together to be contained in the same long shot. And now as before, it is what we see, rather than what we hear, that we are compelled to believe.

The critic in the review above first discusses the director's cinematic style in her use of cinematography to put certain thematic elements in opposition: namely, the disparity between "what we see and what we hear." This is also a major comedic component of the film as well. Her politics—socialism and feminism—are discussed but critic Westerbeck believes them to be subordinate to what she is trying to achieve as a film-maker. Love overcomes politics when given the right environment, but when both are returned to "civilization," the baggage of their former lives seem to be eroding their passion at movie's end.

Woody Allen by now has established himself as an American auteur filmmaker, but unlike so many other directors, he also has a career as a brilliant comic actor. It is in this light that the next review comments on how much his absence in front of the screen in a comedic role has been missed. The following is an actor-driven review of his 1992 hit *Manhattan Murder Mystery* (which he also directed, co-writing the screenplay with Marshall Brickman).

Woody Allen Meets Agatha Christie

It is so refreshing to see Woody Allen off his Bergmanesque schtick of angst, guilt, and pessimism, making funny films again (notwithstanding the very, real anguish of his own personal life). Some of Allen's earlier trademarks as an actor—the neurotic-tinged one-liners, the slapstick ineptitude of his hands when they attempt anything beyond gesturing, the urban and urbane characters that people his comedies of manners—are all present and well-accounted for in *Manhattan Murder Mystery*.

The film marks the reunion of Allen with Diane Keaton. They play Larry and Carol Lipton, yuppieish middle-agers with a son away at college who are in danger of becoming "a pair of comfortable old shoes." Their plight is emphasized when they are invited for a cup of coffee by two new neighbors (the Houses) from their building. Reluctantly, they go for some tedious minutes of simulated interest in his stamp collection and feigned admiration of her high-tech exercise machine. Upon returning to their own apartment across the hall, Carol fears that they too might turn into a "dull, aging couple."

Reciprocation to Mr. and Mrs. House, however, won't be necessary. The next evening the Liptons find paramedics wheeling out the body of Mrs. House. She is dead from a heart attack.

Shocked and concerned about the state of Paul House—who is supposedly too grief-stricken to be comforted—they wonder about the suddenness of the woman's demise. She had been trim and had talked about her exercising regimen while never mentioning her coronary condition. But it is on the next night when they run into Paul—whose responses to Carol's expressed condolences she considers almost "perky"—that the mystery truly unfolds.

Carol is indeed suspicious of Mrs. House's death, but Larry is not interested in pursuing her speculations; indeed, getting a full night's sleep seems paramount among his priorities. The plot soon thickens, and eventually, despite his protests, Larry is dragged into the middle of the suspected foul play. In a number of scenes displaying action, farcical sight gags, and verbal comedy, the Liptons get embroiled in this murder mystery.

Some detectives!—a bumbling, neurotic, paranoid book editor and his wife, a would-be restauranteur desperately looking for excitement in her life. Nick and Nora Charles they are not. Yet the movie has a nice pace, constantly punctuated with gags. Keaton and Allen mesh as nicely as they did in *Annie Hall* and *Manhattan* too long ago. Able support is provided by Alan Alda as Ted, the Liptons' friend, who would like to be a playwright and would also like to bed down Carol. Jerry Adler is well-cast as the initially inoffensive Paul House who proves to be quite sinister and dangerous by movie's end. Anjelica Huston as Marsha Fox, a sexy writer who is on the prowl, serves as Ted's foil. Finally, significant support is furnished by numerous neighborhoods of the Borough of Manhattan at their most charming during early fall. "Autumn in New York" wasn't written for nothing, and Woody Allen sings it louder and better than anyone else.

Woody Allen the actor is emphasized in the first paragraph as distinguished from Woody Allen the auteur-director. This most successful acting reunion opposite Diane Keaton opens the second paragraph which eventually gets into the plot and comical elements of the film. The final paragraph returns to the comical efforts of Allen and Keaton and the outstanding supporting cast.

Lengths

Movie reviews come in all sizes and, as such, function quite differently. The thumbnail sketch is a quick summary of the plot, players, and genre; it usually does not exceed 350 words or so. A piece of medium length is typically anywhere from approximately 400 to 800 words long. Feature length reviews exceed that last number. The longer the review, either the more detailed it becomes or the broader its scope. The John Westerbeck review discussed previously on Lina Wertmuller's *Swept Away* would be a clear-cut example of a feature-length review.

The Quick Summary and Short Review

Some quick summaries, as stated before, give the bare essence of a review. At the other end of this shorter length piece (up to 350+ words) you get a concise review but definitely have more of a feel for the movie. In the short review, the standard conventions of the review are followed but in a more abbreviated form—even if it is as brief as the "thumbnail summary" of a paragraph or two.

Our first example is a thumbnail summary (117 words long) of *Sorcerer*, William Friedkin's 1977 taut adventure thriller.

Sorcerer

Director William Friedkin's *Sorcerer*, a color remake of Georges Clouzot's 1953 thriller, *Wages of Fear*, is just as much a nailbiter as the earlier French version of the Georges Arnaud novel. Four fugitives, in order to escape from a Latin American town, agree to transport ultrasensitive, highly explosive nitroglycerine in a rickety, old truck (ironically christened "Sorcerer") through bumpy jungle roads and narrow mountain passes. Their destination is a raging oil fire which their dangerous cargo would help extinguish. At times, the suspense is painful in its intensity. The international cast, headed by Roy Scheider, also includes Ramon Bieri, Francisco Rabal, Bruno Cremer, Amidou, and Peter Capell. The running time is 122 minutes; the movie is rated PG.

The thumbnail review above consists in large part of important boilerplate about the movie. But also included is premise of the plot and its complication as well as a comparison to an earlier version of the film.

Sorcerer (1977) The rickety truck carrying its delicate yet deadly cargo of nitroglycerine explosives makes its way uncertainly over a treacherous suspension bridge.

Neither the climax nor the resolution is even hinted. The word "nailbiter" and the phrase "the suspense is painful in its intensity" suggest both the genre and its effectiveness within it.

Another short review—this time of 354 words—comments upon the Francis Ford Coppola romantic comedy-drama *Don Juan de Marco* (1995). The unusual film stars Marlon Brando, Johnny Depp, and Faye Dunaway. The essay is written by Jodi Lyn Turchin, a former student at Broward Community College.

Delusion or Reality?

Don Juan de Marco, a film by Francis Ford Coppola, is a study in the complexities of the human psyche. The plot centers around psychiatrist John Mickler (Marlon Brando), and his new patient, a young "delusional" who believes he is Don Juan (Johnny Depp). Mickler is only ten days from retirement when his path crosses Don Juan de Marco's. De Marco isolates himself upon a billboard, demanding a swordfight to end his life. The police call in Mickler, who manages to talk de Marco off the billboard by assuming the identity of Don Octavio de Flores. De Marco places his trust in "Don Octavio" and allows himself to be temporarily institutionalized.

Despite his impending retirement, Mickler insists he be the doctor in charge of de Marco. The chief of staff objects; however, Mickler prevails when de Marco refuses to be treated by anyone except Mickler. Mickler makes a deal with his patient and agrees—against hospital policy—not to administer medication to de Marco for ten days while the patient tells Mickler the story of his life. If, after this period, Mickler does not believe that his patient is really Don Juan, de Marco will agree to be committed and medicated.

During the ten days of treatment, de Marco's tales of his "life" have a profound effect upon the psychiatrist and on his relationship with his wife Marilyn (Faye Dunaway). One scene especially sets Mickler to thinking. This is when de Marco says to him, "There are four questions of value in life: What is sacred? Of what is the spirit made? What is worth living for? What is worth dying for? The answer to each is the same. Only love." It is love that drives de Marco to do what he does, and love that Mickler rediscovers by his interactions with his patient.

Don Juan de Marco is a romantic love story in its own way: a story that leaves the viewer heartwarmed. Coppola's direction is excellent, and Brando's performance as Dr. Mickler is charming. Though Brando steals the film, Depp as Don Juan is believable and entertaining. There seems to be great chemistry between Brando and Depp that makes the film a true delight to view.

Although this review is relatively short, it does cover a number of aspects of the film. The first sentence claims it is "a study of the complexities of the human psyche." The bulk of the review develops that theme. The essay also gives the reader considerable information about the characters and the performances of the actors playing them. We also get an idea of the general movement of the plot and some of the main ideas it posits about love. The final paragraph makes complimentary evaluative statements about the film, its director, and the "positive chemistry" among its cast.

The Standard-Size Review

The medium-length review of a few typewritten pages enables the critic to develop more deeply those aspects of the film and comment upon more fully. All parts of the shorter review are in place; however, they are just treated more extensively.

Irish director Neil Jordan's *The Crying Game* was to some quite controversial, while to many others it was one of the quality films of 1992. The 691-word review that follows discusses some of the movie's more important elements.

Friendship, Love, and the IRA

This Neil Jordan film (writer and director) has two very distinct parts where the first segment inextricably and continuously influences the second. *The Crying Game* is an unusual film, a powerful film. Coming midway in the second section, its great surprise—after the initial shock wears off—does not hinder the audience's increasing absorption with the two central characters and their intensifying relationship.

The first portion of the film takes place in Northern Ireland. Just outside a country fair, an off-duty black English soldier is kidnapped by a number of IRA gunmen. He has been set up by the woman he has just picked up to whom he has been making heavy amorous advances at a secluded spot. The woman, Jude (Miranda Richardson), is a member of the band of irregulars.

The soldier has been taken hostage and placed for safekeeping in an abandoned greenhouse in retaliation for the British internment of a local IRA leader. The words of Maguire (Adrian Dunbar), head of the kidnappers, are chilling: "[He should] be treated as a guest until further developments. . . . Give 'im a cup o' tea."

The captive, bound and barely enduring a suffocatingly thick woolen hood over his entire head, mumbles appreciatively, "Thank you, soldier," when his captor removes the hood. As the hours mount, a wary then friendly relationship builds between Jody (Forest Whitaker) and his guard Fergus (Stephen Rea). Each recognizes the humanity of the other; Fergus, not surprisingly, permits Jody to remain unhooded and his hands unfettered.

Their conversation meanders from the political to the personal with the two often intertwining.

"You're tough, deluded people, and it is not in your nature to let me go," Jody claims.

"I got signed up to get a job," counters Fergus.

"We do our tour of duty and we're finished. . . . If this were all over, [we'd be] having a pint on a rock," Jody ruefully comments. The sequence is reminiscent of a similar confrontation between a captured British soldier and Irish irregular in Edwin O'Connor's troubling short story, "Guest of the Nation."

The men view each other as obedient soldiers without any personal animosity toward each other. In time, Jody trusts Fergus enough to share intimate details of his life and shows his captor a snapshot of his striking lover. Despite the affinity of the two men, the possibility that Fergus may be forced to execute his bound companion is never far from either's mind. In a moment of panic, Jody pleads that Fergus contact his sweetheart, Dil, if his life is taken.

Soon Fergus is ordered to kill Jody. Torn between duty and sentiment, the Irishman allows the British soldier to escape momentarily then desperately chases him through the woods. Before Fergus can make up his mind to shoot to kill or shoot to miss (and thus risk his own life), Jody crashes through a thicket and onto a paved road only to be instantly struck, dragged, and crushed to death by a British personnel carrier en route, ironically, to liberate him.

The movie's second segment has Fergus on the lam from both the pursuing British and his vengeful IRA collaborators (who had been attacked at the hideout and suffered some losses). Altering his appearance somewhat, he flees to England. He goes to Jody's home town and gets a job as a construction worker. Soon he seeks out Dil (Jaye Davidson), keeping his oath to Jody. Dil, indeed, is every bit as beautiful and alluring in person as in the photograph.

In time, Fergus and Dil strike up a friendship, which eventually deepens into a love affair. Their interracial romance takes some unusual twists and turns. But they cannot escape their pasts: Jude, the sole surviving kidnapper, surprises Fergus and threatens harm to Dil unless Fergus participates in an assassination of an English judge.

Suffice it to say, the film ends with Fergus in prison for a crime he did not commit but for which he confessed, to shield Dil from harm. In the last sequence, we see Dil during one of the frequent visits to the incarcerated man, demonstrating the same faithfulness to Fergus that had been shown to Jody.

The review traces how the film comes full circle. Politics directly affects the first portion of the film. This, in turn, leads to an intensification of the human issues and relationships in the lengthy second portion. The climax merges the two with politics strongly impinging on the human story by movie's end. Any evaluative statements are found exclusively in the initial paragraph as are the major credits. Perhaps too much of the plot is detailed in this review; however, the major themes that the film presents are fully developed.

Another standard-sized review is presented next. It is written by Broward Community College student Ann Birr. Her 670-word piece reflects upon the 1996 Anthony Minghella movie *The English Patient* based on the powerful novel by Michael Ondaatje.

Patience Helps in *The English Patient*

As the film opens, pen and brush watercolor drawings of figures floating on a background of sand-colored parchment preview the magnificent yet enigmatic journeys depicted in *The English Patient*. Although the beginning credits of the film capture the audience's focus, viewers must pay strict attention to everything that follows or they will get lost in the convoluted combination of events. The complicated juxtaposition of the present with the past might even cause many theatergoers to return for another viewing of this film which is filled with passion, intrigue, desire, war, violence—Hemingway would be proud of the adaptation Anthony Minghella made of Michael Ondaatje's award-winning novel.

The film actually begins in the middle of the plot with the return of Count Lazlo de Almasy (Ralph Fiennes) in the two-seater plane soaring over the Sahara. The Bedouins below in the desert fire on his plane and cause it to crash. Although the Count survives, most of his body is charred to a crisp. (He refers to himself as "Toast.") Through the Bedouins miraculous care, the Count makes it to a hospital and the care of Hanna (Juliette Binoche), a dedicated nurse who listens to his tales from the past providing the overlay of present with past adventure. Hanna and the Count share a few weeks in a Tuscan monastery while he pieces the puzzle of his past together, and she attempts to mend her psychological wounds from the war. It is 1944 and Hanna's care of the Count is her *raison d'etre*.

Before he became the English patient, the Count was a Hungarian mapmaker and a devoted fan of Herodotus whose volume of work pasted with many mementos survived the crash and sits on the Count's nightstand. As Hanna or Kip (Naveen Andrews), the bomb disposal expert, reads the historic volume aloud to the Count, it provides many leaps into the past: the night in the desert during the burying sandstorm; the Christmas party where Katherine Clifton serves refreshments and feigns a swoon; the overnight waiting in the taxi on the Cliftons' first anniversary; the hotel room where the ill-fated lovers consummate their passion. The main story of the film involves the Count and his affair with his beloved Katherine (Kristin Scott-Thomas) reflected in the entries in the Herodotus scrapbook.

The other story in the complicated plot involves Hanna and her fight to survive. She dedicates herself to the burned patient in the abandoned Italian monastery. Ravaged by the war, her soul (or heart) has deteriorated like the burned flesh of her patient. She listens to Almasy's stories of his lost love in the desert. Hanna's story is equally powerful.

Both characters encounter loved ones who change their lives even more than the war. The complex structure of the film envelops the audience with its vast desert scenes and period shots of the late 30s and early 40s; its haunting music parallels the equally haunting actions of the past and present. Back and forth shifts in the scenes between the arid Saharan desert and the lush Tuscan countryside keep the audience spellbound. The juxtaposition of the contrasting sights and sounds of the past and present magically sweep the viewer into a concrete portrait of one man's subconscious reality. Through a series of flashbacks to the desert, the patient becomes a character of high romantic magnitude whom Hanna finds intriguing. The visual feast of John Scales' cinematography keeps one attentive and hungry for answers to many questions that develop as the plot unfolds. In fact, this film demands the moviegoer's full concentration if all the pieces of the puzzle are ultimately to be fitted together.

The flashback is a device demanding such focus when employed in films and novels. In *The English Patient*, the slightest sound or briefest mention of an object triggers immediate past events in the mind of Count Almasy and thus onto the screen. Although all types of viewers will enjoy this film, those who are avid readers will particularly relish it since this motion picture depends on skills fine-tuned by those who take pleasure in the techniques and sensitivity of printed fiction.

The critic in her review concentrates particularly on the visual aspects of the film together with the use of flashbacks and other structural devices of the plot. It is these techniques that particularly engross those who see the film. This is a "literary" movie that has been adapted from a heavily textured novel. For this motion picture to be best understood and appreciated, the viewer must apply similar techniques to those used when reading a novel critically. The subtle nuances of music, cinematography, and dialogue interwoven with multiple narrative contrivances create a cinematic tapestry that can only be fully appreciated through a contemplative mindset while viewing.

The Feature-Length Review

The feature-length review is long—sometimes the length of an in-depth critique. The main difference, of course, is that it is still a review and follows the restrictions of what it should divulge in terms of boilerplate and plot and what it should not—namely, in most cases, both the climax and finale—since it still operates under the assumption that most of the readership has not yet seen the motion picture. Similar to the critical analysis, however, the feature-length review explores to considerable depth a number of aspects of the motion picture that would be given shorter shrift in a briefer review.

For the feature-length review, we turn to Brian D. Johnson of the Canadian magazine *Maclean's*. It highlights Kevin Costner's 1990 directorial debut in the western epic *Dances with Wolves* from the screenplay by Michael Blake based on his own novel.

Straight-Arrow Hero: Kevin Costner Touches the Native Earth

Studio executives had reason to be nervous about *Dances with Wolves*. For one thing, it is a western. And, aside from the adolescent *Young Guns,* there has not been a hit western in recent memory. In fact, Hollywood's most notorious fiasco, *Heaven's Gate* (1980), was a western. For another reason, *Dances with Wolves* is about Indians, and Hollywood's conventional wisdom has it that Indians are a poor draw at the box office. Even more audacious, the movie is almost three hours long, and much of the dialogue is in the Sioux's Lakota language, with English subtitles. Its director and star, Kevin Costner, insisted on making the final cut, although he had never directed before. There have been a few wisecracks in Hollywood about "Kevin's Gate." But Costner, who spent $2.9 million of his own money to complete the $21-million movie, has acquitted himself admirably. Despite some flaws, *Dances with Wolves* is an epic of astonishing beauty with a rare purity of vision.

While violating almost every Hollywood taboo, Costner has restored some of its most cherished traditions. He has created an adventure with hot-blooded action, breathtaking scenery and a noble theme—a spectacle with the sort of wide-screen grandeur that has become almost extinct. *Dances with Wolves* does for the skies and plains of South Dakota what *Lawrence of Arabia* did for the desert. And in the middle of an unblemished American wilderness, the director has cast himself as an untarnished American hero.

He plays a soldier named John Dunbar, an environmentally friendly frontiersman who befriends the Sioux and rejects the genocidal mission of his own people. Unlike Arabia's Lawrence, however, Dunbar is curiously lacking in psychological torment. He is an uncomplicated hero, ingenuous at the risk of being boring. But his— and the movie's—straight arrow altruism seem uncontrived. And although *Dances with Wolves* enshrines classic Hollywood clichés of white heroism and romance, it also portrays Indians with unprecedented respect and authenticity.

Among the cast are a few Canadian native actors, including Graham Greene and Tantoo Cardinal. In interviews with *Maclean's* last week, they both had strong praise for the director. Said Greene, who has a prominent role as a traditional Sioux medicine man named Kicking Bird: "It was a real treat working with the man. He has a lot of integrity." Cardinal, who plays Kicking Bird's wife, Black Shawl, called the movie "an immense breakthrough in Hollywood's perception of native people."

Adapted by American writer Michael Blake from his own novel, *Dances with Wolves* is a tale of disarming simplicity. It begins with a scene from the Civil War. Dunbar, a Union cavalryman, has been so severely wounded that he wants to die. With great agony, he struggles back to the front lines and makes a suicidal ride in front of a phalanx of Confederate troops. Miraculously, he survives, and is promoted to the rank of lieutenant. "The strangeness of this life," he concludes, "cannot be measured. In trying to kill myself, I was made a hero." As a reward, Dunbar is allowed to choose his next posting. He decides on a far-flung outpost called Fort Sedgewick. "I want to see the frontier before it's gone," he explains. But the fort is just a collection of deserted huts. Undaunted, Dunbar sets up a one-man headquarters and begins a waiting game—waiting for Indians, buffalo and the U.S. Army.

It is a solitary vigil. Slowly, he makes friends with a wolf that visits the edge of the fort. They develop a cautious trust that symbolizes the relationship he will forge with the Indians. After a chance meeting with Kicking Bird, who quickly flees on horseback, Dunbar writes in his journal, "Have made first contact with a wild Indian. The man I encountered was a magnificent-looking fellow."

Behaving more like a boy-scout anthropologist than an army officer, Dunbar decides to seek out the Indians on their own turf. He finds a sympathetic ally in Kicking Bird, and gradually allays the tribe's suspicions. He proves himself by alerting the Sioux to the presence of a buffalo herd—and participating in a hunt, a thrilling spectacle involving thousands of buffalo. He also helps the Sioux fight the marauding Pawnee. But as Dunbar reinvents his identity, he realizes that the white man's onslaught will shatter his new-found utopia.

The narrative trails off in midstream, without a real ending, leaving the strange impression that, even after three hours, the movie could be longer. As it is, the attention to visual beauty leaves some of the characters thinly developed, notably Dunbar's lover. Stands With a Fist (Mary McDonnell) is an orphaned white woman who was adopted by the Sioux. Struggling to remember her mother tongue, she also serves as Dunbar's translator. Their white-on-white romance is unconvincing, their passion forced.

The native characters, meanwhile, are intensely charismatic. In fact, one of the most frustrating things about the movie is that it takes so long to get to know them—and by then it is over. By conventional standards, there is not enough story in *Dances with Wolves* to justify a three-hour epic. Yet the pace seems natural, conveying a sense of real time in a limitless landscape. In keeping with native philosophy, the land is the movie's biggest star. There are long stretches with no dialogue, and when characters do talk, it takes time to connect. But that is what the movie is about—talking across a cultural divide.

The heavy use of Lakota dialogue is especially effective. Costner relied on local Sioux-language instructors during last summer's four-month shoot in South Dakota. And before the cameras rolled, the cast spent about a month learning Lakota, a foreign tongue even to most of the Indian actors. "It puts you on a whole different plane," said Greene. "To speak Lakota in the scenes was like being pure. It's a language that's in tune with the land."

Costner, too, speaks Lakota in the movie. And Cardinal says that he stubbornly resisted the studio's attempt to shoot the script in English. "He's a really tough customer, that Costner," she said. "He's very honest, basically. The way he directed felt absolutely true to me." The movie goes a long way to dispelling stereotypes, she added. "People don't know the beauty of the people I come from—there is incredible inner beauty." Cardinal said that when she began working with Costner, she was reminded of a prophecy by a native chief whose people were being displaced by the building of the railroad across the Canadian Prairies. Recalled Cardinal: "He said, 'The white men are blinded and deafened by greed, but there will be a generation of their children who will be our friends.'"

Earlier films have depicted Indians as ignorant savages. Costner's movie helps redress the balance. Without preaching, it portrays the army as barbaric, the natives as civilized. Its hero is a king of the wild frontier who abdicates. In the age of David Lynch and his *Twin Peaks* cynicism, such single-minded idealism begs disbelief. But in Costner's case, it appears genuine. With *Dances with Wolves*, he has reduced Hollywood formula to an elegant formula of truth and beauty.

Critic Brian Johnson's feature-length review is quite wide-ranging. Besides disclosing some boilerplate and giving the reader an overview of the plot, he touches on a number of aspects of this most ambitious Kevin Costner project. Johnson first comments upon the riskiness of the undertaking: a first-time director demanding and receiving the right to the final cut, a large budget, a genre—the western—that has fallen greatly in box office popularity, a film sympathetic to the Indians at the expense of the U.S. cavalry, a running time of three hours, and considerable dialogue in a language other than English (Lakota) with accompanying subtitles. After ticking off the challenges, he makes an overall appraisal of the film by claiming: "Despite some flaws, *Dances with Wolves* is an epic of astonishing beauty with a rare purity of vision." Costner is shown to violate many Hollywood taboos. yet his film succeeds, nevertheless. He has created, in a sense, an old-fashioned cinematic epic that at once has adventure and cinematographic splendor, while pursuing "noble themes." He compares its breathtaking landscapes of the Great Plains to that of the award-winning cinematography of *Lawrence of Arabia*.

The character of John Dunbar that Kevin Costner portrays is idealistic, altruistic, and honest—characteristics shared by the director in this film. In telling his story, Dunbar/Costner shows an initially fair and sympathetic view towards the Sioux which eventually transforms into one that is empathetic as he shares their life. Costner's decision to have the Sioux characters speak in Lakota with captions further demonstrates his commitment to their perspective.

Because the critic is Canadian and writing for a nationally circulated magazine, he spotlights the Canadian native cast members. Johnson interviews them and shows them to be wholeheartedly supportive of Costner's efforts. Together with his honesty and pursuit of his vision, Kevin Costner has made a western that depicts the Indians with "respect and authenticity" and as far more "civilized" than the "barbaric" American soldiers. Critic Johnson proclaims that the American actor-director has done so with "truth and beauty."

Before its broad discourse on the film review, this chapter first pointed out the two most typical functions of the review: to summarize and evaluate. Consideration of the audience and formulation of the format (including boilerplate) followed. Next the tone and style of reviews were established as well as the word choice necessary to form them. In discussing these concepts, the following types of reviews were introduced: the serious review, the humorous review, the pan, the rave review, and the mixed review. Approaches or points to be emphasized in a review comprised the next section of the chapter and included the plot-driven review; the theme- , idea- , or ideology driven review; and the auteur- or actor-driven review. The chapter's last section covered the varying lengths of a review. These were placed into categories as well, including: the quick summary and short review, the standard-size (medium-length) review, and the feature-length review. To illustrate these concepts, excerpts and complete examples written by professional critics, the author, and college students were provided throughout.

Chapter 4 concerns itself similarly with the critical analysis (or critique).

4

Types of Film Criticism:
The Analytical Critique

The *analytical critique* (also termed the *critical analysis*) assumes that the reader is familiar with the subject in question. In cinema, it would be the particular motion picture that is to be discussed. In broad circulation periodicals—such as newspapers and popular magazines—the critique is far less frequently published than the review.

Audience and Format

The *critique* is normally directed to a somewhat different audience than the review. This audience is often composed of aficionados of film with a background of knowledge about the medium. As a result, the critique is more scholarly in tone than the review, although no research is cited (unlike the documented research paper). Often it is also longer than the review and will develop its thesis in depth. Its title will be fully functional—rather than clever or whimsical which some review titles try to be—and will announce the subject matter and the specific film(s) that are to be discussed in the critique. The title is a key to the paper.

The format differs considerably from the review in what it does and does not require. Boilerplate is restricted to a need-to-know basis. The same is true for the plot summary. The reader is assumed to be already familiar with much of this information. The critique may concentrate on only one portion or sequence in the film and exploit it fully—clearly a different emphasis than in the review. In fact, since the thrust of the critique is so overwhelmingly analytical—with its incumbent explanatory passages—even evaluative comments are optional. The thesis statement is made early in the essay, although not necessarily in the first paragraph. The minor inferences (supporting points) with their accompanying examples—likely from the film itself—make up the bulk of the paper. The longer critical analyses are often divided into subsections which can be so indicated by additional spacing, bullets, subtitles, Roman numerals, or some other clear-cut designation. To summarize, the critical analysis will feature the following:

- Functionally descriptive title including the film's name,
- In-depth development of the thesis and minor inferences with specific examples,
- Acknowledgment of credits limited to those that are relevant,
- Optional plot synopsis and evaluational commentary, and
- Division into subsections for longer critiques and by additional spacing, bullets, subtitles, Roman numerals, or some other clear-cut designation.

Approaches

There is even greater latitude in the critique than in the review: one can discuss anything of interest or importance in a film as long as one's points are justified. Despite this breadth of subject matter, most critiques will either be centered around cinematic technique or cinematic elements, central ideas or topics that the films expose, or characters, actors, or auteurs.

The Cinematic Technique or Cinematic Element-Driven Critique

The technical aspects of filmmaking—the cinematography, sound, music score, lighting, set design, location setting, special effects—all can greatly affect the outcome and impact of a motion picture. Specifically, how any or some of these do so makes for fascinating speculation and development. The success of what has now almost become a television and cable subgenre, "The Making of [supply the name of the first run feature]" is a testament to the interest that this facet of filmmaking engenders.

Below are some sample titles of critical analyses that focus on cinematic techniques or elements:

- The Use of Lighting to Instill and Reinforce Mood in Francis Ford Coppola's *The Godfather*,
- Atmospheric Effects as Supportive Mechanisms for Innovative Choreography in *Singin' in the Rain*,
- The Interplay between Setting and Characterization in Jane Campion's *The Piano*,

- Sergei Eisenstein's Cinematographic Genius in the "Odessa Steps" Sequence of His *Battleship Potemkin,* and
- The Set Design of *Alien* as a Means for Inducing Suspense and Horror.

The following piece is a critical analysis on the influence and effectiveness of a number of literary techniques—namely, foreshadowing, irony, imagery, and symbolism—in Billy Wilder's 1950 *Sunset Boulevard*. This essay was written by former Broward Community College (BCC) student Kimberly Springer.

Effective Literary Techniques in Billy Wilder's *Sunset Boulevard*

The demise of silent pictures brought an end to an era of beautiful faces gracing the silver screen before audiences sitting in quiet darkness. Hollywood had become a progressive town, leaving behind those who could not make the transformation to sound. Careers were finished; images were ruined; and fallen stars were left with only distant memories of their silent achievements now stored away in warehouses. Billy Wilder's *Sunset Boulevard* focuses on one woman's functional demise after the birth of talking pictures. Norma Desmond has never moved beyond Hollywood's transitional period. She is "still waving proudly to a parade that [has] long since passed her by." She has become a monument of the past. Norma and her mansion are described as being "stricken with a kind of creeping paralysis, out of step with the rest of the world." Billy Wilder uses the techniques of foreshadowing, irony, imagery, and symbolism to effectively create a tragic story of one woman's life and one man's death.

What begins as a tale of the ending to one man's life, soon becomes more of a mosaic of its pieces. Throughout the story, the reasons for and the means of Joe Gillis's murder are foreshadowed. A certain uneasy imbalance in Norma's world becomes apparent when, early in the film, Norma requires a proper burial service for her pet monkey by the drained pool. After witnessing this, Joe quietly thinks to himself that, "It was all very queer, but queerer things were yet to come." Norma's seclusion from the outside world signals further problems. She has no real grasp on reality. Norma cannot accept the fact that the world she knew is long gone. The denial she expresses indicates a personal instability. This is proven by Joe's

Sunset Boulevard (1950) The bizarre burial of the pet chimpanzee by Erich von Stroheim witnessed by Gloria Swanson.

discovery that all the mansion doors are without locks because of Norma's suicidal tendencies. When Norma falls in love with Joe, the inevitable happens. Joe's rejection of Norma portends tragedy. All these circumstances foreshadow the same ending: Norma's murder of Joe.

Norma envisions a new opportunity for stardom when Joe arrives on her doorstep. He is not a man of status; but as a writer, he holds the potential to revive her failing career. Joe describes Norma's life as empty. Ironically, Joe slowly becomes one of Norma's possessions and his own life grows as empty as hers. Ultimately, Norma realizes she can no longer bribe Joe for his affection. As a result, she grows frightened at the thought of him leaving her for another woman. If Norma cannot control the dissolution of her career, she would try to control the loss of the next most important thing in her life. Norma, overwhelmed with fear, chooses to murder Joe in order to prevent his leaving. The great irony is that Joe's death leaves Norma without anyone to love. Her decision to murder the one she cherishes is truly ironic, considering Norma's struggle with loneliness after the loss of millions of fans who once adored her. Alone, Norma is left with nothing but surrounding photos of a once stunning and youthful star.

The images associated with Norma and her mansion emphasize her reclusive lifestyle. Her dark-colored hall leads to a shadowed stairway steeped in mystery. The disused pool and tennis court in disrepair symbolize Norma's stagnant life. The outdated car represents her unwillingness to accept the progression of time. The way her hand forms into the shape of a claw signifies her desperation to hold onto what's left in her life. The sunglasses that Norma constantly wears shield her from the light of truth. Yet, just as her mansion was once decorated stylishly with the grounds well-kept, so too was Norma once young of face and slender of figure with a glow that radiated onscreen.

Norma proves to be the product of her own flawed sense of image. As Cecil B. DeMille puts it: "A dozen press agents working overtime can do terrible things to the human spirit." For Norma, the line between fantasy and reality becomes blurred. Rather than a secretive recluse, the audience sees Norma as a lost soul. Wilder's intelligent use of foreshadowing, irony, symbolism and imagery vividly portrays a faded movie queen in a time, place, and circumstance which powerfully depict lost glamour and fame.

After making some historical allusions to the impact of sound on Hollywood's motion picture industry, the essay personalizes the impact down to Norma Desmond. The first paragraph ends with announcing how specific literary devices are used in the film to effectively create a tragic story of one woman's life and one man's death. How director Billy Wilder uses such fictional techniques of foreshadowing, irony, imagery, and symbolism forms the remainder of the piece.

Filmmakers are constantly learning from each other as the art and science of moviemaking expands. Certain masters of the cinema, however, create technical, narrative, and aesthetic breakthroughs that bring the entire industry up to a higher level. One such person was one of the pioneers, D. W. Griffith. His *Birth of a Nation* (1915), based on two Thomas Dixon novels, *The Clansman* and *The Leopard's Spots*, was highly controversial because of the blatant racism of its plot and characterizations. Nevertheless, it had a tremendous impact technically on the young industry. Former Broward Community College student, Jim Sander, offers the following critical analysis on Griffith's early but profound influence on the cinema.

D. W. Griffith's *The Birth of a Nation:* A Precursor to Modern Film

D. W. Griffith's *The Birth of a Nation*, the 1915 epic film examining racial problems in the Civil War period, is a landmark in the history of the motion picture. This work was the first in-depth view of an issue by a motion picture, but that is not the reason it is considered to be a great film. *The Birth of a Nation* achieved its stature by the lasting influence it has had on other filmmakers.

The use of film as a medium for social commentary was not the only revolutionary idea of the time. Griffith chose to reenact certain historical events, such as the signing of the Emancipation Proclamation, to add verisimilitude to the story. Modeled on the Matthew Brady photos of the period, these sequences provide the viewer with a feeling of the times when the story supposedly took place with much more acuity than merely stating dates or alluding to historical events. The addition of such elements made an attempt to bring film out of the "lower" forms of comedy up to an intellectual level akin to literature. Where previous films relied on slapstick, pranks, and happy endings, *The Birth of a Nation* appealed to higher levels of thinking for its impact.

Griffith also employed many techniques to focus the viewer's attention toward precisely what he wanted to be seen. He pioneered the use of close-ups to produce an intimacy that was not felt in earlier films. The subtler emotions of the actors were seen much more easily, and extraneous background information was omitted. These shots allowed the audience to feel a much stronger understanding of the characters than it could have otherwise.

The wide angle shot, also a Griffith creation, allowed vast areas to be shown at one time—such as an entire army marching in a canyon or a mob in the city streets. Depicting such large scenes gave the viewer a sense of the enormity of the events within an historical context, as well as showing just how large some things were—such as armies. Most people at the time of the film's release would not remember the massed armies of the North and the South. The film provided a dramatic simulation to show how unsettling such a sight could be.

In cases where creative close-ups were inappropriate or impossible, Griffith used the vignette, a blackening of the screen except in the area he wished to be concentrated upon. Expanding or contracting the vignette produced an iris effect which shifted the viewer's attention from one area of the screen to another. These devices,

Birth of a Nation (1915)   A wide angle lens shot of military forces engaged in combat resembling the Civil War photographs of Matthew Brady.

along with panning and tilting the camera during the filming of the scene, added a sense of motion to *The Birth of a Nation* that was not seen in films previously.

Griffith pioneered many other advances in camera work. He was the first to film action at night which, considering the film technology of the time, was a great accomplishment. He also was the first to use the technique of "soft" focus, which enhanced the mood for close-ups, toning down harsh lines and smoothing surfaces.

For all Griffith's greatness in controlling the camera, his real genius was in the process of editing. He pioneered the process of "staccato" editing, in which the viewpoint switches between different scenes at an increasingly rapid rate, to increase the suspense of the situation. He also used devices such as fades and dissolves to smooth the transition between one scene and the next.

Perhaps the greatest editing advance by Griffith was the switchback. Using this technique allowed action in two different places, occurring simultaneously, to be shown without resorting to the clumsy dream balloons of previous films. Griffith took this common literary device and applied it to film—freeing himself from the strictly chronological arrangement of simpler films. This device was also used to show the inner thoughts of a character, interrupting the sequence of events to refine an individual character before the action resumed.

A simple but meaningful advance was extending the length of the film. At the time, films were usually quite short—under an hour even at their longest. Nearly two hours long—six times longer than most other films—*The Birth of a Nation* was criticized as a waste of materials and time. Griffith used the length effectively, though, deepening characterization as no other film had done. Not only were the characters more developed, but there were more of them. The cast of main players nearly doubled that of other films of the period.

Griffith is considered a major force in the development of film into what it is today. He used film to do more than entertain. He was not satisfied merely to record images, but to make images that were meaningful. He may not have been commercially successful, or even well-received by the majority of the public at the time, but his contribution to film as an art form continues to be felt today.

His analysis of issues, vivid characterizations, and revolutionary camera and editing techniques were copied and improved upon by the most successful filmmakers of his and later times. *The Birth of the Nation*, combining nearly all his special techniques and new ideas, can be called the ultimate fulfillment of his vision and a blueprint for the best films that came after it. Without D. W. Griffith and his *The Birth of a Nation*, the progress of film to its present state would have been severely limited. Unquestionably, *The Birth of a Nation* is a great example of the art of film.

The critique above concentrates on the innovations brought to the industry by D. W. Griffith in his controversial epic *The Birth of a Nation*. In his Civil War and Reconstruction era two-hour movie, Griffith made film a "medium for social commentary" by reenacting historical events. He introduced a number of camera shots including the close-up, wide angle shot, vignette, and panning and tilting the camera to simulate motion. He also inaugurated outdoor filming at night and soft focusing. His greatest strength was in editing where he used such innovations as "staccato" editing, fades, dissolves, and the switchback. By extending a motion picture's length from twenty minutes to two hours, Griffith was able to add more texture and detail and also to give it greater sweep. Critic Jim Sander points out that although much of the racist tone and characterization of the film can be condemned, nevertheless, the technical and conceptual innovation can be appreciated.

The Idea- or Topic-Driven Critique

Besides studying the various cinematic devices or elements of a film, the critical analysis often explores the ideas evoked from a movie—what the picture says about us, our way of life, our nation, our world. Some films boldly investigate social issues and are political, even propagandistic. Others prefer to look closer to home within the family or within the individual. Hundreds—maybe thousands—of films have been made with larger objectives than merely providing diverting entertainment and reaping the resultant monetary compensation. Many motion pictures are about ideas and concepts—social, historical, political, scientific, and the like. The movie public wants to learn, to ponder, to be ethically affected not just amused—and is willing to pay for it. Sure, the cinema provides well-crafted escapism that grosses multimillions, but it also releases sensitively written, well-acted motion pictures that offer the public more intellectually, morally, and aesthetically.

The critical analysis topics below deal with ideas, concepts, and problems about ourselves and/or our society as they are presented in specific motion pictures.

- The Motifs of Alcoholism and Adultery in *The Best Years of Our Lives,*
- The Retelling of the Orpheus and Eurydice Myth in *Black Orpheus,*
- Mel Brooks' Use of Racial, Scatological, and Sexist Humor in *Blazing Saddles*: Offensive or Liberating?
- Religious Allusions and Symbolism in Bergman's *The Seventh Seal*, and
- Elements of Racism in the Military at Large and on the Army Base Specifically in *A Soldier's Story.*

Joel Schumacher's *Falling Down* (1992) shows that some films, even when excessive, have redeeming qualities. This is an idea film: at times over-sensationalistic and violent; at others, totally unbelievable. But despite its shortcomings, the exceptional performance by Michael Douglas as its Everyman protagonist and the sober social issues it hurls upon the screen make *Falling Down* worthy of discussion. The critique that follows does just that.

Something's Rotten in the State of California: The Golden State as a Microcosm for the Ills of America in Joel Schumacher's *Falling Down*

Falling Down has been pretty much ignored by the critics and the movie-going public. Some would dismiss it as another vigilante movie (à la *Death Wish)* that bewails the ills of contemporary society (shades of *Grand Canyon*) where a normally sane, faceless person refuses to take it any longer and goes berserk (remember *Network*?). The film, directed by Joel Schumacher and written by Ebbe Roe Smith, should be taken more seriously. What it lacks in fresh concepts is more than made up for in the riveting portrayal of the central character by Michael Douglas in easily his most unusual role. The film also deals with a question that our country has been asking, especially since the Rodney King riots of the summer of 1992: Is Los Angeles an unlivable city? Even more worrisome, is L.A. a microcosm of most other large cities in our country—lawless, corrupt, ungovernable, debt-ridden, with public services at the breaking point?

The opening shot certainly seems universally appropriate: cars inching along bumper to bumper and then stopping altogether on a hot, smog-laden freeway. As each car's muffler belches toxic fumes, the camera zooms to one license plate: "California DE-FENS." That tag gives us an insight into the man behind the car's steering wheel. It is Douglas—his crew cut, lined face, and white shirt with its filled pen-holder pocket suggesting a nameless Everycitizen, in this case, a defense industry employee at the end of the work day. His anger and frustration are rising palpably. Finally, he breaks; abandoning his car in disgust, he vows to get home on foot if necessary.

By leaving the purgatory of the freeway, he unwittingly descends into a hell consisting of the many neighborhoods below and surrounding the traffic-choked arteries connecting points of the Los Angeles Basin. His pilgrim's progress to self-destruction has begun.

With each encounter he sinks deeper into the cesspool of the L.A. nether world. His ensuing experiences are a checklist for all that is wrong with contemporary American society.

His first ring of hell is entered when, needing change of a dollar for a telephone call, he walks into a grocery store. When the proprietor—a greedy, distrusting, rude Korean—refuses to do so unless an item is purchased, the conflict begins (soon to escalate out of control). When Douglas is charged eighty-five cents for a can of soda, he feels he is victimized. The shopkeeper, paranoid to begin with, threatens him with a baseball bat. They grapple, the bat switches hands, and Douglas insists that the shopkeeper roll back the prices to 1965. The other refuses. After trashing the store a bit with the weapon, Douglas states, "I'm not the thief, you're the thief," and leaves.

Soon, thereafter, he blunders across a vacant lot and is accosted then threatened by some tough Chicano gang members. Bullying him with their words and posturing, they insist on tribute for trespassing on their turf. Once again, Douglas uses the baseball bat to good advantage defending himself and drives them off.

At last, he finds a commercial street and a public telephone. While making his phone call, the young punks cruise the neighborhood—armed to the teeth with automatic weapons—looking to make a drive-by shooting of the man who beat them up defending himself. Indiscriminately blasting away, they kill and maim a few innocent bystanders, miss hitting Douglas altogether, lose control of their car, and totally wreck the vehicle, resulting in more loss of life.

He boards a bus and passes a well-dressed black man picketing a bank (ironically, the picket is wearing the same tie as Douglas). The African-American is well-educated and has a good job yet has been refused a loan because he is "not economically viable." Eventually, he is arrested for illegal picketing and harassment. The injustice of the event does not escape Douglas.

Next stop, a "survivalist" store, run by a gun-happy Neo-Nazi (Frederic Forrest). The gunshop owner spews racist filth about what's wrong with America, then confides "We're the same, you and me." The reply: "I'm an American and you're a sick asshole." They fight and our hero, increasingly out of control, ends up beating the bigot to death.

At this point, Douglas has unwittingly crossed over and is rapidly becoming what he despises: a person outside the law. This is ironic not only because up to that day he has been so straight, conservative, and law-abiding but also since all these antagonists have been—and his future victims will be—morally bankrupt. As a group they vividly illustrate what is wrong with our country. In a phone conversation with his estranged wife (Barbara Hershey) he confesses, "I'm past the point of no return, Beth. I'm on the other side of the moon, out of contact."

By this time, the police are involved and Douglas' ultimate antagonist is introduced, Lieutenant Prendergast, L.A.P.D. (Robert Duvall). Literally hours away from retirement, he is a law officer who is mild-mannered, not highly respected by his colleagues, henpecked by a half-crazy wife (Tuesday Weld), but has integrity mixed with compassion. It is he who discovers who "DE-FENS" really is:

namely, William Bosler, who had been fired some weeks before from his job of many years as a defense contractor.

As the climactic confrontation between the two approaches, the one-man wrecking party continues. At the gunshop, he dons fatigues—which makes him look more like a P.O.W. than an avenging warrior—and grabs a large satchel which he fills with a small armory of weapons.

He boards a bus and once again he is snarled in traffic. He sees that workers are "fixing" a street. When he asks why, he is rudely informed that nothing is wrong with it (they have to work to justify their inflated budget) and that he should mind his own business. In response, he exercises his taxpayer's indignation by firing an anti-tank gun at some of the crooked contractors' heavy equipment, destroying it.

His travels next take him to a snooty exclusive golf club where two arrogant septuagenarian members try to kick him out. "[He's] not even a member. I don't like the way he's dressed." Bosler responds, "All these beautiful acres fenced in for your little game," and then proceeds to demolish their golf cart, inducing a fatal coronary in one of them.

He then climbs over a fence and enters an opulent estate. Shaking his head, he states, "Plastic surgery built all of this." No further word is necessary to understand his indictment of an excessively vain society that rewards so obscenely for cosmetic services. In yet another call to his terrified ex-wife, he admits that "[he is] obsolete, overeducated, not economically viable." Yet, he desperately, obsessively, wants to get home and celebrate his daughter's birthday—as if magically "everything would be just like it was before."

As Bosler approaches Venice, where his home used to be, his wife flees and Prendergast closes in to talk him into giving up. With ex-wife and daughter watching in horror, the final confrontation takes place on a pier jutting out from the beach. Some excerpts of the dialogue are all-telling:

"He needs help, he's sick," his ex-wife warns.

"You want to see sick? Take a walk around this town," Bosler answers.

Then Bosler's tone switches; he asks the detective: "I'm the bad guy? How'd that happen? I did everything they told me to."

"Hey, they lie to everybody but that doesn't give you any special rights to do what you did today."

The impact of these words shatters Bosler, who has been leaning against the pier's railing. Yet rather than surrender and suffer the indignities of arrest and imprisonment, Bosler—virtually a walking arsenal—draws a plastic toy gun provoking Prendergast to fire in self-defense. As Bosler's lifeless body floats in the shallow sea water, the viewer is left to ponder the two men—one living, one dead—both of them witnesses to the excesses of America: greed, exploitation, hypocrisy, dishonesty, disloyalty, bigotry, brutality.

The film and character of Bosler if taken literally are overdrawn and not believable. However, if taken allegorically as a chronicle of the ills of a city which many view as America's prototypical megalopolis of the future, it presents consequences that we have to ponder: moral, sociological, political, legal, economical, and organizational. Schumacher's *Falling Down* is not a great work of art comparable to John Bunyon's allegorical masterpiece *The Pilgrim's Progress* or Dante Alighieri's *Inferno*; it, nevertheless, like them, gives us pause to look at ourselves and our society . . . and change what we see.

Note that this idea-driven critique goes into considerable detail about the plot. But with each new crisis, the themes and issues of the movie—as indicated by the essay's lengthy title—is broached either with a pungent quote or summary of events that indicates that particular malaise. The last sentence of the penultimate paragraph restates the main points that the movie makes. Then the last paragraph enlarges upon them and gives an overall evaluation of the film.

Character-, Actor-, and Auteur-Driven Critique

Many critical papers about film analyze the characters who people the movies. Often such analyses are either psychological portraits of a character or investigations of what motivates certain characters to take the actions they do. Frequently, the complex and, at times, changing relationships between characters are delved into by the critique.

Some sample titles of critical analyses that focus on aspects of characterization in a motion picture are

- Disco Music as the Defining Agent of Character of Tony Manero in *Saturday Night Fever,*
- The Metamorphosis of Willard into Kurtz to Complete His Mission in *Apocalypse Now,*
- Psychological Profiles of the Jurors in Sidney Lumet's *Twelve Angry Men,*
- The Minor Characters of John Ford's *The Grapes of Wrath* as Indicators of the Mindset Fostered by the Great Depression, and

- "Do as I Say, Not Do as I Do": The Surrogate Father-Son Relationship between Sonny and Calogero in *A Bronx Tale.*

Not all character-driven analyses have to be lengthy. Former Broward Community College student Patrick Baeringer makes some keen observations about Gus Van Sant's 1995 movie about a psychopathic, obsessed personality which also says much about our television-immersed society.

"You're Nobody in America Unless You're on TV": Analysis of a Beautiful Psychopath in Gus Van Sant's *To Die For*

"You're nobody in America unless you're on TV," so says Suzanne Stone Maretta, the central character in Gus Van Sant's satirical, seduction-for-murder film, *To Die For.* Through Suzanne, Van Sant metaphors the allure that fame and recognition hold for the "Television Generations" and the tremendous value placed on celebrity in our society. *To Die For* is a frightening look at our present state of being and the role television plays in standing as a reflection of ourselves. Even more frightening is the fact that Buck Henry's screenplay is based on real events.

Nicole Kidman as Suzanne perfectly portrays a pretty, maniacally-determined bubblehead whose one and only desire is to make it as a top television anchorperson. Just out of college, Suzanne already dons the garb of a professional news anchor. Interminably fake and perky, Suzanne talks about the tricks of the trade and shows her twisted belief in the medium of television.

It is not clear why she marries Larry Maretta (Matt Dillon), the son of an Italian restauranteur. Larry works at his father's establishment, the family business he hopes to own and operate some day. Larry is close to his family, and looks forward to starting one of his own with Suzanne. Her thoughts on children are the opposite of Larry's: she perceives children as being suicide for a woman's career. Larry supports his wife financially while she works as a late night weather girl for a small cable station. When Larry presses the issue of children further, Suzanne opts for having him killed in lieu of divorce, since divorce may mean the loss of her sports car and condominium. She befriends three high school losers whom she met through her teen speakout documentary. She seduces them physically and/or mentally then manipulates them into killing her husband.

To Die For is shot within a documentary-style framework. Through flashbacks and character-narrated interviews, we learn of Suzanne's obsession with becoming a television personality. This and the young widow's complete lack of emotion and remorse clue the Maretta family to her guilt. Larry's sister describes Suzanne as internally without feelings. Warm and bubbly on the outside, inside Suzanne possesses a cold, calculating ruthlessness. Suzanne is able to turn her charm off and on like a switch on the TV camera.

This film explores a phenomenon that occurs when ordinary people allow themselves to be exploited by the ever-increasing and worsening sensationalism of television. All too often, family members of a murder victim are ready and willing to speak to the tabloid press. Barraged by insensitive and probing questions, these suffering people, nevertheless, choose to please the camera rather than demand a respect for their privacy. Is nothing sacred anymore? Not in *To Die For*.

In this modest-length, character-driven critical analysis, the pathology of the protagonist is clearly evidenced. But after discussing her twisted ego and goals, we are asked to consider how much of her excesses are shared by the electronic media industry in particular and, by extension, the general public as well.

Actor-driven critiques are another type of film criticism. They concentrate on the achievements of a player in a particular role or techniques perfected by him or her. When an actor's work is studied as a complete entity, to discern growth or emerging patterns, a comparative analysis format is usually employed. For more on comparative analysis, see Chapter 5.

Below is a listing of critical analysis titles that concentrate on specific actors' involvements in movies:

- Marlon Brando and Method Acting in *On the Waterfront,*
- The Comedic Innovations of Charlie Chaplin,
- The Voice of Teen Angst: James Dean in *Rebel Without a Cause,*
- The Simpleton as Wise Man: Tom Hanks as *Forrest Gump*, and
- Meryl Streep's Subtle, Sensitive, and Multifaceted Interpretation of the Title Role in *Sophie's Choice.*

Blake Edwards was an established maker of clever film comedies from the late 1950s until the middle 1980s. One of his most fortuitous accomplishments was teaming up with comic actor Peter Sellers—who brilliantly embodied the character of Inspector Jacques Clouseau—in the *Pink Panther* series of films.

The actor-driven critique below looks at the genius Sellers had for the unique blend of physical comedy and characterization. These comedic qualities he especially demonstrated in the memorable cinematic creation of Inspector Jacques Clouseau.

Slapstick, Sangfroid, and a French Accent: Peter Sellers as Inspector Jacques Clouseau

We have had other cinema slapstick comedians and other celluloid comic geniuses. Each has had his or her trademarked mannerisms and props. Charlie Chaplin had his derby and rubbery cane and a mixture of impishness and vulnerability as the Little Tramp. Mae West had her walk, that suggestive saunter; her talk, filled with double entendres; and her designs, always out to get men and then put them down. W. C. Fields had that short, fat body and bulbous nose; talking out of the side of his mouth in that singular non-Southern drawl, he was a misanthropic windbag and deflater of all sacred cows—children, pets, motherhood—with clever turns of phrase. To them we add Peter Sellers as Inspector Jacques Clouseau.

No one has taken on a character better than Sellers did with Clouseau. Introduced in 1963 in *The Pink Panther*, the Clouseau character was improved upon in *A Shot in the Dark* (1964) with the introduction of Commissioner Charles Dreyfus (Herbert Lom) his boss and nemesis and Clouseau's comic foil Kato (Burt Kwouk), his Vietnamese houseboy to whom he was teaching karate. Sellers' long-running character appeared in six films of the *Pink Panther* series—the last being released after Sellers' demise and comprising outtakes patched together to become *The Trail of the Pink Panther* (1982). Edwards and Sellers also teamed up for *The Party* (1968) where Sellers devised a character every bit as funny as Clouseau in the person of Hrundi V. Bakshi, a rather inept actor from India who has come to the United States to make it big in Hollywood.

What Sellers demonstrates in the *Pink Panther* films and *The Party* is a magnificent capacity for slapstick physical humor and characterization. Within each of these movies he has developed routines that are identifiable with him alone. Clouseau, in ways, is a throwback to the physical comedy present in the Mack Sennett two-reelers up through Jerry Lewis. Nevertheless, combined with Sellers' genius for vocal mimicry and his ability to totally immerse himself within a character, he was able to invent not only funny film personas but also creations with distinct personalities as well.

In *A Shot in the Dark*, Sellers delineates Inspector Jacques Clouseau, a police detective who is gullible, stupid, incompetent, and physically maladroit; even so, he is quite vain about his sexual charm and detective prowess. Possessing remarkable sangfroid when someone else would be visibly upset, he constantly tries to keep the illusion of order—or at least its outward semblance—despite the obvious reality of the ridiculousness of the moment. Impeccable in dress and appearance—with expensive well-styled clothing, neat haircut, and meticulously trimmed full moustache—he acts as if nothing were extraordinary as he tramps into a luxurious apartment sopping wet (after falling into a fountain while exiting his car) to investigate a murder. He is oblivious to the consequent sloshing noise of his steps and their sodden tracks all over the costly carpeting. In another sequence of the movie, he espouses his forensic theories to Maria Gambrelli (Elke Sommer), the young maid whom everyone suspects of the killing but Clouseau: she is too pretty and engaging in his view. When she suddenly clutches his sleeve, she unintentionally rips it off entirely from the suit-jacket. After momentarily noticing the now useless material hanging on his arm and then dispensing it, Clouseau continues his monologue not visibly upset and totally ignoring the absurdity of his sartorial situation.

A Shot in the Dark has numerous farcical moments. Some have even become standard features in the remainder of his *Pink Panther* films, among them: his ongoing karate matches with Kato and his persecution at the hands of Commissioner Dreyfus. The Inspector knows little about karate—as his stylized karate chops would indicate, yet he insists on teaching Kato the martial art and instructs him to attack without warning any time of the day or night. Kato takes this to heart and assails his teacher in the dead of night. But Clouseau is ready, having gone to bed wearing his heavy canvas karate kimono. They grapple, with the Inspector knocking out his valet unintentionally. These sudden assaults occur throughout the movie—each at an even more inappropriate time. Yet, on each occasion, Clouseau's shortcomings in self-defense are outmatched by his servant's ineptitude in the attacks.

If Clouseau always keeps his cool, Dreyfus is the opposite. Being reduced to a gibbering, maniacal killer by film's end, he is desperate to the point of insanity to rid himself and his department of the bumbling investigator forever.

Another aspect of Sellers' ingenious characterization is his accent and inventive mispronunciations. When Maria hits her head, what results is a "bwemmp" (bump); those creatures that fly at night and eat clothing are "mewths" (moths). Whether his accent is accurately French or falls short is not the point: it is funny and consistently maintained. (The same can be said for the lilting singsong of his Hindu thespian in *The Party.*)

There are other comedic instances throughout the film. As mentioned before, the receptions to both *The Pink Panther* and its immediate sequel *A Shot in the Dark* were strong enough to inspire the producers to cultivate it into a movie series. Perhaps the greatest compliment to Sellers was that after his death in 1980, *Curse of the Pink Panther* (1983) featured a successor but flopped badly enough to end the series permanently. Obviously, it was neither the clever gags, the plots, nor the concept that had made the series such a huge moneymaker. Rather, it was the unique qualities of Peter Sellers which captured increasingly large audiences as he molded and refined this memorable cinematic product in film after film: Inspector Jacques Clouseau.

By tracing the course of a number of films in which Peter Sellers appeared and the roles he embodied in them, his genius for zany characterization and physical comedy is showcased. Although the emphasis has been on the *Pink Panther* series, it should be obvious that his unique abilities extended to his other films as well.

The auteur-driven critical analysis concentrates on certain trademarks, quirks, or talents that have become synonymous with a filmmaker. This is an area that may also be served by the comparative analysis. However, in the analytical critique, we are restricted to techniques or qualities as evidenced in one specific work. Sample critical analysis titles that center on the filmmaker would be:

- Sam Peckinpah's Excessive Use of Violence in The *Wild Bunch,*
- A Story Told from Four Points of View: Akira Kurosawa's *Rashomon,*
- The Concept of Auteurism as Exemplified by Francois Truffaut in his *The 400 Blows,*
- The Widescreen Epic as Defined by David Lean in *Lawrence of Arabia,* and
- Race, Romance, and Rock n' Roll in 1963: The Hilarious Yet Venomous Satire of John Waters' *Hairspray.*

Once again we turn to Jim Sander, former BCC student, for his thoroughgoing treatment of Alfred Hitchcock's classic *The 39 Steps*

(1935). Alfred Hitchcock, the master of suspense, made a number of excellent plot-driven thrillers in England before emigrating to the United States in 1939 where his success and influence grew even more so. Formulas that he developed in England, he continued and expanded upon once he got to Hollywood. Sander concentrates on those techniques and patented devices that make Hitchcock the *sine qua non* model for any director of the suspense/thriller genre.

The "Hitchcockian" Elements of *The 39 Steps*

Alfred Hitchcock's production of *The 39 Steps* is only one of his many masterful creations, but it contains many elements that make it a uniquely interesting motion picture. This early example of Hitchcock's visually intensive storytelling set a mark for his future films to strive after. The "Hitchcockian" elements ensure that *The 39 Steps* will continue to enjoy a large audience for years to come.

The most noticeable feature of the film is its blistering pace. The only time the action stops is to let the characters (and the audience) have a breath or two while the suspense of the plot is elevated to an even higher level. Action sequences occur not only in static confined spaces but in crowded public places. This adds the complication of ordinary passersby interfering with the characters, both pursuer and pursued. In the instance of the chase onboard the train, this sense is raised to an extreme level. Richard Hannay (Robert Donat) finds himself hanging onto the outside of the passenger car as the countryside blurs by him at an alarming rate as he is suspended from his precarious perch inches above the trackbed.

Instead of limiting the story to a single set path, Hitchcock allows a myriad of subplots to enter the main storyline, serve their purpose, and leave—having never been really completed. This practice keeps viewers guessing about who will be the next important character to emerge. For example, when we first meet Anabelle Smith (Lucie Mannheim), we are sure she will be the heroine of the picture only to have her murdered in the first quarter hour. A passing kiss to keep Richard from being detected by the police introduces us to Pamela (Madeleine Carroll), who will return later as a substantial aid to our fleeing friend.

Plotlines and trains are not the only things that move quickly in *The 39 Steps*. Even the camera motions are fast. Instead of focusing on one area of the frame for a long time to emphasize its importance, the camera pans quickly by or cuts rapidly to another image. By forcing viewers to be looking for details without having

The 39 Steps (1935)   Robert Donat stifles Madeleine Carroll's scream in Alfred Hitchcock's suspense thriller.

their presence become ostentatious, Hitchcock keeps the action alive even when nothing exciting is happening. The blurring motion of street signs, barely readable, is a much more stylistic way to show a change of setting than a simple narrative statement or still shot.

Suspense and mystery are perhaps the most notable elements of a Hitchcock film. *The 39 Steps* is not the exception. From the very beginning we are kept wondering. At first, we ask who fired the shots in the traveling show during Mr. Memory's (Wyle Watson) act. Once that enigma is solved, we learn that the seemingly ordinary woman is a secret agent who is trying to prevent valuable information from leaving the country. Before the mystery of the nature of that information can be solved, she is murdered—which makes for another mystery. The wary anticipation of being unsure of who is a friend and who is an enemy that Richard feels is conveyed to the viewers.

Hitchcock used unique visual scenes to heighten suspense and exhibit ordinary events in a more stimulating manner. Instead of showing two men attempt to catch the train on which Richard is escaping tire and then fall back, we see only the men's running feet and the shadow of the train accelerating away from them. We notice silhouettes of police officers waiting to search the train as it enters the station as the first sign that Richard has not gotten away quite yet.

Other visual effects add interest to otherwise dull scenes. The sense of motion created by moving the camera had begun to lose some of its impact as moviegoers became more sophisticated, so Hitchcock added other subtle devices to increase interest. The reflections that appear: first, from a woman's jewelry as the train speeds away from her and, next, from a cigarette case offered to Richard by the hostess of the party—where he meets the enemy agent with the missing finger—give a sense of flair to a scene that is visually dull but has plot significance nonetheless.

Audio cues are also an important part of Hitchcock's films. The background conversations that are barely audible and often truncated give additional information about the place and time; occasionally, they also provide comic relief. Less subtly, sounds can furnish transitions between otherwise unrelated scenes. The scene where Anabella's body is discovered starts with the landlady screaming at the top of her lungs. A quick cut to a train blowing its whistle, the same train that Richard is fleeing on, links the two events in a mutual time frame.

One Hitchcock trademark that is noticeably absent from films of today (some would say regretfully absent) is the lack of onscreen violence. This is not to say that there is none at all, but rather that its severity is less than in contemporary movies. We do not see Anabella have a knife thrust into her spine with a virtual explosion of gore as we would more than likely see today; we merely see her stagger into Richard's arms and collapse, a bloody butcher's blade protruding from her back. There is little or no blood elsewhere; the process is remarkably clean—still shocking without being nauseating. In the final scene where Mr. Memory is shot, he is obviously in pain and near death, but we are spared the gushing geysers of blood that modern filmmakers feel compelled to use to make wounds appear real.

The 39 Steps is a motion picture that both transcends the changes in film and celebrates a time before the use of elaborate special effects. It is a pioneering effort that takes a staple of the printed literary world—namely, the murder mystery—and puts it into the visual medium of film. Hitchcock's artistic craft remains enjoyable today both for its timelessness and, paradoxically, for its nostalgia.

Each of the critic's paragraphs has introduced at least one element of Alfred Hitchcock's genius that made him during his lifetime the master of the suspense thriller. Enough of Hitchcock's skills were evidenced in this discussion of *The 39 Steps* that no other film by him had to be mentioned. Jim Sander also makes some trenchant implications about how the genre has declined somewhat since the great director's passing from the scene.

The approach of this chapter has been similar to that of the preceding one on the review. Again, the audience and format were first considered. Approaches to the critical analysis followed, where different emphases were given including: the cinematic technique, or cinematic element-driven critique; the idea- or topic-driven critique; and the character- , actor- , or auteur-driven critique. As in the previous chapter, numerous illustrative excerpts and examples have been provided.

Chapter 5, in similar fashion, expounds on the comparative analysis.

5

TYPES OF FILM CRITICISM:
THE COMPARATIVE ANALYSIS

The *comparative analysis,* like the critical analysis, assumes that the reader is knowledgeable about the movies or people in question. The range of topics is limitless. Essentially, the writer finds similarities between two or three or even four things, makes some statements about them, and then backs up these assertions in the bulk of the paper.

Audience and Format

Typically, the audience for a comparative film analysis would be students of film or those interested in the cinema with a broad background and deep knowledge about motion pictures. Like the critique, the comparative analysis is more scholarly in tone than the review although, again, no research is cited. Because at least two films or directors or actors are compared on any number of aspects, the comparative analysis is usually longer than the review. Most often it submits a thesis and develops it in depth. Like the critical analysis, its title is fully functional, descriptive, and sometimes lengthy. It announces the subject matter and the specifics that will be compared and developed.

Like the critique, the format of the comparative analysis differs from the review in what information is necessary and what is not. Boilerplate is restricted to the bare essentials, and the essay may assume considerable background information already familiar to the reader. The same is true for the plot summary. Again, the reader's familiarity with the plot is assumed so plot summarization may be brief. The comparative analysis will concentrate mainly on those portions of the film relevant to the thesis. Since so much of the comparative piece is analytical and explicatory, there may be less focus on evaluative commentary.

In the comparative analysis, the thesis is made early in the essay, although not necessarily in the first paragraph. The minor inferences (supporting points) with their accompanying examples make up the bulk of the paper but follow a structure somewhat different than the critique (critical analysis). The paper will either emphasize the similarities of the aspects being compared or contrast their differences. Occasionally, the paper will first discuss the parallels and then switch to those points that differ. (A more detailed discussion of the structure—namely block or point-by-point—will be discussed in the next subsection.) Like the longer critical analysis, the comparative analysis can be divided into subtitled subsections. To summarize, the comparative analysis features the following:

- A functionally descriptive title including the film's name,
- An in-depth development of the thesis and subordinate points with specific examples,
- Two or more major points compared with the emphasis being either on their similarities, differences, or one then the other,
- Acknowledgment of credits limited to those that are relevant to the essay,
- Optional plot synopsis and, in same cases, a less evaluative bent,
- Longer critiques, possibly broken into different subsections often subtitled, and
  A structure that is either block or point-by-point.

Structure

Structurally, the comparative analysis differs from the critical analysis because the critique uses a more standard format which has the thesis followed by development of the minor inferences. With the comparative analysis, however, the writer has the option of either employing *block style* or the *point-by-point style*. Either of the two styles (structures) appear after the introduction, which includes the *thesis statement*. The formulas provided below illustrate the differences between the two styles.

Block Style

The block style initially introduces the entire thesis statement—which is often derived from the title—and contains the *thesis* together with the *minor inferences* which elaborate upon it. Then, if block style is employed, the writer first develops the points (Point 1, 2, 3, below) about the first half of the thesis (Film A, below). Next, in a corresponding fashion, the writer develops those same points in regard to the second half of the thesis (Film B, below).

BLOCK STYLE
Thesis Statement = Thesis + Minor Inferences
Thesis (Films A and B) + Minor Inferences (Points 1, 2, 3)
Film A: Point 1, Point 2, Point 3
Film B: Point 1, Point 2, Point 3

Using this formula, we can come up with a topic that uses comparative analysis as a means of developing it. The title below is an example:

Terrence Mallick's *Badlands*
and Oliver Stone's *Natural Born Killers*:
Parallel Motifs of Alienated Youth,
False Heroes, and Violent Endings

The above title would be converted into block style by first discussing *Badlands* (1973) in terms of the shared motifs of alienated youth, false heroes, and violent endings. Then, in similar fashion but in a separate section, conversing about *Natural Born Killers* (1994) along the same lines.

Film A: Point 1, Point 2, Point 3
Badlands: alienated youth, false heroes, violent endings

Film B: Point 1, Point 2, Point 3
Natural Born Killers: alienated youth, false heroes, violent endings

Admittedly, there are additional similarities between these two movies in terms of plotlines, set pieces, characterization, geographic locale, and the like. A complete comparative analysis of the two films would contain numerous variables showing similarity. However, for simplicity's sake, only three variables were selected to illustrate the concept of comparative analysis and how it could be applied to a cinematic topic.

Point-by-Point Style

In point-by-point structure the same thesis statement is used but its elements are turned around. We start with Point 1 (the first minor inference) and discuss in it terms of Film A; then we treat Film B in a similar manner. The same procedure is used for elaborating on Point 2 and then Point 3. The formula looks like this:

POINT-BY-POINT STYLE
Thesis Statement = Thesis + Minor Inferences
Thesis (Films A and B) + Minor Inferences (Points 1, 2, 3)
Point 1:   Film A   Film B
Point 2:   Film A   Film B
Point 3:   Film A   Film B

Using this formula, we can see how we would first be discussing "youthful alienation" and how it applies to *Badlands* and then consider the same motif's use in *Natural Born Killers*. We would then focus on "false heroes" and how that motif is shown in the Mallick film followed by Stone's treatment of it. Finally, "violent endings" would be considered in *Badlands* and then in *Natural Born Killers*.

Point 1:	Film A	Film B
alienated youth:	*Badlands*	*Natural Born Killers*
Point 2:	Film A	Film B
false heroes:	*Badlands*	*Natural Born Killers*
Point 3:	Film A	Film B
violent endings:	*Badlands*	*Natural Born Killers*

Approaches

As with the critique, a number of topics can be looked at in a comparative manner. Directors' styles can be compared. Benchmark films from the *oeuvre* (works) of an established star can be contrasted, highlighting his or her growth from bit player to sought-after commodity commanding millions per film. An actor's transition from light comedy to serious dramatic roles can be analyzed and his or her effectiveness compared in each. Cinematic techniques and special effects moving into obsolescence because of computer-driven imaging and such are other areas ripe for comparative analysis. Why a certain cinema genre has arrived, flourished, waned. and disappeared can be developed through comparative study of causal factors and the environment necessary for nourishment. The approaches listed below are only partial; there are other means and topic areas just as appropriate.

The Movie-to-Movie Comparative Analysis

Often movies are compared for common elements or are contrasted for their effects on audiences. The topics that can be selected for comparative papers are vast. Below are some sample titles that give some indications of directions one can go when writing a comparative analysis of film:

- Cinema's Depiction of the Iniquitous Power of Television as Portrayed by Elia Kazan and Budd Schulberg's *A Face in the Crowd* and Sidney Lumet's *Network,*
- Fifty Years of Film Noir as Represented by *The Big Sleep* (1946), *Chinatown* (1974), and *Seven* (1995),
- Michael Cimino's *The Deer Hunter* and *Heaven's Gate*: Why One Worked and the Other Flopped,
- The Changing Portrayal of the American Indian in the Western Movie: From *Stagecoach* to *Dances with Wolves*, and
- Italian Postwar Neorealism: Three Representative Motion Pictures.

One movie can be shown as the logical outgrowth of another. Former BCC student Arlene Mandel has compared two of the most influential documentaries of all time: Leni Riefenstahl's masterly piece of Third Reich propaganda *Triumph of the Will* and Alain Resnais's heartbreaking film of Auschwitz *Night and Fog*. Using the block format, she first looks at the earlier Riefenstahl film (1936) and then at the Resnais cinematic document (1955) as the tragic aftermath: the Nazi death camp.

The Rise of the Third Reich and Its Horrible Legacy: Riefenstahl's *Triumph of the Will* and Resnais's *Night and Fog*

The comparative nature of this paper is implied and self-explanatory. Leni Riefenstahl's documentary helped bring about the rise of Hitler's Third Reich and World War II. All acts have consequences. In a way, the Leni Riefenstahl documentary of the 1934 Nuremberg Rally had the concentration camp at Auschwitz as its logical end one decade later. The Alain Resnais film is a testament of the ultimate horrors brought about by that regime.

Triumph of the Will

The Nazis more than any other group realized the unlimited potency of film in a generation addicted to the cinema. In addition to propaganda films using carefully picked actors to show Aryan Supremacy and the superiority of Hitler's policies, the regime produced an epic so accomplished in musical and compositional elements of film that *Triumph of the Will* is considered one of the greatest documentaries of all time.

The subject of *Triumph of the Will* was the 1934 Nazi Congress in Nuremberg, but its true purpose was to mythicize Hitler and show him as the god of the German people. The preparation for the 1934 Nuremberg Rally, the arrival of Hitler, the marches, and the speeches make up this documentary with its title suggested by Hitler himself. Ecstatic faces stare up at Hitler as the sun catches his head like a halo. By using dramatic editing, Riefenstahl has the people become a dehumanized mass.

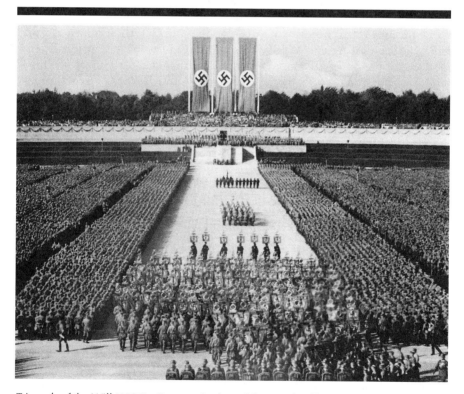

Triumph of the Will (1935)   Panoramic shot of thousands of brownshirts massed in formation at the Nuremberg Rally.

Leni Riefenstahl's film expresses her central belief in the endurance and prevalence of the human spirit. In *Triumph of the Will*, a political rally film, it is Adolf Hitler who is the individual who stands out against the crowd. The crowd is subservient to the leader. The individual is depicted as an unidentified part of a regimented multitude, implying that emotion is superior to reason.

When seen today, *Triumph of the Will* reminds us of Hitler's plans for creating a German renaissance through Nazi Party unity and military strength. It now recalls memories of a madman whose ideas of rebirth led to genocide; it reminds us of the unspeakable evil, of the stillness that lives now in the ruins of Dachau, Buchenwald, Mauthausen, Auschwitz, Treblinka, and Belsen. It reminds us that man can be irrational, that people can follow false gods, and that it is all too possible to make hell seem like heaven.

Triumph of the Will is the documentary as propaganda. It transforms the actual reality of 1934 Party disunity and chaos into a massive spectacle of regimentation, unity, and fidelity under the Fuehrer. The film is faithful to the outright lies on which it is focused—succeeding in making those lies seem like the truth.

Triumph of the Will is the official film record of the 1934 Nuremberg Rally of the National Socialist Party. The film does not preserve a chronological record of the numerous meetings, separate rallies, and diverse speeches; nor does it capture what historically we have come to see as the central experience of Nazism in 1934. But Riefenstahl's task was to make a film of the Party rally, not a documentary of the prevailing social conditions. Her film is true to the perceived reality of Nuremberg, however dishonest and misleading that convention may have been. Although not an accurate chronological record of events, it is, nevertheless, a valid cinematic expression of the Nazi mystique.

The major theme of *Triumph of the Will* is the godliness of Hitler as he imposes his will over the mass of ordinary Germans. But there are several themes subordinate to it, including: (1) the German heritage and tradition maintained in the Nazi order; (2) the importance of communal work and cooperation; (3) the mysticism of the Nazi Party. The film suggests that the party is the legal and spiritual heir to the legacy of the German nation. Through the medieval architecture of Nuremberg, the folk music, and the emphasis on Hitler's wide public support, the film reinforces the continuity between Germany's past and present (1934). The film also demonstrates that the group effort is the right way, the only way. The crowds are always unified, even in solemn tributes. Riefenstahl uses such visual contrasts as day with night, young with old, joy with sorrow, light with dark, children with soldiers, ancient city with modern rally, specific actions and words of individuals with the monolithic appearance and behavior of crowds, and, finally, Hitler with his followers.

There is no in-depth substance in *Triumph of the Will* either in words or action, only fleeting impressions of organized meetings, precision displays of marching, and self-congratulatory speeches. Yet it is their cumulative effect that is so convincing.

Riefenstahl presents Hitler, a figure of national importance, as a leader of great historical significance to the destiny of Germany. In this sense she is recording history. The epic and heroic forces of the film always center around Hitler. The triumph of his will represents the triumph of the German collective will to rise from the ashes of Versailles phoenix-like and lead Europe.

The world of Hitler's storm troopers was the outgrowth of his elite corps of youth. His warriors, bent on global domination, were the fruit of one man's conception—not the inevitability of time and space. It is this world that Hitler envisioned that Leni Riefenstahl through her film helped create.

Night and Fog

Alain Resnais' *Night and Fog* forces us to confront the implications of Auschwitz for the future. It resurrects the hellish life of the prisoners with concentrated imaginativeness and leaves us looking over our shoulders for those among us capable of administering another such system. A great deal of *Night and Fog* is composed of the Nazis' own film archives that contributed such damning evidence in this Alain Resnais documentary.

Night and Fog incorporates poetic, impassioned, yet disciplined narration with a superb musical score. Through the imaginative use of these two elements as well as the compilation footage, Resnais exposes the foundations of the death camps: that minority who are always ready to carry out orders that brutalize other human beings. This film is harrowing—not only for what it shows, but for the vision of the remainder of the 20th century that it raises.

The documentary tours the remnants of Auschwitz in the middle 1950s; however, intercut with this retrospective cinematic visit are black and white archival material of the horrors that took place there not too many years before. The carefully controlled commentary, as well as the sad but gentle music, stands in stark contrast with the newsreels of the concentration camp victims: the past intrudes upon the present; memory precludes forgetting.

Once setting in motion the official destruction of what Nazi ideology called the "racially valueless" children, Hitler then turned to the medical murder of the surviving Jewish people. Various gases were tried, and the accepted procedure evolved into one that was relatively simple and convincingly deceptive. The people were told to undress; the women and girls had their hair cut off—later to be woven into cloth. In groups of twenty to thirty, the inmates of the camp were brought into a chamber disguised as a shower room. The doors and windows of the room were sealed, and the "patients," who believed they were there for showers, were instead gassed to death by the doctor on duty. To make room for the next load, the bodies were tossed out right away, and thrown into large ditches, to be burned later either in the crematoria or in the open air.

Although *Night and Fog* is in French with English subtitles, it is a film that is easy to understand. One can clearly see the pain and suffering written on the faces of the people in the concentration camps. The film is quite moving as well as horrifying. Consequently, *Night and Fog* is considered the single most powerful documentary ever made about man's capacity for destroying his kin.

A documentary film such as *Night and Fog* needs to be seen by everyone to remind people of the evil that once took place. People throughout the world, from one generation to the next, must never forget what Hitler and his forces did to millions of people. Only by constant reminders, such as documentaries like *Night and Fog*, can succeeding generations be made aware of the tragic end result of one man's tyranny.

In a block-style comparative analysis, the critic has paralleled two documentaries about the Hitler Era. She argues how Leni Riefenstahl's *Triumph of the Will* aided and abetted the rise of the Third Reich. Conversely, Alain Resnais' *Night and Fog* bears witness to the horrendous effects of the establishment and growth of that regime.

The Literary Work-to-Movie Comparative Analysis

Many movies over the years have used novels, short stories, or plays as their literary sources. As we have already discussed, some adaptations have been literal, others faithful, while some—at best—have loosely based literary antecedents. Immediately following is a list of titles for comparative papers based on the adaptation of literary works into movies.

- Many Faces and Interpretations of Shakespeare's *Hamlet*: Portrayals by Laurence Olivier, Nicol Williamson, and Mel Gibson,
- Elements in Common between Two Literal Adaptations of American Dramatic Classics: *The Glass Menagerie* and *Death of a Salesman,*
- The Books Work but the Movies Do Not: *The Bonfire of the Vanities* and *King Solomon's Mines* (the remake);
- Hemingway's Short Stories Transposed onto the Screen: *The Snows of Kilimanjaro* and *The Old Man and the Sea*, and
- True to the Spirit of the Depression: Adaptations of John Steinbeck's *The Grapes of Wrath* and *Of Mice and Men.*

What follows is a short comparative analysis using an informal point-by-point structure on director Michael Mann's motion picture of *The Last of the Mohicans* (1992) and the James Fenimore Cooper novel upon which it is loosely based.

What Price Action?

Hollywood, not surprisingly, has done it again. In the remaking of the 1936 movie of James Fenimore Cooper's romantic classic *The Last of the Mohicans*, today's moviemakers have jam-packed the film with action and special effects while taking generous liberties with plot and characterization. Perhaps "romantic" is the operative word here, for its associations were quite different back in 1826 when the book was published. Romanticism involved selfless quests and idealized notions of love between men and women. Sexual passion and its graphic depiction were not found on the pages of the typical romantic tome. Having just finished reading the Cooper opus, this critic made the mistake of viewing the film soon thereafter at the local moviehouse. Thus, the Hollywoodization of the storyline was particularly disconcerting. Despite Cooper's overblown 19th century prose and turgid explications, the original plot was captivating and should have been more closely adhered to in this widescreen epic by Michael Mann (director, producer, and co-writer). Yes, the same Michael Mann who made his mark with *Miami Vice*, that flashy television series notorious for its stylized violence, stylish automobiles, and styles of fashion.

The tale unfolds in 1757 in the pre-Revolutionary colony of New York: the French and Indian War is already of three years' duration. The French and their Indian allies are on an offensive, sweeping down from Canada and attacking outposts and farms across the area north of Albany up through the Adirondacks to the shores of

Lake George. The actual historical incidents involved are the attack on the British-held Fort William Henry, its ignominious surrender, and the subsequent massacre of its troops and civilians by the Huron henchmen of the French. It is up to Cooper's fictitious creation Hawkeye (played unconvincingly by Daniel Day-Lewis) and Chingachgook and his son Uncas—his two Mohican bloodbrothers—to rescue the hostage daughters of the defeated English commandant and avenge the slaughter. As one can expect, there are numerous chases, skirmishes, ambushes, and panoramic battle episodes, but it is in the particulars of the plot and its persona that Mann strays from the text in yielding to box office blandishments.

Hawkeye has always been pictured as a nonsexual hero by Cooper—somewhat of a chivalrous knight in buckskin. Mann, however, has him "making it" with Cora, the elder captive daughter (adequately acted by Madeleine Stowe), in one of the scenes where she is free, twenty-one, and very willing. True, there is no onscreen bunkroom nude scene here at the fort, but by the principals' suggestive dialogue and promising glances, such offscreen capers are more than hinted.

Cora, in the book, is murdered by a treacherous Huron warrior in the novel's finale. Her sister Alice, though, survives to eventually find happiness in England. In the movie, however, Alice chooses suicide rather than submit to any additional Huron indignities during her capture, whereas Cora and Hawkeye, in the film's final sequence, stand together on a rocky crag facing the setting sun and pondering their future.

Major Heyward, the young, gallant English officer that Cooper portrays as a man just a shade less heroic than Hawkeye, is always a willing, helpful collaborator of the woodsman in the quest to free the sisters. Yet Mann depicts him as stupid, devious, arrogant, and vindictive—whose only positive act is his heroic death. In the movie, his love for Cora is spurned; in the book, his affections are always directed to and ultimately returned by Alice.

Despite its betrayal of the text and its indifferent acting—with the exception of the masterfully cast Wes Studi as the malevolent Huron antagonist Magua—the film does have a number of admirable qualities. The cinematography and special effects are exemplary. The battle scenes—both the siege of the fort and the surprise attack from the woods—are well-choreographed and authentic, even down to the differing types of European artillery and assorted Indian weapons employed. The action is fast-paced and doesn't give one time to ruminate on the script's inadequacies. The book (at times exhaustingly so) puts the events in both historical and anthropological perspective. The film hardly makes the effort to do so. This has probably added to its overall positive reception by audiences as a historical spectacle . . . unless, of course, you have just read the book.

The essay above has discussed a film based on a novel that is also a remake of an earlier cinematic version of the book. The thrust of the critique is the castigation of the director and screenwriter for the excessive liberties they took with the original literary work. Wanton disregard for plot and characterization are the film's greatest flaws. Such trampling upon the author's intentions would especially harm the viewer who was knowledgeable about the written source, James Fenimore Cooper's *The Last of the Mohicans*. Most of the paragraphs that follow the introduction through contrast give specific instances of such abuses.

The Comparison-of-Individuals Comparative Analysis

Another fertile area for comparative analysis concerns those individuals—directors, actors, characters—involved in movies. Comparative studies can be made on such subject areas as:

- Two different actors playing the same or a similar role in two different films,
- Two different styles of directors, and
- The same theme but in separate films by the same director.

The following is a representative listing of titles for comparative papers based on individuals in the cinema:

- Racism in America as Perceived by the Films of Spike Lee,
- Humphrey Bogart and Robert Mitchum as Philip Marlowe: Interpretive Differences in *The Big Sleep,*
- Mel Brooks and Woody Allen: Two Comedic Auteurs,
- Femme Fatales of the Nineties: Sharon Stone and Linda Fiorentino, and
- The New Wave of Truffaut and Godard: Similarities and Differences.

The comparative essay below by former Broward Community College student Debra Wade discusses the portrayal of women in motion pictures. She looks at two relatively recent films: Mike Nichols' *Working Girl* (1989) and Donald Petrie's *Grumpy Old Men* (1993).

How Women Are Portrayed in Movies

The implied message broadcast on the silver screen has been that for a woman to be successful in the professional arena, she must be emotionally tough and verbally terse. She must be able to hide her feminine form by dressing conservatively. A woman must appear more like a man in her attire yet retain her femininity.

Another strongly implied message is that for women, middle age is not a time of productivity. It is often shown as the time for a woman to begin winding down her life. It is rarely seen as a time of growth. It is most often represented as a time of looking to the past, mourning what has been lost.

The characters are often portrayed by much younger women playing the parts of middle-aged women. These characters are often depicted as bastions of wisdom or as babysitters for their grandchildren. They are rarely pictured as having a successful career outside their family or an active sex life. They are often displayed as insecure and fearful of losing their attractiveness. However, two movies that depart from the way women are usually interpreted in film are *Working Girl* and *Grumpy Old Men*.

In *Working Girl*, the lead character Tess, played by Melanie Griffith, is initially portrayed as a "sex kitten." By her style of dress and use of language, her seeming lack of education and class are evident. But, as her character develops, it becomes clear that Tess has been working to improve herself. She has been going to night school and doing independent study.

Tess shows initiative in presenting a well-thought out idea to management in hopes of moving into a management level training program. Through the twists of the storyline, she finds herself in the position to take advantage of an opportunity to promote her investment idea. She adjusts her speaking style to one that is more professional. She "borrows" a more conservative wardrobe to showcase her attractiveness, but she uses her education and her keen business savvy to gain professional inroads in a male-dominated arena.

Throughout the film, Tess remains softly feminine but fiercely professional. Her sexuality is appealing, but it is not the key to her success.

In the film *Grumpy Old Men*, the feminine lead Ariel, played by Ann-Margaret, is a decidedly middle-aged widow. The two male leads, John and Max, played by Jack Lemmon and Walter Matthau, respectively, are senior citizens well into retirement.

Though she is a widow and middle-aged, Ariel embraces life. She is intelligent: a college professor. She is creative: a sculptress. Above all else, she is a lover of life and ardently sexual. This character is soft and feminine, intensely sexy, yet definitely thick in the waist. She is outrageous, sassy, and loves to take risks. Her approach to life is a zesty one. She isn't the least bit concerned with what the neighbors think. She delights, in fact, in stirring things up.

Throughout this movie, these characters deal with the sexual urges too often ascribed to the young. Many of the humorous moments of the movie result from the antics of two aging men who are blasted out of their retirement and dropkicked back into the competitive sexuality of their youth. As John and Max deal with the fears and worries of dating, the feminine lead is shown as confident of her sexuality and indulgent of the foibles of her suitors.

Tess in *Working Girl* departs from traditional depiction by being sexy but intelligent and competent. Tess isn't determined to get ahead at the cost of her femininity nor is she willing to back down. She can and does fight for herself. In so doing, this character demands and receives respect.

Ariel in *Grumpy Old Men* departs from the typical mature woman portrayal by being very feminine and very sexual. Ariel is confident in herself and embraces life. She shows us that age and sexuality are a matter of attitude.

These two films depart from the way women are presented in films. They show a young woman succeeding without primarily using her sexuality and a mature woman reveling in the success of her sexuality. In both films, sexuality, femininity, and intelligence operate quite independently of each other. Both characters—Tess and Ariel—demonstrate that femininity at any age is a quality to be reveled in, a quality to be celebrated.

In her comparative essay, the critic establishes how women are typically portrayed in most film roles. After defining how the "successful" businesswoman and the middle-aged woman are traditionally depicted in the movies, she introduces two films that depart radically from these stereotypes. The remainder of her essay goes on to comment how *Working Girl* and *Grumpy Old Men* shatter many clichés about women characters in the cinema. Her critique is mainly written in a loose block structure; yet final summarization verges on the point-by-point mode. Nevertheless, it does works. By the end of this comparative work, we have a clear indication on how the two women differ markedly from their celluloid sisters.

The Original-to-Remake-or-Sequel Comparative Analysis

"Imitation is the highest form of flattery." "You can't argue with success." These two adages serve as introductions to our final area for comparative analytical study: the many remakes and sequels created over the years of original films that met with some degree of success, either critically or financially. Hollywood, during the last twenty years or so, has been especially prone to repeatedly mine the motherlode. A movie hit is analyzed and converted into a formula that is repeated over and over again—often with diminishing returns. In most cases, the sequel is not as good as the original expressly because the formulation of what was originally a unique concept could only be brought to fruition once, not a second time.

Remakes recognize a good story. The rationale behind making them is that it is the right time for a new generation of filmgoers to see a movie classic renewed. Or, it could be viewed as a good star vehicle to showcase whoever happens to be hot that year. Whatever the motive, remakes, because they are contemporary, can appeal to new viewers; conversely, they are often resisted by older viewers, enamored with the earlier version and its stars. Occasionally, a remake of a foreign language film will be produced which might have had relatively little exposure in the United States. Examples would be Martin Brest's *Scent of a Woman* (1992) from the 1976 Italian film of the same name by Dino Risi, Jim McBride's *Breathless* (1983) from Jean-Luc Godard's 1961 French New Wave film (also of the same title), and William Friedkin's 1977 *Sorcerer*, the remake of H. G. Clouzot's 1955 *The Wages of Fear*.

Below is a list of titles for topics comparing original films with sequels and remakes.

- A comparison of Shakespeare's *Richard III:* 1955 and 1995,
- *Rocky* and Its Sequels: The Continuation of a Myth,
- From Comic Book Pages to the Big Screen: The *Batman* Films,
- *King Solomon's Mines:* A Misconceived Change in Tone in the Remake, and
- The *Star Wars* Trilogy: Formulas for Box Office Success.

The motives behind remakes vary although a healthy profit margin is a universally shared inducement. The comparative study that follows looks at the film noir classic *The Big Sleep* (1946) by Howard Hawks and compares elements of it with the 1978 remake by Michael Winner.

Same Title, Different Time and Place:
The Original and the Remake of *The Big Sleep*

English director Michael Winner decided it was time for a British cinema version of American mystery novelist Raymond Chandler's *The Big Sleep*. More than three decades had passed since Howard Hawks' original film noir hit. Winner assembled a mixed Anglo-American cast and shot the film in color in contemporary London rather than the black and white Los Angeles of 32 years earlier. It takes some getting used to.

The Big Sleep of 1945 has always epitomized the 1940s film noir. It stars Humphrey Bogart as Philip Marlowe, private investigator—one of the detective icons of the genre. Marlowe has an office in Los Angeles. Shot in black and white, the interior setting is always suffused with shadows. Exterior settings are usually at night, with wet streets and rain. Greater Los Angeles in 1945 is a sprawling, horizontal city—with alleys running in back of low buildings and one-story bungalows rather than between tall edifices. Expressways and boulevards like arteries and veins link countless suburbs, but L.A. has no true heart. The physical decay, seediness, and wasted space are mirrored by the morally decayed, seedy, and wasted lives that Marlowe encounters in his world.

A totally different physical atmosphere is created by a sunny London, which seems a misnomer but, in this instance, is not. It is London's summer rather than L.A.'s. To the blue skies are added the achingly green manicured lawns of an English estate. London is one of the world's largest cities and one of its densest. Its public transportation—omnibuses, cabs, and the underground—play an important role in the city's life: They link its sections and neighborhoods tightly with each other and the city's center, creating an ambiance at variance with the private automobile-addicted Los Angeles where public transportation is a mirthless joke.

The colors in London are vibrant. Thus an important mood element—the murkiness, shadows, dimness, and play of light and dark in the original—is negated. An interior sequence shows the detective's bedroom done up in color-coordinated sheets, comforter, blanket and accessories: surroundings that the 1945 Marlowe would not possess, much less want. Somehow, the tough, lonely detective of author Chandler and the tough, independent shamus of director Hawks would not care about what blend of colors would "make" a bedroom. Also gone is the memorable L.A. office of Marlowe with

The Big Sleep (1946)   Humphrey Bogart as Philip Marlowe hides in the shadows of his office.

those venetian blinds forming the sinister diagonal lines across the walls and ceiling.

The plot in both versions, at times, makes no sense, and perhaps Raymond Chandler never intended it to, for *The Big Sleep* is a novel of characterization, setting, and mood. Howard Hawks honored this closely enough to gain the novelist's approbation. What Chandler would have felt about director Winner's liberties can only be speculated—Chandler having died in 1959. The setting and mood decidedly differ in the two films.

According to critic Janey Place, Chandler sees Marlowe as a man who walks down mean streets but is far more noble than the places he visits. He envisions the detective as a loner untarnished morally despite the depravity of the people he deals with daily and is unafraid of them or the situations they induce. He is above the world he chooses to travel through; he is not of that world but outside it. At times, he is hardboiled in his words; on other occasions, he philosophizes about this world and those who people it, even poetically. Hardbitten on the surface, he can show deep compassion:

The Big Sleep (1978)   Robert Mitchum as private investigator Philip Marlowe chats with James Stewart as the infirm General Sternwood in the Michael Winner remake.

for Harry Jones, the little man with misplaced loyalties; for General Sternwood, the aging and infirm widower remorseful at having failed in the upbringing of his two daughters. Distrustful of women, Marlowe shows some vulnerability to the elder Sternwood daughter as she changes and proves trustworthy to him in the end. The earlier cinematic Marlowe is especially faithful to the Chandler creation. The major change being the Hollywoodization of the romance between Marlowe and Vivian Sternwood (Lauren Bacall). In the later movie, the sexual relationship somewhat alluded to in the earlier is now more graphic (it is R-rated) with Robert Mitchum's Marlowe linked with Charlotte Sternwood, played by Sarah Miles. (For some reason, the character's name has been changed from "Vivian" to "Charlotte.") The other Sternwood daughter—whom Winner renames "Camilla" (from the earlier "Carmen")—is here played by Candy Clark. Her performance portrays the younger daughter as mad, nymphomaniacal, and kooky, whereas Martha Vickers' Carmen of the Hawks film is promiscuous, provocative, and psychotic: a femme fatale in the making. In all three cases (the book and both movies), the younger sister is resisted by Marlowe, who's morally outraged at her attempted seduction of him.

Humphrey Bogart and Robert Mitchum play Marlowe in the respective versions. They bring two different approaches to the character. Bogart, in the role, presents a different presence than Mitchum. Film critic Janet Maslin sees Bogart as more "swaggering and suspicious" whereas Mitchum is more "unflappably calm and world weary" in his interpretation of the private investigator. Thus, when Marlowe philosophizes, the lines are especially effectively delivered by Mitchum.

Remakes are never judged on their own merits alone. They are always compared to the original by the critics and the public. Whether this is fair or not does not really matter. Producers and directors realize the mindset of the public and the professional reviewers: they rationalize that although the knives of commentary will be especially whetted, so will the curiosity of comparison and it is the latter as much as the former that will effect their profit margins.

Remakes of movies are excellent grist for critical comparative analysis. The comparative critique above has evaluated and commented on the two versions of the film noir classic *The Big Sleep*. The structure is decidedly point-by-point. The critic first looks at the setting, ambiance, and mood of the original and then juxtaposes those elements with the later version. He then shows that the plot for both films is hard to follow and not very logical. With two very different actors playing the role of Philip Marlowe, it is pointed out how disparate their interpretations of the private investigator are; also mentioned are the dissimilarities between the other two sets of players.

Sequels face the same biases of remakes and a comparable anticipatory interest. Although a number of years, even decades, may pass between the original and the remake, the time span between the original and the sequel is usually much shorter. *A Shot in the Dark*, for example, was released just a few months after its precursor, *The Pink Panther,* finished its first run. Few expect the sequel to be as good as the film it is emulating, and yet everyone wants to see it just to prove that point. At times, though, the sequel is every bit as worthy as the original: witness the accolades for *The Godfather II* or *The Empire Strikes Back.*

Usually, sequels come hot on the heels of the originals and keep coming, if showing a profit. Whenever possible, as much of the original crew—both in front and behind the camera—is kept for the sequel. Contract commitments and salary demands of some of the cast because of newly found marketability force replacements. This and the often perceived need to rush the new product to theaters before the interest of the fickle public wanes result in sequel productions that are markedly inferior. As stated before. formula often substitutes for creativity as repetition replaces craft.

Most atypically. the acclaimed *The Last Picture Show* (1971) by Peter Bogdanovich had to wait almost two decades before being followed by its more modestly received sequel *Texasville* (1990). This is highly unusual since a sequel usually appears no more than a year or so after a successful original. Both films are based on the novels by Larry McMurty, who wrote the screenplay for the earlier film. The analysis that follows compares the two films.

Same Place, Different Time:
The Last Picture Show
and Its Belated Sequel *Texasville*

Most of the team was back in place with Peter Bogdanovich again at the helm. No longer the boy genius of *The Last Picture Show* and having experienced a number of bumps along his directorial road, it was time to return to his roots (of success, at least) and tap them for the hit that would re-establish his career.

Simply stated, it didn't work out that way. The lack of the sequel's success—both critically and at the box office—resulted from a number of factors. One factor no one could control was age: would the characters be as interesting and their lives as compelling to the viewer thirty years later? Many of the original cast was back in their roles: Jeff Bridges (as Duane Jackson), Timothy Bottoms (Sonny Crawford), Cybill Shepherd (Jacy Farrow), Cloris Leachman (Ruth Popper), Randy Quaid (Lester Marlow), and Eileen Brennan (Genevieve). The original, *The Last Picture Show*, was set in the 1950s. And if there is one major failing of *Texasville* set in the 1980s, it is that the lives of these same characters after three decades just do not elicit the same degree of empathy as they did before. They have all changed—and not only physically. The texture and look of the film has changed. The town itself has grown somewhat and changed. The point of view has changed. The tone has changed. The theme has changed. And with all that change, much has been lost.

The Last Picture Show was centered around Sonny, whereas *Texasville* revolves about Duane. In altering the point of view, a ripple effect is created upon other aspects of the film. The tone, once serious and wistful as Sonny himself, now effects the whimsical, ironic humor of Duane. The isolation, loneliness, and slowness of life's passage infused the earlier film. Its "slice of life" style affected the view-

The Last Picture Show (1971) Cybill Shepherd and Jeff Bridges as young lovers.

ers. Although nostalgic for the audience, it was not so for the characters who weren't reflecting on their lives back in the 1950s but living them.

The Last Picture Show was about the aches of young unrequited love, the tests of friendship, the mystery and pain of sexuality, and the devastation of loss through death. There are far fewer rites of passage in the later film. Not too many fresh wounds, just many scars. Everyone is hardened, cynical, blasé, selfish, and tired. Sonny, although the mayor of Anarene, proprietor of a convenience store, and owner of some other enterprises, considers himself a failure. He is also losing his mind: not being able to keep up with the events of the day and disappearing suddenly from his shop to sit within the burned-out shell of the old movie theater, he watches moving pictures in the sky. Duane has become rich running an oil business, but presently is millions in debt. Now he fills his idle hours—and there are many of them—by sexually servicing all but one of the town's unhappy wives and recent divorcées: his own missus Karla (Annie Potts). A theme of sexual anomie and moral bankruptcy abounds in the film. Everyone is talking about sex or engaging in it, but no one is finding true pleasure in it—much less love. A spate of unintended pregnancies are the consequences of this lasciviousness, but no one seems to take them that seriously.

The opening sequence sets the tone and theme. In a hot tub, behind an enormous house plunked down in the midst of the sterile North Texas prairie, sits Duane firing an enormous pistol at an expensive, brand new doghouse. He blasts it to smithereens for no logical reason. His boredom, aimlessness, and the uselessness of his possessions are apparent. His family is rotting from moral decay. His first daughter has two little kids, is divorced, and is working on the fiancé of the week with perhaps another pregnancy in the offing. His older son Dickie (William McNamara) is engaged to be married but has gotten one neighbor's wife pregnant and prefers the estranged wife of another. He has also been jailed for speeding eight-five miles an hour through a school zone. Duane and Karla's pre-teen twins are spoiled brats, fighting with each other and showing no respect for any of the adults around them. Karla is, in turn, angry, sharp tongued, and runs off to shop when provoked.

Ruth Popper is now Duane's loyal secretary wasting her good advice on her boss who "because the oil business has gone belly up

Texasville (1990) Jeff Bridges and Cybill Shepherd reprise their roles from *The Last Picture Show* twenty years later.

[has] nothing . . . to do but sleep with any woman [he] can find." Over the years, well after her husband's death, Ruth has never rekindled the romance that she once shared with Sonny and one wonders why.

Two events are to bring conflict and genuine change to the movie. But both fall short. The first is the return of Jacy to Anarene. The second is the centennial celebration for "Texasville," the forerunner of Anarene, to which the film builds in a meaningless climax. Jacy returns to Anarene—if only temporarily—to recover from the death of her little boy. Having lived in Italy for years as a third-rate actress, she hopes to convalesce from her loss at the site of her earliest triumphs as richest and prettiest girl in town (and also its most selfish and heartless). She soon engages in mental/emotional dueling with Duane as she co-opts his wife, children, and dog. At one point in the film, she and Karla actually appear for a pageant rehearsal in identical outfits that they bought together during a shopping spree. The embers between Duane and Jacy—always smoldering—never burst into flame, however. Perhaps Duane no longer does "know how to fall in love [or back in love] with anybody." And perhaps Jacy, despite her strong feelings for Duane, still has not outgrown her tendency to play with the emotions of numerous others at the same time. She accompanies Duane to Odessa where he is desperately seeking to make a financial deal and stay solvent. They get a motel room but have a totally non-sexual encounter (or so it appears)s. She is watching a game show on television while giving him some nickel philosophizing and a psychological insight into herself which the film never develops further. She states:

> Game shows are what life's really like. You win things that look really great at the time but turn out to be junk and you lose things you may want to keep forever just because you're unlucky.

Does she mean Duane or the dead child or both? She continues to lead Duane—and the audience—on: we expect something passionate to develop between them but it never does. Just a number of wistful glances for what was and what might have been. She says such words as: "I feel like we're the Adam and Eve of this town" and "You're scared to death you'll feel something you can't control." Yet such mixed signals lead nowhere. By the film's last reel, Duane and Karla are slouching toward reconciliation and Jacy is preparing to return to Europe. At movie's end, we see a number of knowing glances between Jacy and Duane, Duane and Karla, and Karla and Jacy. What they know Bogdanovich certainly doesn't share with the audience.

Texasville sorely misses those characters who have died off: Ruth's husband, Jacy's mother, Sonny's kid brother, and Sam the Lion, the philosopher king of the tiny 1950s town now grown to considerable size by the 1980s. Those characters, their conflicts, and, the relationships they engendered brought a serious, somewhat tragic element to the earlier film. This is totally missing from the sequel. The characters' flaws as shown and discoursed over in *Texasville* are too excessive to avoid self-parody. Unfortunately, the causal subtext behind them that would make the film more believable and fulfilling is neither viewed nor discussed sufficiently.

This lengthy comparative analysis of an original and a sequel initially is cast in the point-by-point mode. However, midway it segues mainly into a critique of *Texasville*, the sequel to *The Last Picture Show*. The critic points out that a number of factors contribute to the flaws of the later film. These factors have to do with change—and the changes in the sequel do not work. Among these alterations are: the aging of the actors (most of the original cast are reprising their roles); the setting (same place but three decades later); the point of view (the original centered around Sonny, the sequel revolves around Duane); the tone (previously serious and wistful, now whimsical and ironic); and the themes and motifs (in the former: unrequited love, friendship, sexuality's pain and mystery, and devastating loss through death; in the latter: cynicism, selfishness, tiredness, sexual anomie, and moral bankruptcy). Taken altogether, these factors make for a sequel that is inferior to the original.

Again the audience and the format have been initially considered. Then, in a departure from the previous two chapters on the review and the critique respectively, specific structural options were presented: namely, block style and point-by-point style. Approaches to the comparative analysis followed next. They included movie-to-movie comparative analysis, literary work-to-movie comparative analysis, comparison-of-individuals comparative analysis and original-to-remake-or-sequel comparative analysis. As before, a full complement of excerpts and complete examples have been furnished.

Chapter 6 studies in depth the documented research paper. The chapter ends with two entire sample essays and their respective works cited pages.

6

TYPES OF FILM CRITICISM:
THE DOCUMENTED RESEARCH PAPER

The documented research paper is the most formalized means of critical written expression. Not only are ideas, opinions, and theories of the writer necessary, but they now must be backed up by the views of "experts" on film and perhaps even those individuals involved directly in the making of the movie(s) discussed. To gather such material, the writer must seek these secondary sources from books, periodicals, personal interviews, videos, filmstrips, cassette tapes, CD ROMs, and the Internet to access Web sites. The approach should be methodical and well-planned before being undertaken. Once an outline is drawn up, the researched material amassed is culled for information that will be used and documented accordingly. When the draft is written, in-text citations must be incorporated and a "works cited" page drawn up. The remainder of this subsection will address portions of the process in greater detail.

Deciding on a Topic

Much time can be saved if you have some idea of your topic before beginning research. Ideally, it should either be on an aspect of film about which you either have some previous knowledge as a base to build upon or a subject area that interests you greatly—be it a film, director, actor, or period of cinema. If you cannot select your own subject and a list of titles or topics is imposed on you, again, opt for what you know best or what interests you most from among them.

Length of Paper

The length of your research paper will either be externally decided—the professor requires a 10-to-15-page research paper or one of 1,500–2,000 words. Or, its length will be internally determined: how much time you have to devote to doing research—including viewing some films or videos—and then converting that to a written document.

Subject Area: Neither Too Broad nor Too Narrow

Probably more important than length is determining the adequacy of your topic to the given assignment and the time you will allot yourself to work on it. If the project is a 1,500-word paper (approximately five to six pages) a topic such as "The American Western" would be too broad and general. One could literally write a 600-page tome on such a topic. Conversely, one would be hard put to write a 2,000-word research paper (seven to eight pages) on "The Symbolic Impact of the Train Whistle in *High Noon*"—on such a subject, one or two pages would suffice. You should back up your points and assertions with multiple sources, but not so many as to lead to boring repetition. The sample topics below are for an assignment of from 1,500–2,000 words. Actually, with each of the sample topics below, if you were to choose to write a paper of at least double that length, you could fairly easily. To do so, you would go into greater detail and increase the number of variables covered or being compared. Yet notice, however, that the titles are specific enough to be focused yet broad enough to avoid being overly repetitive. The following titles can be appropriately covered in a research paper of from 1,500 to 2,000 words or one much longer:

• An Overview of Contemporary Film Noir: The Same Themes, Moods, and Characterizations but Shot in Color;
• The Many Accents of Meryl Streep: A Gifted Actress's Genius for Characterization as Evidenced in *Out of Africa, Sophie's Choice, A Cry in the Dark*, and *The Bridges of Madison County;*
• Truffaut and Godard: Interaction with and Influence on Each Other and the French New Wave;
• Dashiell Hammett's Sam Spade and Raymond Chandler's Philip Marlowe Compared: Two Detectives of the 1940s; and
• From Idealistic Country Lawyer to Unscrupulous Political Demagogue: The Corruption of Willie Stark in *All the King's Men.*

Note that some of the topics could also be developed as critical analyses whereas others could be better served with a comparative analysis format. Regardless of approach, the research information you have gathered will be interwoven into your text by means of quotations, cited paraphrases, and summaries supplementing and supporting your own insights and opinions.

The Outline

Once you have arrived at a specific topic for your research essay, you are ready to draw up a working outline. But before. you take this step, first convert the topic into a detailed title with the specific movie(s) or person(s) as part of it. Once done, you are then ready to turn your title into a thesis statement.

Thesis Statement

As stated before, the complete thesis statement has three intentions, thus, subsequently, parts: a *subject*, a *thesis* (the *statement* regarding the subject), and *minor inferences* (evidence of *support* for the statement). Often, in fact, the title of the research paper will reflect the complete thesis statement. Returning to the titles immediately above, we will repeat and then convert two of them into thesis statements:

Title:	An Overview of Contemporary Film Noir: The Same Themes, Moods, and Characterizations but Shot in Color as Seen in *Body Heat*, *Seven*, and *L.A. Confidential*
Subject:	Contemporary film noir
Statement:	Has comparable themes, moods, and characterizations (as classic film noir)
Support:	Evidenced in such relatively recent color productions as *Body Heat, Seven,* and *L.A. Confidential*

Similarly, we can convert the title about Meryl Streep's gifts at playing roles of non-American characters.

Title:	The Many Accents of Meryl Streep: A Gifted Actress's Genius for Characterization as Depicted in *Out of Africa, Sophie's Choice, A Cry in the Dark*, and *The Bridges of Madison County*
Subject:	Meryl Streep
Statement:	Has a talent for characterization through her remarkable adoption of foreign accents and mannerisms
Support:	This is vividly depicted in such films as *Out of Africa, Sophie's Choice, A Cry in the Dark,* and *The Bridges of Madison County;*

or

Support: This is vividly depicted sd she plays a Danish writer in *Out of Africa*, a Polish refugee in *Sophie's Choice*, an Australian mother in *A Cry in the Dark*, and an Italian farmwife in Iowa in *The Bridges of Madison County*.

Mapping Main Points, Subordinate Points, and Examples

Once the title has been converted into a complete thesis statement, the outline can be drawn since it flows out of the thesis statement components. With the thesis statement reached, building a working outline follows. The term "working" is used because the outline is somewhat incomplete and will be adjusted as research dictates. Initially, there will be certain holes in the outline that will be filled in with the selection of the secondary sources (criticism found in periodicals, books, online, etc.) to be incorporated into the paper.

The typical outline is both sequential and hierarchical. The outline is *sequential* if it builds in an orderly fashion that emanates from the thesis statement. In some cases, it is chronological and follows a pattern of elapsed time: the first event is analyzed, then the second, the third, and so forth.

The outline is *hierarchical* if it denotes that there is a pecking order to the steps of the outline. The outline is not, a ten-step process, for example, with each step being of equal weight. Instead, some steps are subordinate to others or are outgrowths or examples of other steps. Essentially, your paper makes some main points (the major supportive statements or *minor inferences*). These main points are the First Level (using Roman numerals) and each would be the *topic sentence* of its paragraph. Each of these *main points* contain a number of *subordinate points* which elaborate upon them. These comprise the Second Level and are represented by capital letters. Finally, *specific examples* or *illustrations* are used to further clarify the subordinate points. These examples to the subordinate points are the Third Level; they are designated by Arabic numerals.

Notice in the following outline that the movement goes from the most important point to the least important and from the most general and abstract point to the most specific. What follows is a conceptual schematic of the outline format:

LEAD-IN/INTRODUCTION
THESIS STATEMENT WITH ITS MAIN POINTS (MINOR INFER-
ENCES)
   I. FIRST MAIN POINT
       A. Subordinate Point
          1. Specific example
          2. Specific example
       B. Subordinate Point
          1. Specific example
          2. Specific example
  II. SECOND MAIN POINT
       A. Subordinate Point
          1. Specific example
          2. Specific example
       B. Subordinate Point
          1. Specific example
          2. Specific example
 III. THIRD MAIN POINT
       A. Subordinate Point
          1. Specific example
          2. Specific example
       B. Subordinate Point
          1. Specific example
          2. Specific example
       C. Subordinate Point
          1. Specific example
          2. Specific example
CONCLUSION

The outline is useful for a number of reasons. The following suc-
cinctly lists its most important attributes:

- Helps organize one's thoughts,
- Enables one to plan and develop well-thought arguments,
- Points out those areas that are weak or need later data,
- Serves as a guide to keep the writer focused and not wander off on a tangent,
- Arranges material sequentially and hierarchically showing the interconnectedness of its parts, and
- Makes the research phase more efficient.

Now, we will look at a working outline with the emphasis on the thesis statement, followed by its main supportive points, its subordinate

points, and its specific examples. Note that the lead-in/introduction and conclusion sections are indicated but not developed; they will be addressed in a later subsection. The title for the research paper is the following:

HOLY SACRAMENTS AND DEADLY SINS: THE CORLEONES
AND THE INTERPLAY BETWEEN RELIGIOUS RITUAL
AND VIOLENT "BUSINESS" AT DIFFERENT TIMES
AND PLACES IN *THE GODFATHER*

This title we can easily convert into a thesis statement and, subsequently, break that down into its subject, statement, and support.

THESIS STATEMENT: Over the years and in different places, the lives of the Corleones are characterized by the interplay between religious ritual and violent "business" in *The Godfather*.

Subject: The lives of the Corleone family in *The Godfather*

Statement: are characterized by the interplay between familiar or religious ritual and violent "business"

Support: in different times and places.

LEAD-IN/INTRODUCTION
THESIS STATEMENT: Over the years and in different settings, the lives of the Corleones are characterized by the interplay between religious ritual and violent "business" in *The Godfather*.

  I. 1945, Long Island, New York
    A. Carlo and Connie's wedding
      1. Eating and drinking of guests and family
      2. Singing by Mama Corleone and guest
      3. Dancing of Vito Corleone and the bride
    B. Don Corleone conducting business
      1. Don Corleone listens to requests
        a. grants favor to Bonasera, an undertaker
        b. grants favor to Johnny Fontaine, his godson
        c. refuses favor to Solozzo, another "capo"
      2. Violent actions soon follow as a consequence
        a. Bonasera's daughter is avenged
        b. Fontaine's enemy is threatened and concedes
        c. Don Corleone is seriously wounded by Solozzo
        d. This leads to other violent acts

II. 1948, Corleone, Sicily
   A. Michael and Apollonia's wedding and honeymoon
     1. Marching from the church with brass band
     2. Dancing in the square to their music
     3. She learns English and driving
   B. Assassins try to kill Michael
     1. Apollonia starts car and it blows up
     2. Michael flees back to the United States
III. 1955, Manhattan and Long Island
   A. The christening of Carlo and Connie's baby
     1. In church as Michael takes ritual oaths as the infant's god-
        father
   B. Numerous ambushes and assassinations occur that very day
     and night
     1. The killings of Barzini, the Tattaglias, and other enemies
        from the other crime families
     2. Murder of Carlo
CONCLUSION

Amassing and Culling Data

After the working outline is completed, it is time to shift gears into the research mode. Using both hard data (books and periodicals) and soft data (computer databases, the Internet, CD ROMs)—all available at the college library—the writer is ready to amass relevant data pertaining to the paper. Then he or she will speed-read the multiple sources and glean material from them. Only those specific sources that will be used are photocopied (if possible). By having an outline as a guide, those sources that are repetitive or do not address the subject are able to be discarded, whereas those that will be quoted from or paraphrased are kept.

Hard Data: Books and Periodicals

The bulk of the sources are still probably going to be generated from books, journals, newspapers, and other periodicals. Yet as more and more libraries reduce their hard-copy sources available and convert to microfilm and microfiche, paper printouts of the articles will be available rather than photocopies. Often newspaper articles are gathered for a given year and bound and are thus made available for photocopying.

Soft Data: Databases, the Internet, CD ROMs

In many instances, soft data derived from electronic databases also can be converted into paper copies. This is true for local library databases as well as data from the World Wide Web on the Internet. Data on a computer screen—which would include most CD ROMs—can also be converted from a monitor screen into a paper copy.

Such paper copies are useful because they offer portability as well as verification of the source. In the system of photocopying and color coding, that will be discussed in the next subsection, this verification process vouches for the authenticity of the sources and helps prevent plagiarism.

Photocopying and Color Coding

The system of photocopying and color coding was designed to streamline the documentation process of the research paper. It has three main benefits:

*   A means of avoiding plagiarism,
*   An economical alternative to bibliography cards,
*   An efficient equivalent to note cards.

Avoiding Plagiarism

Plagiarism has many faces. For those who willingly and dishonestly try to pass off another's work or words as their own, little can be done to prevent their deeds. Instructors must be vigilant to discover such actions and apply harsh measures sanctioned by the department head and the dean to censure the offender. However, too many students commit plagiarism by accident or out of ignorance. The system described in the ensuing paragraphs is devised to prevent most instances of plagiarism since those pages, paragraphs, sentences, and phrases that are quoted, paraphrased, or summarized are photocopied for the instructor's perusal and are part of the research paper package.

A folder is used to hold in one pocket the final typed research paper to be submitted. In the other pocket, photocopies or computer printouts of the actual sources are gathered into stapled packets and inserted into it. To keep down expense and waste of paper, only those pages of a chapter or article or other source that are actually adopted for quoting, paraphrasing, or summarizing are copied. In a ten-page article that begins on page 87 and ends on page 96, for example, only material on pages 87, 88, and 96 is used. Therefore, to create a *source packet* only those three pages are photocopied and stapled together, with the lowest page number (87) first and the highest (96) last, regardless of where they will be used in the paper. On the first page (87), the name of the article or title of the book and its author(s) should be written across the top in colored ink (if either does not already appear there); the same should be done for the actual page number if it is not already printed. The other pages stapled to it should have their page numbers written down if not already printed.

The process does not stop at this point. Color coding is applied to indicate how the source entry is being used: that is, either as a quote, a paraphrase, or a summary. A given photocopied page may have two to four entries: a quoted phrase, a paraphrased sentence or two, and a summarized paragraph. To indicate the differences among the three, the following color codes and marking conventions should be incorporated:

- Paraphrase: yellow highlighter over words, sentence, or passage;
- Quote: blue underlining of words, sentence, or passage; and
- Summary: red brackets at beginning and end of passage or paragraph.

Thus, that page with the four entries would have the quoted sentence underlined in blue, the two sentences paraphrased highlighted in yellow, and the small paragraph that is summarized bracketed in red. Sometimes a paragraph summarized or paraphrased also contains a sentence that is quoted within it. If paraphrased, the paragraph would be highlighted in yellow with the specific sentence quoted within also underlined in blue ink; if summarized, the paragraph would be bracketed in red, fore and aft, with the quoted sentence still underlined in blue.

This helps the instructor greatly: when he or she reads the research paper and wants to check the authenticity and accuracy of the student's source, it is right there. The photocopy vouches for both. How well the student paraphrases or summarizes can also be judged since the original is available for immediate comparison. The internal (in-text) citation which follows every paraphrase, quote, or summary easily directs the instructor to the exact photocopied source page in the other pocket of the folder.

Alternatives to Bibliography Cards and Note Cards

Rather than separate index cards for each bibliographic source, a complete alphabetized listing of every source used in the paper should be kept. This will become the works cited section that constitutes the last page(s) of the paper.

Note cards are obviated by the photocopy/color code system. In the standard system, any sentence or passage used as a source has to be handwritten or typed on index cards, then numbered, with some bibliographic information also entered on these cards. The stack becomes ever more cumbersome and unwieldy as the separate sources increase and the individual entries accumulate. Instructors dread the rubberband suddenly snapping and cards scattering every which way. The photocopy subsystem eliminates much of the drudgery of the old method; the color-coding subsystem—when done correctly—clearly indicates how the entries are being employed in the text of the research paper.

Documentation Features

In order to conduct research, one must seek sources—books, articles, and such; then one must cull the pieces for those that will contribute to the paper; finally, one must skillfully incorporate those findings into the work. In addition, the research paper will include one additional—but major—step: the orderly documentation of the sources used. This is done with *in-text citations* and a *works cited* section. Both use Modern Language Association (MLA) conventions of style.

If doing a paper about film, you must separate the *primary sources* (the films themselves) from the *secondary sources* (criticism about the film from books, magazine articles, newspaper reviews, CD ROMs, and Internet data) when organizing the works cited page. The procedures for using in-text citations and compiling a works cited listing are described in the subsections that immediately follow.

In-Text Citations (MLA)

In writing a research paper about film, you use the same MLA conventions that would be observed for any other type of critical essay on literature. After each quote, paraphrase, or summary from a secondary source, a citation providing minimal information—namely, author and page—is furnished as a quick reference. Author and page alone are sufficient to both direct the reader to the works cited page—which offers the full citation—and guide the reader to the appropriate photocopy which authenticates that part of the original document being discussed.

After a quoted passage, a parenthetical reference (in-text citation) is inserted *after* the closing quotation mark but *before* the period. This is indicated by bold print in the following sentence:

"The movie was compared in its romantic sweep and power to the operas of Verdi and the great epic novels of the nineteenth century" **(Giannetti & Eyman 412).**

An extended quotation of four lines or more uses a slightly different convention. The quote is indented to a special margin on the left, quotation marks are discarded since they are understood, and the parenthetical in-text citation (in bold print) *follows* the period.

> Commerce and art are not necessarily the deadly enemies they are often said to be. *The Godfather* was the highest-grossing movie in history and is still among the all-time box office champions. Yet the movie, along with its sequel (most critics regard them as a single work), is also one of the most critically admired of the contemporary cinema. **(Giannetti & Eyman 411)**

A paraphrase or summary dispenses with the quotation marks, since the source, although referred to, is not quoted directly. Although the ideas or opinions are restated in the writer's own language and the sentence structure is altered, the source (in bold print) must still be attributed. The preceding short paragraph can be restated as follows:

> Commercial success and artistic integrity are not mutually exclusive. One of the highest grossing motion pictures in history, *The Godfather* . . . also captured rave reviews from many esteemed critics and film historians. **(Giannetti & Eyman 411)**

However, if only a sentence is paraphrased, the period moves *outside* the parenthesis. In the example below, the authors are mentioned before the paraphrase; when this occurs, only the page (in bold print) is given. In *Flashback: A Brief History of Film,* Louis Giannetti and Scott Eyman claim that commercial success and artistic integrity are not mutually exclusive **(411)**.

Since none of this should be new to any student who has taken or is taking English Composition (ENC 1101, English 101, or the like), the best source for the intricacies of in-text citations would be a textbook that includes extensive discussion and examples of MLA writing style such as James D. Lester's *Writing Research Papers: A Complete Guide* or the appropriate section of any reputable college writers' handbook.

Works Cited (MLA)

The works cited section functions in the same manner as a bibliography. It too is arranged alphabetically rather than in the sequential order that the secondary sources appear in the body of the research paper. If a book's sources are cited, entries are listed by initially furnishing the author's last name, then first name and initial for the first component of the citation. The next part provides the title—in italics or underlined—and the edition (unless it is the first edition, where it goes unmentioned). The site of the publisher comes next, with the publishing house following, and then the year of publication. You will note that each part of the citation is ended with a period. The full citation for the Giannetti and Eyman text is as follows:

Giannetti, Louis and Scott Eyman. *Flashback: A Brief History of Film*. 3rd ed. Englewood Cliffs, N.J.: Prentice Hall, 1996.

For a periodical, such as a journal or newspaper, the full citation has a different format. A daily newspaper citation begins with the author—last name, first name, middle initial; then the title of the article in quotation marks; followed by the name of the publication; the complete date of the issue by day's date, month, and year; the edition (if there is one), and the section and page number. Below is a sample of a daily newspaper citation:

Canby, Vincent. "The Godfather." *The New York Times* 16 Mar. 1972, 56.

Again, a writers' handbook should be consulted for the exact type of publication and the particular variables that come into play for each individual work to be cited. It is better not to rely on your memory for all the citations since most of them will differ somewhat from each other.

So far we have been referring to secondary sources. For primary sources, you list alphabetically by film title. The components in their proper order are: the film title, the director, the distributor, and the year released. The following listing would be a works cited with seven primary sources:

Ben-Hur. Dir. William Wyler. Metro-Goldwyn-Mayer, 1959.

Bronx Tale, A. Robert De Niro. Savoy Pictures, 1993.

Carmen Jones. Dir. Otto Preminger. Twentieth Century-Fox, 1954.

How Green Was My Valley. Dir. John Ford. Twentieth Century-Fox, 1941.

Manhattan. Dir. Woody Allen. United Artists, 1979.

Seventh Seal, The. Dir. Ingmar Bergman. Janus Films, 1958.

Sorcerer Dir. William Friedkin. Paramount Pictures and Universal Pictures, 1977.

The First Draft

The first draft of the research paper contains all the elements of the final draft except that it will need editing, contain corrections, require some deletions and, possibly, a few additions. The first draft includes: the title page; the lead-in or introduction, which usually culminates in the thesis statement; the body, including the development of the minor inferences (supporting points) of the thesis statement; the conclusion with its final remarks or posing of questions; and the works cited page(s).

The Title Page

The title should be typed approximately one-third down the page and should be centered (it may or may not be in all capitals). It should be double spaced which makes it more readable. The title should be detailed enough to name the subject of the paper and main point(s) to be made about it. If movie titles are involved, they should be underlined or italicized. The name of the research paper's writer would follow, centered about an inch below. An inch below that would appear the title of the course, course number, and section; below that the instructor's name followed below by the date of submission. These last three lines would be centered.

The Lead-In or Introduction

As with any good piece of writing, you need a lead-in or a series of lead-ins before establishing the thesis and developing the minor inferences. If the paper will be eight or ten pages, the reader's interest must be captured and then gradually led to and presented with the main thrust of the paper. The lead-in paragraph or section can use numerous tactics to attract and keep the reader: shock, statistics, facts, an anecdote, sweeping statements, fascinating details, opinions—obviously, the approach varies greatly. Eventually, however, the reader will be smoothly guided to the thesis statement. The thesis statement usually ends the introduction phase or is embedded in a paragraph fairly close to its termination.

If we select the topic on *The Godfather* about the interplay between family and religious rituals and the family business of crime, the lead-in or introduction could first mention other memorable films that featured rituals, such as weddings, as integral parts of them: for example, *Father of the Bride, A Member of the Wedding, The Deer Hunter*, and *Steel Magnolias*. Then a segue would follow to an in-depth descriptive paragraph of the first wedding in *The Godfather*. Eventually, we would mention how, despite the revelry, the hundreds of guests, the opulent setting and the like, business is, nevertheless, conducted almost throughout the entire nuptial festivities.

The Body

The body is the largest section of the paper and is the natural outgrowth of the thesis. It develops each minor inference presented by the thesis and supports each inference by furnishing detailed examples, adding specific information, providing documented critical opinions, and the like.

The Conclusion

The concluding remarks are as important as the introduction. They do more than just rehash the thesis statement and voice the obvious. Effective concluding remarks may also raise questions, mention ramifications, or discuss ensuing results of what has been presented and discussed.

Works Cited

The section provides a full set of information on those quotes, paraphrases, and summaries that have been cited in the text. The works cited page validates critical references which have added weight to the insights of the writer of the research paper. Specific aspects of this section have already been discussed.

The Final Draft

What follows is a final draft of a research paper: from the first page through the works cited page, inclusive. However, you will note that the margins are much narrower than the other complete reviews and analyses that have previously been presented in this book. Occasional commentary in the right-hand margin "analyzes" the analysis, commenting upon the motives behind and the methods used in preparing this final version of a comparative research paper.

1

Holy Sacraments and Deadly Sins: The Corleones
and the Interplay between Religious Ritual
and Violent "Business" at Different Times
and Places in *The Godfather*

The concept and result were daring: a motion picture three hours long with all the stops pulled out—expenses, cast selection, and locations. Francis Ford Coppola, director and co-screenwriter with author Mario Puzo, ultimately take Puzo's gangster novel *The Godfather* and convert it into a sweeping epic of twentieth century America, fusing such elements as crime, family, business, wealth, and power. These interrelated motifs Coppola uses to weave a rich cinematic tapestry against which to document the rise and fall of one fictitious Italian American extended family.

The end result is a classic: one of the great achievements in cinema. It drew huge audiences, yet also commanded great critical acclaim including numerous Academy Awards—foremost being the Oscar for Best Picture of 1972.

Although *The Godfather* may be the apotheosis of the gangster film, it not only raises the standard of the genre but transcends it, thus helping define the American experience. Its theme links crime with business, drawing parallels between them. American organized crime and American enterprise mirror each other. Leslie Taubman perceives *The Godfather* as

> A quintessential gangster film that elevates
> the longstanding popular genre to the high-

Side annotations:

Title very expressive of the main thrust of the film.

Lead-in provides the "hook" to capture the reader's interest by presenting the film's daring concept.

In mentioning the great success of the film, it is hoped that the reader's interest is quickened.

Introduces one element of the thesis.

2

A series of quotes and paraphrases followed by known critical authorities: the first being noted film reviewer Leslie Taubman.

est level of art. [It] portrays a Mafia organization [as] a malevolent extension of the ethics of capitalism and . . . free enterprise. . . . Its Sicilian-American "family" serves as a metaphor for corrupt big business and government. (638)

Quote and paraphrase by critic Vincent Canby.

Yet Vincent Canby sees it "[depicting] a sorrowful American dream as a slambang, sentimental gangster melodrama" (11). In a later piece, he likens the Corleones to the "robber barons" of many leading nineteenth century American industries (56).

Quotes and paraphrases by Gerald Mast and Bruce F. Kawin.

To Gerald Mast and Bruce Kawin, it is "a monumental American epic about the conflict between doing business and living [by] meaningful values—a conflict built into the very familial and economic structure of American society" (448). Coppola believes American enterprises as having "dark undersides": conflicts between conducting profitable business with the values necessary to do so. Rather than a deadly disease on the nation, the Mafia should be considered as symptomatic of the way America conducts its economic and political affairs (448).

The film is great not solely through thematic strength and accompanying political, historical, economic, sociological, and psychological musings. It also uses several cinematic devices to remarkable effect. These relate to the themes symbolically, while simultaneously producing memorable cinematographic sequences and narrative episodes. In the film, the lives of the Corleones are marked by the

3

interplay of religious rite and violent "business." In different times and places, religious rituals are often performed simultaneously to orgiastic gang violence as retribution, policy statement or naked grab for power. The remainder of this paper explores how the movie achieves these ends by discussing its effect narratively and pictorially as it connects its shocking themes and symbols.

Juxtaposing the sacred with the profane commences at once. It is the summer of 1945. In his dark, sinister office, mob kingpin Vito Corleone (Marlon Brando) holds court during his daughter's wedding at the family's Long Island estate. Customarily, the bride's father grants favors to those who ask in the midst of the reception (Taubman 639).

Full thesis of the research paper is introduced.

Denotes the objectives of the paper.

The theme is announced in the topic sentence and then developed by a narrative example from the film. Paraphrase of Taubman's insight into Italian wedding customs.

The Godfather (1972) Marlon Brando as Don Vito Corleone conducts "business" in his cavernous office during his daughter's wedding celebration.

4

First seen is the local undertaker Bonasera (Salvatore Corsitto), whose daughter has been raped and mutilated by two men. All attempts to get them arrested and punished by the police have been fruitless, so, in desperation, he beseeches the don for justice.

The sequence is fascinating: despite the emotional explosiveness of the issue, both Bonasera and Corleone show verbal restraint as they go through the ritualistic moves from explication to supplication to admonition to ultimate conciliation.

The lengthy paragraph is peppered with snatches of dialogue from the film.

Bonasera begins stating "I believe in America . . ." and recounts details of his daughter's assault, disfiguration, and then failure of the American legal system. Don Vito chides him for seeking the police rather than trust him in the first place. Bonasera is further berated for never inviting the don to his home nor "[wanting] my friendship and to be in my debt. Now you come . . . the day my daughter is to be married." The irony is strong—a man asking aid for his daughter rendered unmarriageable because of facial scars and internal damage. The aggrieved father, now penitent, swears fealty and friendship to the don. Corleone agrees to help him if he would return a favor, if asked, sometime in the future. Bonasera agrees, they embrace, and terrible justice is to be meted out to the two offenders.

Next, Vito's godson Johnny Fontane (Al Martino), a singer trying to break into the movies, asks the don for help. Again, Don Vito accedes. In this and other instances, Corleone employs intimidation, extortion, battery, and even murder to gain

5

loyalty comparable to a feudal knight with his vassals. An "exotic code of honor [set] within a terrible system of rewards and punishment" is delineated, provoking violent events in locales as diverse as New York, Hollywood, Las Vegas, and Sicily (Canby, March 12, 1972, 11).

Short quotes and para- phrases of Canby's views.

Business completed, Vito leaves his den, emerging into sunlight to dance with his daughter at the lawn party in the spacious family compound in Long Beach. The dour, powerful don momentarily becomes the smiling, cavorting clan patriarch, proud of his family.

Another side of Don Vito Corleone— considerably warmer—is exhibited.

Cinematographer Gordon Willis, in shooting both major scenes of the wedding, uses variation of light and darkness effectively. The irregularly-shaped office with its patterned shadows, contrasts with the bright sunlight and dazzling hues of the merry-making outside. The effect, both visually and thematically, "reflects the nature of the family and of the man who is warm and generous and is also a murderer" (Taubman 642).

Lighting is used not only to enhance the mood but to furnish sym- bolic and thematic overtones.

Quote by Taubman.

As Mama Corleone (Morgana King) entertains, singing Italian folk songs, Solazzo (Al Lettieri), another "capo," suggests that Vito join him in introducing drugs to the business of the five crime families. Corleone refuses—not because of moral scruples—but because it would threaten his friendly ties with politicians and judges. They could discount gambling pursuits but could not ignore his ventures into the narcotics trade.

Despite the ongoing nuptial fes- tivities, seeds of the central con- flict of the film are sown that will grow as the movie progresses.

Not taking kindly to the rebuff—despite its courteous delivery—Solozzo, soon thereafter, tries to kill Corleone. Nearly succeeding, his men seriously wound the don. His son Sonny (James Caan) takes over the family and a full-blown gang war results. Sonny is ambushed and murdered at a highway tollbooth while enroute to avenge pregnant sister Connie (Talia Shire), who has again been brutally beaten by her husband Carlo (Gianni Russo).

It is now up to Michael (Al Pacino), the Dartmouth-educated and decorated war hero, to assume the mantle of family leadership and the "business." Kept totally away from criminal activities by his father—who hoped he would someday become a United States senator—it is now up to the youngest son to gain vengeance. He arranges to meet with Solozzo and the corrupt police captain McCluskey (Sterling Hayden) at a small Italian restaurant in the Bronx to talk peace. Instead, using a pistol concealed in the men's room, Michael shoots them point blank then escapes to Sicily. The gang war continues back home.

Protected by Don Tomassino (Corrado Gaipa), long a friend of Vito, Michael has two bodyguards assigned to him at all times. One day, during his customary trek through the countryside, he comes upon a beautiful young woman. Hit at once by the "thunderbolt," all thoughts of Kay Adams (Diane Keaton), his betrothed back home, evaporate as love-smitten Michael declares his serious intentions to the girl's father.

Their courtship is very traditional. Everywhere he and Apollonia (Simonetta Stefanelli) go, a horde of her female chaperones and his bodyguard duo follow. After the wedding ceremony, the entourage

Major change of setting from New York to Sicily serves to amplify the thesis.

7

leaves the church. A procession with a brass band follows the connubial pair as it walks through the town's narrow, winding streets to its square where the reception is held. The newlyweds dance to the band's music and offer sweets to those special guests attending.

Life is idyllic for awhile. Michael teaches his wife English and driving. Then she is killed by a car bomb-intended for him—when sitting behind the wheel alone to demonstrate her skill. He returns to America realizing that life is even more dangerous in Sicily than in the United States. Again, we have the juxtaposition of the sacred—as before, a marriage—intermingled with the profane—a Mafia feud-related killing.

The pattern of the sacred and the profane continues.

Michael becomes the new godfather. Soon after his return, he resumes the relationship with Kay, eventually marrying her. The film's climax takes place in 1955 at a cathedral in Manhattan. It is the third instance of the commingling of a religious rite with mob-related atrocities. Michael and Kay are at the christening of Connie and Carlo's baby as godparents. A series of intercuts take us from the golden-light-suffused ceremony with its organ music and priest's liturgical drone to a string of brutal slayings and back again.

To Joseph M. Boggs, the sequence's irony builds with each cut, reaching its zenith when Michael affirms his belief in God, pledging "to renounce Satan" while a spate of killings he has ordered occur simultaneously. At ceremony's end, he makes his final and most cynical decision: to have

Criticism by Jos. M. Boggs highlights the terrible irony of the baptism ritual as it is juxtaposed with a series of killings that occur those very moments.

8

the infant's father, his brother-in-law Carlo—whom
he holds responsible for Sonny's death—killed. His

Paraphrase of
Boggs'
statement.

power as both head of his immediate family and the
extended crime family is underscored. It comes as no
surprise that when Kay later asks if he were responsible for Carlo's murder, he tells her not to ask

Michael has
become a
consummate
liar.

about the family's business, then lies convincingly,
"No."

9

WORKS CITED

Primary Sources

The com-
plete listings
of the critical
sources
used and
cited in this
paper.

Godfather, The. Dir. Francis Ford Coppola. Paramount
  Pictures, 1972.

Secondary Sources

Boggs, Joseph M. *The Art of Watching Films.* 4th ed.
  Mountain View, CA: Mayfield, 1996.

Canby, Vincent. *The New York Times* 12 Mar. 1972, II,
  1. Rpt. *The New York Times Film Reviews (1971-
  1972)* 233-34.

——. "Godfather, The." *The New York Times* 16 Mar.
  1972, 56. Rpt. *The New York Times Film Reviews
  (1971-1972)* 235.

Mast, Gerald and Bruce F. Kawin. *A Short History of
  the Movies.* 5th ed. New York: Macmillan, 1992.

Taubman, Leslie. "The Godfather." *Magill's Survey of
  Cinema: English Language Films Series.* Ed.
  Frank N. Magill. 1, Vol. 2, EAS-LON. Englewood
  Cliffs, NJ: Salem Press, 1980. 638-43.

Research Paper: *Gandhi* and the Critics

This chapter concludes with a research paper written by Broward Community College professor Gloria D. Johnson, Ph.D., for a film workshop that she attended in 1984. It presents and comments upon some of the professional critical reaction to Richard Attenborough's *Gandhi*, released in 1982. Notice that this is a straightforward analysis of some representative professional criticism of a highly acclaimed motion picture. Dr. Johnson uses a series of quotes and paraphrases to back her assertions. (The original title page of her paper has not been included.)

Johnson 1

Gandhi and the Critics

It has always been a mystery to me how man
can feel themselves honored by the humiliation of their fellow human beings.

These words from Gandhi's autobiography, quoted
in Louis Fischer's biography *The Life of Mahatma
Gandhi*, became the impetus for Sir Richard Attenborough's determination to make a film on this nonviolent spiritual and political leader of India,
according to Edward Parks in the December 13, 1982,
issue of *Smithsonian* (29). More than twenty years
passed before Attenborough's "unflagging will" produced the $22 million *Gandhi*, which he hoped would
"demythologize and demystify his subject, thus
restoring him to human dimensions," reports Richard
Schickel in "Triumph of a Martyr's Will" (*Time*, Dec.
6, 1982, 97).

The success of Attenborough's undertaking was
debated (and still is being debated) with enthusiasm
and energy by American film critics from its first
showings in December 1982. *Newsweek*'s Jack Kroll,
writing a special report which he titled "A Magnifi-

---

cent Life of Gandhi," begins with words of praise:
"There are very few movies that absolutely must be
seen. Sir Richard Attenborough's *Gandhi* is one of
them" (Dec. 13, 1982, 60). And "Stanley Kauffmann on
Film" in *New Republic* claims that the movie "epito-
mizes" Gandhi's life (Dec. 13, 1982, 26). *America's*
Richard A. Blake concludes in "Mythmaking" that

> with all its limitations "Gandhi" is a supe-
> rior film that can be recommended without
> hesitation. It does exactly what its makers
> wanted it to do. It gives a loving, histori-
> cally accurate and entertaining portrait of
> one of the great figures of the 20th cen-
> tury. (Dec. 18, 1982, 392)

However, in his final sentence, Blake tempers his
evaluation, saying that he "only wishes that they
had wanted to do more with their film" (392).
Pauline Kael begins her review in *The New Yorker* by
recalling that when she left the showing of *Gandhi*,
she "felt the way the British must have when they
left India: exhausted and relieved." She complains
that the movie lacks a "dramatic center; in compensation, the action all seems to take place in the
dead middle of the screen." She goes on to say that
the picture is not impressive: "It isn't a disgrace—
it just isn't much of anything" (Dec. 27, 1982, 72).

The range of evaluations of Attenborough's
skills as director of *Gandhi* are as varied as the
overall pronouncements of the film. Blake admits
Attenborough takes a tremendous step forward in sep-
arating Gandhi from the myth surrounding his life,

but that eventually Attenborough commits the same errors that others have in paying homage to this unusual man. Although Attenborough recreates "the human personality with brilliance," he ultimately employs it "as a symbol representing rather vague and undefined values." Blake believes that the Gandhi whom Attenborough has so "lovingly" resurrected is "a perfect secular humanitarian rather than a Hindu mystic" (392). Blake is annoyed that Gandhi is portrayed as a man with no "philosophic and religious" beliefs. If the viewers are to understand the true Gandhi, are to be able to separate him from the myth, he argues, then his philosophy and religion must be explained—otherwise the viewers will perceive "their values and motivations in Gandhi" just as, Blake thinks, "Attenborough and Briley did in the first place" (392).

What were Gandhi's motives in staying in South Africa after his confrontation with the conductor about his riding in a first-class train car which ended in his being thrown from the train, Blake asks (392). Why did he transform himself into "a model civil-rights activist," enduring police brutality while exhorting the people to set fire to their loathsome identification papers? Why did he find "such strong solidarity with the poor and oppressed after his smug exchange with the conductor?" What caused Gandhi to embrace a theory of passive resistance in order to gain civil rights? From what sources did he draw the moral courage to bear the flogging by the police? Blake maintains that the viewers are given no answers to these questions, that they are "led to intuit some sort of grand humanitarian impulse, a sense of fair play and justice or even revenge" (392). Later, in India, Gandhi took the loin cloth and the spinning wheel to represent his oneness with the villagers. "With no religious or philosophic explanation for his behavior," Blake reasons, the viewers decide that

> he wants to be seen as a selfless man of the people for reasons known to him alone. Even his facts are presented as purely political tactics and his sexual abstinence as a form of self-discipline for political trials to come. (392)

Gandhi (1982) Ben Kingsley as Mahatma Gandhi in a loincloth at his spinning wheel.

Nevertheless, Blake admits that despite Attenborough's negligence in portraying "the inner workings" of Gandhi in "his spirituality," he is "remarkably successful" in handling "the complexities of Indian society" in the final period of British sovereignty in India. Attenborough does not depict "white hats and black hats. . . . No one has a monopoly on righteousness," Blake asserts (392).

Stanley Kauffmann, like Blake, has mixed responses to Attenborough. He bluntly states Attenborough is "not a first-class director," adding that because "good art filters experience . . . through the persona of the artist," and that because "no such filtering is wanted . . . with the Gandhi story," no first-class director would consider filming Gandhi (26). Kauffmann, however, does credit Attenborough for doing "virtually all that sincerity, dedication and professional competency could do" (26). He goes on to say that in addition to the admitted "omissions and selected emphases," by the director, there are "condensations" and several alterations in details, such as the fact that Gandhi's remains were dropped into the Ganges from a military amphibious craft, not from Attenborough's flower-laden boat" (26). Nevertheless, Kauffmann believes that Attenborough has abstracted the essence of Gandhi's life, that the director has clearly revealed the major milestones in Gandhi's journey, and that "the sunsets over Indian rivers, the great fields fringed with far mountains, the crowded cities, the street battles, the train jour-

neys, the government palaces, the immense funeral
procession" are filmed with validity (26).

    Schickel, like Blake and Kauffmann, has both
positive and negative remarks about Attenborough. He
praises him for his "unflagging will," but he cannot
do the same for his "directorial skill." Schickel
describes the director's skill as "traditional-
stately." His treatments of the landscapes in India,
Schickel complains, is "predictable" rather than
exciting (97). (One notices that Kauffmann praises
Attenborough for the validity of his landscapes.)
And the savage confrontations between Gandhi's disciples and British colonial soldiers, Schickel complains about also: although "competent and
craftemanlike," they lack "excitement" (97).

    Schickel goes on to say that these complaints
matter very little, that "the refusal to be flashy
finally seems to be the earnestness of Attenborough's obvious idealism," and of "his apparent
desire to both demythologize and demystify" Gandhi,
thereby "restoring" him "to human dimensions." He
concludes by praising Attenborough for his "stylistic self-denial" which causes the viewers to concentrate on "a persuasive if perhaps debatable vision
of Gandhi's spirit, and on the remarkable actor who
has caught its light in all its seasons" (97).

    In contrast to Schickel's denouement of Atten-
borough's film lacking excitement, Kroll praises
Attenborough's skill, pointing out that *Gandhi* is
"miraculous" because of its freshness and electric-
ity, and its ability to move the audience (60).

Kroll goes on to say that Attenborough handles his
subject "with a mixture of high intelligence and
immediate impact" (60). He further praises the
director for the "brutal gravity" with which he
forcefully stages such events as Gandhi's Salt March
to the Sea, and his fasts in reaction to his followers' use of violence when they are confronted with
it, and General Dyer's slaughter of the unarmed,
nonviolent protesters (61).

Although Kroll agrees with Schickel that Attenborough's style is traditional, Kroll views this
"old-fashioned" style as perfect for the "no-tricks,
no-phony psychologizing quality" which Attenborough
wanted (61). Kroll further praises the director of
the film's

> strong clear narrative that carries in
> remarkable balance Gandhi's revolutionary
> ideas, the paradoxes of his character, the
> overwhelming energy generated by the huge
> masses of people that Gandhi arouses, the
> spectacles and drama of his audacity and the
> ironic climax of his life as the indepen-
> dence he had helped win from Britain
> explodes into savage civil war between Hin-
> dus and Muslims. (63)

Although most critics find some redeeming feature about Attenborough's directing, Kael can discover none. She points out that the director has
been praised for his "old-fashioned movie" (for
example, Kroll), but that he directs this film in
his usual way. She accuses him of directing in "the

tradition of orderly, neat imagery: in his India
even poverty is clean and barbered." She goes on to
complain that even his "sensibility is conventional," and sarcastically describes this
"respectable" picture as glossing over several of
the main happenings in his community life and tidy-
ing up "his rather kinky domestic relations." For
her, the film is a "schoolbook Life of Gandhi" (73).

Kael further excoriates Attenborough for not
letting the audience know what Gandhi is thinking.
(Blake, as stated earlier, also makes this com-
plaint.) The viewers never really understand him,
she adds (72). In fact, Kael maintains that the
audience can't tell what goes on in anybody's head.
She refers to Gandhi as a "one-man independence
movement": he is never involved in a dialogue about
nonviolence—he simply decrees it (73). Kael also
proposes, in another caustic remark, that the only
drama that Attenborough has created in the movie of
Gandhi and his disciples is in their courage when
they commit civil disobedience and "allow themselves
to be beaten, maimed, and killed" (73). Kael does
not even seem to admire the historical Gandhi. She
accuses him of utilizing his martyrdom as a strat-
egy—"pushing guilt on everybody and getting his
way." She compares him with the proverbial Jewish
mother: "he's using the same diabolical tricks"
(73).

Perhaps Kael makes one positive comment about
Gandhi in three words: "Kingsley is impressive"
(72). Other critics—Blake, Kroll, Schickel, and

Kauffmann—can hardly contain themselves with their laudatory descriptions of Ben Kingsley's talents. Indeed, they have no negative criticisms. Blake describes Kingsley's acting as "a fitting memorial to Gandhi." Blake maintains that Kingsley is "equally magnificent" as the youthful barrister in South Africa and as the aged Mahatma in India (392).

Kroll refers to Kingsley's acting as possibly "the most astonishing biographical performance in screen history" (60). He praises Kingsley for brilliantly representing "the inner and outer odyssey of Gandhi":

> The clipped British overlay to his speech
> gradually disappears, to be replaced by the
> assertive lilting Indian rhythms. The new
> voice, the shaved head, the half-naked body,
> at once vulnerable-looking and powerful—all
> this reflects both a new spiritual disci-
> pline and the most effective image-making
> power of any 20th century leader. (61)

Schickel extolls Kingsley's ability to age approximately fifty years during the movie persuasively, singling out the actor's "subtleties of movement" as opposed to the makeup process. He further praises Kingsley's amazing "spiritual presence":

> His Gandhi is no mystic, but a man with a
> practical political sense, an almost sly
> awareness of other men's motives and how
> they might be levered to advance his own
> cause, and above all, a sense of self-irony.
> (97)

Schickel also describes Kingsley's performance as implying that the Mahatma's leadership talents were not so much a result of his being unlike other people but from his realization that he was, indeed, "like them, with only the force of his will to set them apart." As Schickel concludes, "He was an example self-made, not born" (97).

"He is simply fine" are the words of Kauffmann in beginning his commendatory remarks about Kingsley (26). He credits Kingsley with understanding the basic "truth" of Gandhi's "dynamics":

> Gandhi could not lose. He knew he might be killed, he knew he would certainly be hurt and jailed, he knew his political causes might fail, but he could not lose because he had invested all his being in his beliefs. (27)

The other characters in *Gandhi* are treated negligibly. So is the author of the screenplay, John Briley, who eventually won an Oscar in 1983 for his screenplay. Attenborough, Kingsley, and the film itself demand all of the critics' attention. And when one considers that Attenborough, Kingsley and *Gandhi* won the major motion picture Academy Awards for 1983—Attenborough for his directing, Kingsley for his acting, and *Gandhi* for being the best picture of the year—one can understand the focus of the critics' attention, even though quite often they are condemning rather than extolling.

One main point, however, that several critics have made needs to be challenged. Blake and Kael

both complain that Attenborough does not give the
viewers the "inner workings" of Gandhi, that he does
not let them know what Gandhi is thinking. It is
obvious that no one really knows with certainty what
was going on in the real Gandhi's mind. In order to
be true to his historical character, the director
cannot impose his personal inferences on Gandhi's
character. He simply has to show him as he was
observed by others and as he was recorded in history. How can one really know Gandhi? Could one even
know the fictitious Citizen Kane?

Although the critics have been very incisive
in their judgments, one main point they have
neglected, and it is the salient point of *Gandhi*.
Kroll touches on the matter when he claims that
Attenborough throws a mighty challenge to his viewers by picturing Gandhi as "the most profound and
effective of revolutionaries, creating out of a
fierce personal discipline a chain reaction that led
to tremendous historical consequences" (63-64).
Kroll even goes on to say that world problems being
what they are today—"deep political unrest, economic
dislocation and nuclear anxiety"—viewing *Gandhi* is
"an event that will change many minds and hearts"
(64). It will do much more.

Kroll summarizes world problems almost too suc-
cinctly. Most people today are filled with fear as
they consider the threat of nuclear holocaust, the
seemingly uncontrollable drug problem, the nebulous
economy, the extreme poverty in the midst of extreme
wealth, the continuing racial tensions, and the lack

of integrity in leadership positions, to name a few. People have a sense of futility at the ballot box, they have a helpless feeling that no one is in control, that the world is slightly askew with no one having the power to set it straight again. They ask themselves, "What can I do?" And they answer, "Very little." But seeing Sir Richard Attenborough's dynamic *Gandhi* can give them hope. It does not matter that the viewers really understand the inner workings of Gandhi's mind. It does not matter that Attenborough was inaccurate or careless in his delineation of some of the minor events in Gandhi's life. It does not matter that he portrayed Gandhi almost as a saint when the evidence testifies to an imperfect man. It does not matter that Pauline Kael does not seemingly admire the Gandhi who once lived. What does matter is that Gandhi did live and that the viewers of *Gandhi* have been dramatically reminded of how he—just one person—a slight man with a bald head, a loin cloth, and a spinning wheel—with no political office and no great wealth—challenged the strength of the British Empire and won. This is an historical fact, not a fictional presentation on the screen. And the powerful way in which the film presents this fact to the viewers should give them hope that other persons with the will, the courage, the wisdom, and the moral integrity that Gandhi possessed can by the force of their personalities conquer "princes and principalities" if necessary to prevent men from honoring themselves "by the humiliation of their fellow beings."

Johnson 13

WORKS CITED

Blake, Richard A. "Mythmaking." *America* 18 Dec 1982,
     392.

Fischer, Louis. *The Life of Mahatma Gandhi* London:
     Jonathan Cape, 1951.

Kael, Pauline. *The New Yorker* 27 Dec 1982, 72-73.

Kauffmann, Stanley. "Stanley Kauffmann on Films."
     New Republic 13 Dec 1982, 26-27.

Kroll, Jack. "A Magnificent Life of Gandhi."
     Newsweek 13 Dec 1982, 60-64.

Parks, Edward. *Smithsonian* 13 Dec 1982, 29.

Schickel, Richard. "Triumph of a Martyr's Will."
     Time 6 Dec 1982, 97.

A

Documentation of Primary and Secondary Sources of Works Cited

Chapter 1. Preparation for and the Process of Film Criticism

Primary: Film

African Queen, The. Dir. John Huston. United Artists, 1951.

Babette's Feast. Dir. Gabriel Axel. Panorama/Nordisk/Danish Film Institute, 1987.

Gone with the Wind. Dir. Victor Fleming. Metro-Goldwyn-Mayer, 1939.

Secondary: Published Film Criticism

(None used.)

Chapter 2. Style and Structure in Film Criticism

Primary: Film

Amadeus. Dir. Milos Foreman. Orion Pictures, 1983.

American Graffiti. Dir. George Lucas. Universal Pictures, 1973.

Avalon. Dir. Barry Levinson. Tri-Star Pictures, 1990.

Awakenings. Dir. Penny Marshall. Columbia Pictures, 1990.

Bang the Drum Slowly. Dir. John Hancock. Paramount Pictures, 1974.

Black Orpheus. Dir. Marcel Camus. Lopert Films, 1959.

Bodyguard, The. Dir. Mick Jackson. Warner Brothers, 1992.

Body Heat. Dir. Lawrence Kasdan. Warner Brothers, 1981.

Breathless. Dir. Jean-Luc Godard. Films Around the World, Inc., 1961.

Carmen Jones. Dir. Otto Preminger. Twentieth Century-Fox, 1954.

Closely Watched Trains. Dir. Jiri Menzel. Sigma III, 1967.

Diner. Dir. Barry Levinson. Metro-Goldwyn-Mayer/United Artists, 1982.

Forrest Gump. Dir. Robert Zemeckis. Paramount Pictures, 1994.

Glengarry Glen Ross. Dir. James Foley. New Line Cinema, 1992.

Gone with the Wind. Dir. Victor Fleming. Metro-Goldwyn-Mayer, 1939.

Honeymoon in Vegas. Dir. Andrew Bergman. Columbia Pictures, 1992.

Of Mice and Men. Dir. Gary Sinese. Metro-Goldwyn-Mayer, 1992.

Platoon. Dir. Oliver Stone. Orion Pictures, 1986.

Porgy and Bess. Dir. Otto Preminger. Columbia Pictures, 1959.

Quest for Fire. Dir Jean-Jacques Annoud. ICC-Cine Trail/Belstar/ Stephan Films, 1982.

Schindler's List. Dir. Steven Spielberg. Universal Pictures, 1993.

Shadows. Dir. John Cassavetes. Lion International Films, 1961.

Shop on Main Street, The. Dir. Jan Kadar and Elmar Klos. Museum of Modern Art, 1965.

Sneakers. Dir. Phil Alden Robinson. Universal Pictures, 1992.

Sophie's Choice. Dir. Alan J. Pakula. Universal Pictures, 1982.

Tin Men. Dir. Barry Levinson. Buena Vista, 1987.

Twelve Angry Men. Dir. Sidney Lumet. United Artists, 1957.

Secondary: Published Film Criticism

Crowther, Bosley. "Black Orpheus." *The New York Times* 22 Dec. 1959, 41+. Rpt. *The New York Times Film Reviews (1959–1968)* 3163–64.

——. "Breathless." *The New York Times* 8 Feb. 1961, 26. Rpt. *The New York Times Film Reviews (1959–1968)* 3239.

——. "Closely Watched Trains." *The New York Times* 16 Oct. 1967, 59. Rpt. *The New York Times Film Reviews (1959–1968)* 3707.

Greenspun, Roger. "American Graffiti." *The New York Times* 13 Aug. 1973, 21+. Rpt. *The New York Times Film Reviews (1973–1974)* 93-94.

Pearson, Harry, Jr. "Forrest Gump." *Films in Review* Nov. 1994, 60–61.

Weiler, A. H. "Twelve Angry Men." *The New York Times* , 15 Apr. 1957, 24. Rpt. *The New York Times Film Reviews (1949–1958)* 2978.

Chapter 3. Types of Film Criticism: The Review

Primary: Film

Best Years of Our Lives, The. Dir. William Wyler. RKO, 1946.

Big Carnival, The (Ace in the Hole). Dir. Billy Wilder. Paramount, 1951.

Crying Game, The. Dir. Neil Jordan. Miramax Films, 1992.

Dances with Wolves. Dir. Kevin Costner. Orion Pictures, 1990.

Die Hard. Dir. John McTiernan. Twentieth Century–Fox, 1988.

Distant Thunder. Dir. Satyajit Ray. Cinema 5, 1973.

Dog Day Afternoon. Dir. Sidney Lumet. Warner Brothers, 1976.

Don Juan de Marco. Dir. Francis Ford Coppola. New Line Cinema, 1995.

English Patient, The. Dir. Anthony Minghella. Miramax Films, 1996.

Few Good Men, A. Dir. Rob Reiner. Columbia Pictures, 1992.

First Blood (Rambo). Dir. Ted Kotcheff. Orion Pictures, 1982.

Good, the Bad, and the Ugly, The. Dir. Sergio Leone. United Artists, 1966.

Home Alone. Dir. Chris Columbus. Twentieth Century–Fox, 1990.

Home Alone 2: Lost in New York. Dir. Chris Columbus. Twentieth Century–Fox, 1992.

In the Company of Men. Dir. Neil LaBute. Sony Pictures Classics, 1997.

Lawrence of Arabia. Dir. David Lean. Columbia Pictures, 1962.

Lethal Weapon. Dir. Richard Donner. Warner Brothers, 1987.

Mad City. Dir. Costa Gavras. Warner Brothers, 1997.

Manhattan Murder Mystery. Dir. Woody Allen. TriStar Pictures, 1992.

Natural Born Killers. Dir. Oliver Stone. Warner Brothers, 1994.

Pulp Fiction. Dir. Quentin Tarantino. Miramax Films, 1994.

Scent of a Woman. Dir. Martin Brest. Universal Pictures, 1992.

Sorceror. Dir. William Friedkin. Paramount Pictures/Universal Pictures, 1977.

Swept Away (By an Unusual Destiny in the Blue Sea of August). Dir. Lina Wertmuller. Cinema V, 1975.

Thousand Acres, A. Dir. Jocelyn Moorehouse. Touchstone Pictures, 1997.

Tootsie. Dir. Sydney Pollack. Columbia Pictures, 1982.

True Lies. Dir. James Cameron. Twentieth Century–Fox, 1994.

You Can't Take It with You. Dir. Frank Capra. Columbia Pictures, 1938.

Your Friends and Neighbors. Dir. Neil LaBute. Grammercy, 1998.

Z. Dir. Costa Gavras. Reggane Films, 1969.

Secondary: Film Criticism

Adler, Renata. "The Good, the Bad, and the Ugly." *The New York Times* 25 Jan. 1968, 33. Rpt. *The New York Times Film Reviews (1959–1968)* 3731.

"Best Years of Our Lives." *Boxoffice* 7 Dec. 1946. Rpt. *Boxoffice Online Reviews* Online. 10 Sep. 1998.

http://www.boxoffice.com/cgi/getclassic.pl?f...F\x20LIVES&search page=classic.html

Canby, Vincent. "Distant Thunder." *The New York Times* 12 Oct. 1973, 32. Rpt. *The New York Times Film Reviews (1973–1974)* 116.

Crowther, Bosley. "The Best Years of Our Lives." *The New York Times* 22 Nov. 1946, 27. Rpt. *The New York Times Film Reviews (1939–1948)* 2146–47.

Ebert, Roger. "Your Friends and Neighbors." Online. *Chicago Sun-Times* 8 Oct. 1998.

http://www.suntimes.com/ebert/ebert_reviews/1998/08/082103.html

Hatch, Robert. "Films." *Nation* 11 Oct. 1975, 347+.

Johnson, Brian D. "Straight-arrow Hero: Kevin Costner Touches the Native Earth." *Maclean's* 19 Nov. 1990, 58–59.

Kroll, Jack. "Media Is the Monster: Hoffman and Travolta Go Live on the Evening News." *Newsweek* 17 Nov. 1997, 90.

Mermelstein, David. "The Best Years of Our Lives." Online. *Mr. Showbiz Movie Guide* 10 Sep. 1998.

http://www.mrshowbiz.com/reviews/moviereviews/movies/35214. html

Nugent, Frank S. "You Can't Take It with You." *The New York Times* 2 Sept. 1938, 21. Rpt. *The New York Times Film Reviews (1932–1938)* 1527.

Rosenbaum, Jonathan. "You Can't Take It with You." Online. *Chicago Reader: On Film Brief Reviews* 11 Sept. 1998.

http://onfilm.chireader.com/MovieCaps/Y/YO/09610_YOU_CANT_ TAKE_IT_WITH_YOU.html

Sam. "You Can't Take It with You (1938)." Online. *At-A-Glance Film Reviews* 11 Sept. 1998.

http://www.rinkworks.com/movies/m/you.cant.take.it.with.you.1938 .shtml

Schickel, Richard. "The Infirmities of Our Age: Shakespeare's *Lear* Gets Updated in *A Thousand Acres*. Result: Just Another Dysfunctional Family." *Time* 22 Sept. 1997, 93.

Westerbeck, Colin L., Jr. "Robinson Crusoe." *Commonweal* 10 Oct. 1975, 470–71.

Chapter 4. Types of Film Criticism: The Analytical Critique

Primary: Film

Birth of a Nation. Dir. D. W. Griffith. Museum of Modern Art, 1915.
Falling Down. Dir. Joel Schumacher. Warner Brothers, 1992.
Party, The. Dir. Blake Edwards. United Artists, 1968.
Shot in the Dark, A. Dir. Blake Edwards. United Artists, 1964.
Sunset Boulevard. Dir. Billy Wilder. Paramount Pictures, 1950.
39 Steps, The. Dir. Alfred Hitchcock. Gaumont-British, 1935.
To Die For. Dir. Gus Van Sant. Columbia Pictures, 1995.

Secondary: Film Criticism

(None Used.)

Chapter 5. Types of Film Criticism: The Comparative Analysis

Primary: Film

Badlands. Dir. Terrence Mallick. Warner Brothers, 1973.
Big Sleep, The. Dir. Howard Hawks. Warner Brothers, 1946.
Big Sleep, The. Dir. Michael Winner. United Artists, 1977.
Grumpy Old Men. Dir. Donald Petrie. Warner Brothers, 1993.
Last of the Mohicans, The. Dir. Michael Mann. Twentieth Century–Fox, 1992.
Last Picture Show, The. Dir. Peter Bogdanovich. Columbia Pictures, 1971.
Natural Born Killers. Dir. Oliver Stone. Warner Brothers, 1994.
Night and Fog. Dir. Alain Resnais. Argos Films, 1955.
Texasville. Dir. Peter Bogdanovich. Columbia Pictures, 1990.
Triumph of the Will. Dir. Leni Riefenstahl. Museum of Modern Art, 1936.

Working Girl. Dir. Mike Nichols. Twentieth Century–Fox, 1988.

Secondary: Published Film Criticism

Maslin, Janet. "The Big Sleep." *The New York Times* 15 Mar. 1978, C19. Rpt. *The New York Times Film Reviews (1977–1978)* 182.

Place, Janey. "The Big Sleep." *Magill's Survey of Cinema: English Language Films Series.* Ed. Frank N. Magill. 1, Vol. 1, A-EAS. Englewood Cliffs, NJ: Salem Press, 1980. 162–164.

Chapter 6. Types of Film Criticism: The Documented Research Paper

Primary: Film

Gandhi. Dir. Richard Attenborough. Columbia Pictures, 1982.

Godfather, The. Dir. Francis Ford Coppola. Paramount Pictures, 1972.

Secondary: Film Criticism

Blake, Richard A. "Mythmaking." *America* 18 Dec. 1982, 392.

Boggs, Joseph M. *The Art of Watching Films.* 4th ed. Mountain View, CA: Mayfield, 1996.

Canby, Vincent. "Godfather, The." *The New York Times* 16 Mar. 1972, 56. Rpt. *The New York Times Film Reviews (1971–1972)* 235.

———. *The New York Times* 12 Mar. 1972, II, 1. Rpt. *The New York Times Film Reviews* 233-34.

Fischer, Louis. *The Life of Mahatma Gandhi.* London: Jonathan Cape, 1951.

Giannetti, Louis and Scott Eyman. *Flashback: A Brief History of Film.* 3rd ed. Englewood Cliffs, NJ: Prentice Hall, 1996.

Kael, Pauline. *The New Yorker* 27 Dec. 1982, 72–73.

Kauffmann, Stanley. "Stanley Kauffmann on Films." *The New Republic* 13 Dec. 1982, 26–27.

Kroll, Jack. "A Magnificent Life of Gandhi." *Newsweek* 13 Dec. 1982, 60–64.

Lester, James D. *Writing Research Papers: A Complete Guide.* 8th ed. New York: HarperCollins, 1996.

Mast, Gerald and Bruce F. Kawin. *A Short History of the Movies.* 5th ed. New York: Macmillan, 1992.

Parks, Edward. *Smithsonian* 13 Dec. 1982, 29.

Schickel, Richard. "Triumph of a Martyr's Will." *Time* 6 Dec. 1982, 97.

Taubman, Leslie. "The Godfather." *Magill's Survey of Cinema: English Language Films Series.* Ed. Frank N. Magill. 1, Vol. 2, Eas-Lon. Englewood Cliffs, NJ: Salem Press, 1980. 638–43.

B

Quizzes, Questions, Essays, and Research Projects

Reviewing Chapter 1. Preparation for and the Process of Film Criticism and Glossary of Cinematic Terms

I. Quiz: Cinematic Terms

1. A _____ is an abrupt break from one continuous set of images to another.
2. The _____ is the individual who plans a scene and then shoots it.
3. _____ is the arrangement of actors, three dimensional objects, and other visual components that form the image within a frame.
4. The planning and directing of the actors' movements and positions prior to filming is _____.
5. An image, object, or idea repeated throughout a film usually for thematic effect is a _____.
6. The _____ is a synonym for a director who has the power to put his or her individual stamp on a film usually by also doing the editing, writing, or producing.
7. The _____ is the basic category of motion picture.
8. The basic unit of filming is the _____ .
9. _____ _____ movies are characterized by low-key lighting, pessimism, violence, corruption, and betrayal.
10. The _____, a series of interrelated shots, is unified in action or established location and time.
11. The _____ is narration off the screen.
12. The various photographic, artistic, animated, computerized machi-

nations filmed to approximate reality are termed _____
_____.

13. The _____ shot is one that has the subject filmed by a camera mounted on a moving vehicle.

14. A _____ shot is characterized by jumpiness and is used to follow a character moving through a crowd.

15. The _____ is a series of interrelated scenes that establish a certain prolonged effect with a decided beginning, middle, and end.

16. Music used in a movie is collectively called its _____ .

17. The _____ _____ is the movie storyline broken down to its individual shots often with technical instructions.

18. _____ _____ are neither music nor dialogue but lend realistic noise to a scene.

19. A _____ _____ is one taken from a mounted camera moving vertically on a fixed axis.

20. A soundstage decorated for shooting or any other site prepared for filming to occur is a _____.

II.   Questions

1. What are the differences between the review and the critical analysis (critique)?

2. What are the reasons that one critiques or reviews a movie?

III.   Essay and Research Projects

1. Select any film or video and describe specifically the procedures you have followed and the raw data you have gathered prior to writing the first draft of a critical piece on that cinematic work.

Reviewing Chapter 2. Style and Structure in Film Criticism

I.   Quiz: Matching Directors with Their Films

Name	**Characteristics**
_____1. Alan J. Pakula	A. *Texasville*

_____2. Milos Forman
_____3. Andrew Bergman
_____4. Penny Marshall
_____5. Sidney Lumet
_____6. George Lucas
_____7. Steven Spielberg
_____8. Marcel Camus
_____9. Victor Fleming
_____10. Barry Levinson
_____11. Jean-Luc Godard
_____12. John Hancock
_____13. James Foley
_____14 Jiri Menzel
_____15. John Cassavetes
_____16. Peter Bogdanovich
_____17. Mick Jackson
_____18. Jean-Jacques Annoud
_____19. Lawrence Kasdan
_____20. Otto Preminger
_____21. Jan Kadar
_____22 Robert Zemeckis
_____23. Gary Sinese
_____24. Phil Alden Robinson

B. *Twelve Angry Men*
C. *Black Orpheus*
D. *Carmen Jones*
E. *Glengarry Glen Ross*
F. *Bang the Drum Slowly*
G. *Sophie's Choice*
H. *Quest for Fire*
I. *Sneakers*
J. *Body Heat*
K. *The Shop on Main Street*
L. *Closely Watched Trains*
M. *Of Mice and Men*
N. *The Bodyguard*
0. *Honeymoon in Vegas*
P. *Schindler's List*
Q. *Breathless*
R. *American Graffiti*
S. *Diner*
T. *Gone with the Wind*
U. *Amadeus*
V. *Forrest Gump*
W. *Awakenings*
X. *Shadows*

II. Questions

1. List a number of items that make up "boilerplate.
2. What is meant by being subjective about a film?
3. What is meant by being objective about a film?

III. Essay and Research Projects

1. Select a film and write two paragraphs about it subjectively. Then treat the same film objectively.
2. Write a 200-word précis of a film ofyour choice.
3. Write three introductory paragraphs on the same film of your choice but for three different audiences.
4. Write three introductory paragraphs on the same film of your choice but of three different lengths.

Reviewing Chapter 3. Types of Film Criticism: The Review

I. Quiz: Movies and Their Genres

A. comedy   E. western   I. horror
B. melodrama   F. science fiction   J. romance
C. mystery   G. animation   K. epic
D. action thriller   H. biography   L. documentary

Note: Some of the films below may combine genres.

Genre	Selection
1. ————	*Tootsie*
2. ————	*Distant Thunder*
3. ————	*Diehard*
4. ————	*Lethal Weapon*
5. ————	*True Lies*
6. ————	*Home Alone / 2*
7. ————	*The Good, the Bad, and the Ugly*
8. ————	*The Best Years of Our Lives*
9. ————	*You Can't Take It with You*
10. ————	*Dog Day Afternoon*
11. ————	*Scent of a Woman*
12. ————	*A Few Good Men*
13. ————	*Swept Away*
14. ————	*Manhattan Murder Mystery*
15. ————	*Sorcerer*
16. ————	*Don Juan DeMarco*
17. ————	*The Crying Game*
18. ————	*Alien*
19. ————	*Dances with Wolves*
20. ————	*Amadeus*

II. Questions

1. What do you do to adjust to an audience in a written piece of criticism?
2. What is the assumption about the reader that the writer of a movie review makes?
3. When panning a film, what must you avoid?
4. What do you discuss in a plot-driven review?

5. What do you discuss in a theme- , idea- , or ideology-driven review?
6. Distinguish between an actor-driven and an auteur-driven review.

III. Essay and Research Projects

1. Write a review on any film of your choice; make sure to include boilerplate, a plot synopsis, points for development, and an evaluation.
2. Write a review on one of the films that we've seen in class. Include all the features of Question 1.
3. Write a short review on any movie of your choice (under 100 words). Then write a review on the same movie in 300–500 words.
4. Write a pan of a film adopting either a humorous or serious tone.

Reviewing Chapter 4. Types of Film Criticism: The Analytical Critique

I. Multiple-Choice Quiz: Movies Discussed in This Chapter

1. ____ One of the motifs of *Sunset Boulevard* is the demise of (A) the star system (B) major studios (C) silent movies and the effects it had upon Hollywood.
2. ____ Prior to coming to Hollywood, Joe Gillis worked as a(n) (A) door-to-door salesman (B) English teacher (C) journalist in the Midwest.
3. ____ D. W. Griffith's *Birth of a Nation* showcased a myriad of cinematic innovations, among them (A) reenactment of historical events, close-up shots, and wide-angle shots (B) sound, color, and editing (C) sound, the dissolve, and editing.
4. ____ *Falling Down* has in it elements of (A) *Death Wish, Citizen Kane,* and *The 39 Steps* (B) *Death Wish, Grand Canyon,* and *Network* (C) *Rambo, True Lies,* and *Die Hard.*
5. ____ Among the societal issues discussed in *Falling Down* that show America in trouble are (A) crime, greed, corruption (B) illiteracy, immigration, abortion (C) bigotry, acid rain, class warfare.
6. ____ *To Die For* is an example of a (A) thriller (B) comedy (C) satire.
7. ____ In *To Die For,* Suzanne is obsessed with (A) a desire to escape to Brazil (B) becoming a television personality (C) revenge for a childhood slight.
8. ____ Peter Sellers is closely identified with his creation of (A) the Little Tramp (B) Inspector Jacques Clouseau (C) the misanthropic windbag and deflator of all sacred cows.
9. ____ Peter Sellers' comedic strong points are (A) one-liners and

story telling (B) facial mugging and contortionistic body movements (C) slapstick physical humor and characterization.

10. Alfred Hitchcock's *The 39 Steps* is noted for its (A) blistering pace and suspense (B) changing exotic locations and graphic violence (C) wry humor and predictable plot lines.

II. Questions

1. What is the major assumption that the critical analysis makes that differentiates it from the review?
2. What do you discuss in a cinematic technique- or cinematic element-driven critique?
3. Name some other ways that the critique differs from the review.
4. What do you discuss in an idea- or topic-driven critique?
5. What do you discuss in a character-, actor-, or auteur-driven critique?

III. Essay and Research Projects

1. Write a critique on any film of your choice; make sure to include all the elements of that format of criticism.
2. Write a critique on one of the films that we've seen in class. Include all the features of Question 1.
3. Submit five sample titles each of critical analysis studies that focus on
- Cinematic techniques or elements,
- Societal problems,
- The actor or auteur, and
- Characterization.

Reviewing Chapter 5. Types of Film Criticism:
The Comparative Analysis

I. True-False Quiz: Audience, Format, Structure, and Approaches

1. _____ Like the analytical critique, the comparative analysis assumes that the reader is not familiar with or has not seen the film in question.

2. _____ Research is always done and formally cited in the comparative analysis.
3. _____ The title of the comparative analysis is often whimsical and clever rather than being descriptive of the topic.
4. _____ A well-written comparative analysis will often mix point-by-point and block structures.
5. _____ In the comparative analysis, the thesis statement is usually made early in the paper.
6. _____ A medley of thesis statements and minor inferences is one of the more popular structures of the comparative piece.
7. _____ The movie to movie approach lends itself nicely to a comparative analysis paper.
8. _____ Directors' or actors' styles are better to be treated in a research paper format.
9. _____ Comparative papers that study adaptation of literary works into movies are rare because they are so ponderous.
10. Remakes and sequels are synonymous terms in the film industry.

II. Questions

1. Write a block-style outline to compare two films.
2. Write a point-by-point style outline to compare the same two films.
3. What does a movie-to-movie approach attempt to do?
4. What does a literary work to movie approach attempt to do?
5. What is the difference between a remake and a sequel?

III. Essay and Research Projects

1. Write a comparative analysis of any two films of your choice. Make sure to be consistent in your structure.
2. Write a critique on any two films that we've seen in class. Make sure to be consistent in your structure.
3. Submit five sample titles each for comparative analysis studies that have the following approaches:
   - Movie to movie,
   - Literary work to movie,
   - Comparison of individuals: actors or auteurs,
   - Original to remake, and
   - Original to sequel.

Reviewing Chapter 6. Types of Film Criticism: The Documented Research Paper

I. Matching Quiz

Terms

A. thesis statement
B. sequential
C. hard data
D. plagiarism
E. the Internet
F. outline
G. minor inferences
H. color coding

I. documented
J. thesis
K. photocopying
L. works cited
M. hierarchical
N. subject area
0. subject

1. In the formal research paper, not only must critical sources be used but they must be _____.
2. After selecting a topic, an _____ must be drawn up and followed.
3. The final portion of the research paper is the _____ _____ page.
4. Length of the paper is an important consideration, but so is _____.
5. Before you can start on the outline, you must craft a plausible _____.
6. It is composed of three parts: a _____, a _____, and _____.
7. The typical outline is both _____ and _____.
8. _____ is considered newspapers, magazines, books, and other printed matter.
9. Various data bases, CD ROMs, and _____ are examples of soft data.
10. Attributing something that another has written or created as your own is an example of _____.
11. An alternative to bibliography cards and note cards is a system _____ and _____.

II. Questions

1. What considerations must you make when deciding on a topic for a research paper?
2. Come up with ten different descriptive titles for a research paper.

3. Take five of those titles and break them down into subject, statement, and support.
4. Discuss the many faces of plagiarism.
5. How would you avoid plagiarism?

III. *Essay and Research Projects*

1. Write a complete outline for one of the titles listed in Question 2 where main points, subordinate points, and examples are mapped.
2. Go to the library or the Internet to find at least five critical articles for one of the titles that you have selected immediately above. Then transfer these sources into a works cited page in MLA format.
3. Write a complete introduction with its lead-in(s) for the title that you have above.

GLOSSARY OF CINEMATIC TERMS

This text uses numerous terms that relate to the moving picture. They are common enough, but since assumptions of shared knowledge can be dangerous, the following definitions enable every reader to be familiar with the cinema terminology used in these pages.

angle   The position of the camera in relation to the subject being filmed. If the camera is above the subject, it is at a high angle; if beneath, it is at a low angle.

auteur   The director (who often also is the screenwriter) as the primary creator of film art who is involved in every aspect of the filmmaking process and thus gives each work his/her distinctive style.

backlighting   Lighting emanating from behind the actors thus putting them into heavy shadow or even silhouette in the foreground.

blocking   The planning and directing of the actors' movements and positions prior to filming.

cinematographer   The individual who plans a scene (usually with the director) and then shoots it.

close-up shot   A shot of a character's head or face, for example, that fills the screen.

composition   The arrangement of the actors, three dimensional objects (manufactured and natural), and other visual components that form the image within a frame.

crane shot   A shot taken from high above the characters and the action by using a mechanical crane.

cut   An abrupt change (break) from one continuous set of images to another.

deep-focus shot   A shot with the visual field in sharp focus: foreground, background, and everything in between.

dissolve   A slow fading out of one shot followed by the slow fading in of another where the images are superimposed at midpoint.

editing The act of putting together (splicing) images of film that have not been shot sequentially.

fade A transitional effect (also called fade-out/fade-in) where the last image from the previous scene fades to black then gradually, as the light increases, becomes the first image of the next scene.

film noir A genre of mainly American mystery films of the 1940s and 1950s characterized by a pessimistic tone, low-key lighting, and motifs of violence, betrayal, deception, and corrupted passion.

frame Like composition in its concern with the elements within a shot; however, here the emphasis is with the borders of that shot.

freeze frame The reprinting of the same frame a number of times giving the effect of freezing the action into a still photograph on the screen.

full shot A medium long shot that shows a complete person from head to foot.

genre A category of motion picture, such as the western, the comedy, the melodrama, the action epic.

hand-held shot A shot that follows a character moving—usually through a crowd—using a hand-held camera and characterized by a jumpiness not present in a mounted camera.

long shot A shot taken at considerable distance from the subject.

medium shot A shot of a person from the knees or waist up.

mise-en-scène All the theatrical elements necessary in composing a scene to be filmed: props, sets, lighting, sound effects, costumes, make-up, actors' placement (blocking).

montage A series of abruptly juxtaposed shots using short, edited sequences and music, often interrelated by theme and/or events, denoting the passage of time.

motif An image, object, or idea repeated throughout a film usually to lend a thematic effect.

narrative The storyline or sequential plot of a film.

New Wave A group of young French directors during the 1950s. Among them are Francois Truffaut, Jean-Luc Godard, and Alain Resnais, whose films are characterized by shooting scripts written directly for the screen, urban location shooting, improvisation, naturalistic acting, and allusions to earlier films.

pan shot A shot taken from a mounted camera moving horizontally on a fixed axis.

period piece A film that does not use a contemporary setting but rather that of an earlier historical era.

point of view Either a subjective (first-person) or objective vantage from which everything is observed and interpreted. The subjective viewpoint would be from the perspective of one of the characters. The objective viewpoint would be more neutral and not from any one character's perspective.

prop A three-dimensional object used by an actor or present on a set.

reaction shot A shot of a character's reaction to what has been said or done in the previous shot.

scenarist The person who adapts a literary source for a movie by writing the screenplay, or who writes a script directly for a film; a screenwriter.

scene A series of shots unified in action or established location and time (setting).

score Music—either originally composed for the film or not—used in a motion picture.

sequence A series of interrelated scenes that establish a certain prolonged effect with a decided beginning, middle, and ending.

set A soundstage decorated for shooting or any other site prepared for filming to occur.

shooting script The movie storyline broken down to its individual shots, often with technical instructions.

shot The basic unit of filming, which is the unedited, continuously exposed image of any duration made up of any number of frames.

sound effects Sounds—neither musical nor dialogue—that are made to realistically approximate a desired noise.

special effects Various photographic, artistic, animated, or computerized effects that are filmed to approximate reality or produce a sense of the surreal.

star An actor, actress, or celebrity having great popular appeal.

star system Filmmaking that capitalizes on the mass commercial appeal of certain performers to assure maximum box-office appeal.

star vehicle A film produced with maximum publicity to demonstrate the talents or appeal of a specific star.

symbol As with literature, a device in which an object or event means more than its narrow literal meaning.

tilt shot A shot taken from a mounted camera moving vertically on a fixed axis.

tracking shot A shot of a subject filmed by a camera mounted on a moving vehicle.

voice-over Narration offscreen while a series of shots unfold onscreen.

zoom shot An ongoing shot through a stationary camera where through the continuous action of the lens, a long shot can very rapidly convert to a close-up as zoom in. A close-up reverting to a long shot is a zoom out.

CREDITS

Photo Credits

Page 6, Photofest; page 14, Shooting Star International Photo Agency; page 17, New Line Cinema/Shooting Star International Photo Agency; paage 32, Everett Collection, Inc.; page 37, Photofest; page 58, Shooting Star International Photo Agency; page 63, Photofest; page 73, Ron Batzdorff/Everett Collection, Inc.; page 87, Everett Collection, Inc.; page 92, Archive Photos; page 106, Kobal Collection; page 109, Epic (Courtesy Kobal); page 122, Shooting Star International Photo Agency; page 130, Kobal Collection; page 141, Everett Collection, Inc.; page 142, Shooting Star International Photo Agency; page 145, Everett Collection, Inc.; page 146, Columbia (Courtesy Kobal), Photographer: Richard Foreman; page 165, Paramount (Courtesy Kobal); page 174, Everett Collection, Inc.

Text Credits

Adler, Renata. "The Good, the Bad, and the Ugly." Copyright 1968 by The New York Times. Reprinted by permission.

Ansen, David. "A Powerful Duet from the Heartland: Pfeiffer and Lange Triumph in 'A Thousand Acres.'" Copyright 1997 by Newsweek. Reprinted by permission.

Baeringer, Patrick, J. "You're Nobody in American Unless You're on TV: Analysis of a Beautiful Psychopath in Gus Van Sant's *To Die For*." Copyright 1998. Reprinted by permission.

Baeringer, Patrick, J. "The 'Hitchcockian' Elements of *The 39 Steps*." Copyright 1998. Reprinted by permission.

"Best Years of Our Lives." Copyright 1946 by Boxoffice. Reprinted by permission.

Birr, Ann L. "Patience Helps in *The English Patient*." Copyright 1999. Reprinted by permission.

Canby, Vincent. "Distant Thunder." Copyright 1973 by The New York Times. Reprinted by permission.

Crowther, Bosley. "The Best Years of Our Lives." Copyright 1946 by The New York Times. Reprinted by permission.

Ebert, Roger. "Your Friends and Neighbors." Copyright 1998 by Universal Press Syndicate. Reprinted by permission.

Hatch, Robert. "Films." Copyright 1975 by The Nation. Reprinted by permission.

Johnson, Brian D. "Straight-Arrow Hero: Kevin Costner Touches the Native Earth." Copyright 1990 by MacLean's. Reprinted by permission.

Johnson, Gloria Dunn. "*Gandhi* and the Critics." Copyright 1999. Reprinted by permission.

Kroll, Jack. "Media is the Monster: Hoffman and Travolta Go Live on the Evening News." Copyright 1997 by Newsweek. Reprinted by permission.

Mandel, Arlene. "The Rise of the Third Reich and its Horrible Legacy: Riefenstahl's *Triumph of the Will* and Resnais's *Night and Fog.*" Copyright 1998. Reprinted by permission.

Mermelstein, David. "The Best Years of Our Lives." Copyright 1998 by Mr. Showbiz Movie Guide. Reprinted by permission.

Nugent, Frank S. "You Can't Take it With You." Copyright 1951 by The New York Times. Reprinted by permission.

Rosenbaum, Jonathan. "You Can't Take it With You." Copyright 1998 by Chicago Reader: On Film Brief Reviews. Reprinted by permission.

Sander, Jim. "D.W. Griffith's *The Birth of a Nation*: A Precursor to Modern Film." Copyright 1998. Reprinted by permission.

Springer, Kimberly. "Effective Literary Techniques in Billy Wilder's *Sunset Boulevard.*" Copyright 1998. Reprinted by permission.

Stoddard, Sam. "You Can't Take it With You." Copyright 1998 by At-A-Glance Film Reviews. Reprinted by permission.

Schickel, Richard. "The Infirmities of Our Age: Shakespeare's Lear Gets Updated in *A Thousand Acres*. Result: Just Another Dysfunctional Family." Copyright 1997 by Time Life. Reprinted by permission.

Wade, Deborah Foster. "How Women Are Portrayed in Movies." Copyright 1998. Reprinted by permission.

Westerbeck, Colin L., Jr. "Robinson Crusoe." Copyright 1975 by Commonweal. Reprinted by permission.

INDEX
OF TITLES AND NAMES